T0146665

The FLYING DRUM

The Mojo Doctor's Guide to Creating Magic in Your Life

Bradford Keeney, PhD

ATRIA BOOKS
New York London Toronto Sydney

BEYOND WORDS
Hillsboro, Oregon

ATRIA BOOKS
A Division of Simon & Schuster, Inc.
1230 Avenue of the Americas
New York, NY 10020

BEYOND WORDS
20827 N.W. Cornell Road, Suite 500
Hillsboro, Oregon 97124-9808
503-531-8700 / 503-531-8773 fax
www.beyondword.com

Managing editor: Lindsay S. Brown
Editor: Julie Steigerwaldt
Copyeditor: Ali McCart
Proofreader: Jennifer Weaver-Neist
Cover Art: Mark Bryan (artofmarkbryan.com)
Design: Devon Smith
Composition: William H. Brunson Typography Services

First Atria Books/Beyond Words hardcover edition April 2011

ATRIA BOOKS and colophon are trademarks of Simon & Schuster, Inc.
Beyond Words Publishing is a division of Simon & Schuster, Inc.

For more information about special discounts for bulk purchases,
please contact Simon & Schuster Special Sales at 1-866-506-1949 or
business@simonandschuster.com.

The Simon & Schuster Speakers Bureau can bring authors to your live event.
For more information or to book an event, contact the Simon & Schuster Speakers
Bureau at 1-866-248-3049 or visit our website at www.simonspeakers.com.

Manufactured in the United States of America

10 9 8 7 6 5 4 3 2 1

Library of Congress Cataloging-in-Publication Data

Keeney, Bradford P.
   The flying drum : the mojo doctor's guide to creating magic in your life / Bradford Keeney.
       p.   cm.
   1. Medicine, Magic, mystic, and spagyric.   2. Shamanism.   I. Title.
   RZ999.K44   2011
   615.5'3—dc22

                                                                2010042455

ISBN 978-1-5827-0288-9
ISBN 978-1-4516-1066-6 (ebook)

The corporate mission of Beyond Words Publishing, Inc.: *Inspire to Integrity*

Dedicated to Hillary Stephenson, the extreme mojo love of my life. I adore you with all my heart and soul.

CONTENTS

That's the thing with magic. You've got to know it's still here, all around us, or it just stays invisible for you.

—Charles de Lint, fantasy author and Celtic folk musician

INTRODUCTION

*B*efore I introduce you to the flying drum, be prepared to know that what I am about to share is incredible and unbelievable: *I own a drum that has been observed to fly.* Made from an oval wooden frame covered with the bladder of a polar bear, this drum, originally called a *qilaat*, started flying in the Arctic over one hundred years ago when it belonged to a historically renowned Inuit-Eskimo shaman. (Wait, there's more!) The flying drum is only one magical object from the whole collection of long-lost mojo that has recently made its return.

Mojo is, in a word, magic. I don't mean sleight of hand trickery or adolescent renderings of fantasy. Authentic magic, or the old French word *magique*, is defined as "the art of influencing events and producing marvels." It signifies the complex mystery behind experiential transformation, whether pursued for reasons of health, wealth, freedom, relationship, spiritual wisdom, inspiration, or happiness. Though often associated with special charms, amulets, or objects, mojo also refers to all forms of ability that can influence and help bring forth a desired change. "To have one's mojo working" means that good things are happening for you—luck is on your side.

Originally rooted to African healing traditions, the word was introduced to the general public through the lyrics of blues songs recorded in the 1920s. Blues queen Ma Rainey sang about going to

Louisiana to get a "mojo hand" so she could "stop these women from taking my man." Guitar legend Robert Johnson sang about mojo being used in card games while Lightnin' Hopkins, Sonny Boy Williamson, and Blind Willie McTell sang about its impact on love, relationships, and how to handle the blues.

Anyone with self-confidence and assuredness is said to have mojo. It provides a basis for belief in one's natural skills in any situation, including the capacity to bounce back from negative and traumatic events. Mojo underlies the expression of creativity, charisma, life force energy, and the special uniqueness that empowers everyday life. Mojo makes you both socially cool and expressively hot, and is regarded as the unseen force that is responsible for personal magnetism, natural leadership, and spirited presence. It is the one quality that matters most in bringing forth exceptional meaning, ecstatic joy, and tremendous success.

**Mojo underlies the expression of creativity, charisma,
life force energy, and the special uniqueness
that empowers everyday life.**

Before you wonder whether you should go further with these stories of mojo and magical objects, it may be worth mentioning that I carry some respectable credentials as a scholar and therapist. As a matter of fact, I was just elected president of the Louisiana Association for Marriage and Family Therapy. There is nothing special about this position, though some outside observers may think there is something unusual about my holding it. Being an atypical therapist is not a serious problem where I live because Louisiana is not your typical state.

We not only have a state flower but we also have a state reptile—the alligator. So don't be surprised if the state therapist is a witch doctor. This part of the Deep South never stops savoring the many contradictory tastes of its deep-fried experiences. Our cultural gumbo holds Cajun healers, turtle hunting, ghost stories, right-wing evangelical churches, the Southern Decadence gay festival, Mardis Gras parades, hot sauce, voodoo dolls, root doctors, swamp boats, political corruption, gambling, organized crime, hurricanes, king cake, bayou swamps, gospel, zydeco, blues, and jazz. You can drink and party all night long on Saturday and dance down the church aisles on Sunday morning. Or not. Whatever and however you choose to express yourself, you can do it here and be cool because whatever happens "ain't nobody's business if I do," as the Fats Waller Big Easy mantra is sung on Bourbon Street.

Where else could a mojo doctor be a licensed therapist and elected president of a state organization that attends to the professionals who are on the front lines of our most heated moral and practical issues, from abortion to divorce, gay rights, runaway kids, sexuality, alternative lifestyles, courtship, childbirth, child rearing, leaving home, elder living, and bereavement, not to mention all the tricky symptoms and problems associated with depression, anxiety, eating disorders, emotional and behavioral issues, social hassles, and madness? I have spent a career masked as a therapist and have worked with almost every imaginable mess and form of suffering people can get themselves into. And I have done this while secretly dispensing swamp mojo and the assorted magical know-how of various ancestral traditions.

Am I really a mojo doctor—someone who draws upon unexplainable mysteries to help people change? Am I a witch doctor because I specialize in mojo? It actually sounds weird to be called that, but there is a truth to this name. Admittedly, I was initiated in several doctoring ways in Africa, including the world's oldest living culture, the Bushmen of the Kalahari Desert. There I am called "the big doctor" because I am big in stature compared to their small physical size and because they regard me as holding the expertise of their healing knowledge.

In Louisiana, I am known as a therapist, marriage therapist, family therapist, or creative therapist—whichever name best serves the clients, whether they are in need of personal healing or are therapists wanting to enliven their practices; my card does not say I am a mojo doctor. It mentions only that I am a licensed marriage and family therapist, and that I am a professor and the Hanna Spyker Eminent Scholars Chair in Education at the University of Louisiana, Monroe. With Hillary Stephenson, I am also co-founder and co-director of Circulus: Innovations for Creative Transformation, a consortium of practitioners, artists, cultural tricksters, and scholars devoted to studying innovative ways of personal and social change.

You might be tempted to say that I am a professor and therapist by day and a mojo doctor at night, but it's actually more intertwined than that. I regard all therapists as striving mojo doctors. Some therapists have learned to access mojo and others have not been as lucky, but all disseminators of the talking cure are part of an ancient art whose most noble purpose is to help clients find their own mojo. Not only do people carry within themselves all the necessary capacities for healing, growth, and making meaning but their mojo also sits inside them, waiting to be asked to spring into action. A good mojo doctor knows how to wake up another person's mojo. Once you grab hold of your own personal magic or feel grabbed by it, there is little to no need for the doctor. This is true until you again forget where you hid your mojo—then I may need to make another house call.

What I do as I go about each day of my professional clinical practice and teaching career is directed by what I learned from the original mojo traditions. African traditional practitioners are not called witch doctors except by outside observers. Among the Bushmen, you are called a *n/om-kxao*, whereas the Zulu, the largest ethnic tribe in southern Africa, respectfully address you as a *sangoma*. I am both, but that is not the end of my calling cards. I have also been initiated and given the official status of a traditional practitioner in other cultures around the world, including the ancient samurai tradition of *seiki jutsu* in Japan, where I was pronounced the successor and custodian of its teaching by its most revered elder practitioner, Ikuko Osumi, sensei. Among the Guarani Indians of the Amazon, the shamans regard me as a grandfather shaman who receives the holy songs and dreams of their spiritual tradition. The traditional healers of Bali accept me as a fellow practitioner, while in Mexico I am called a *curandero* and *nagual* by folk healers and a prophet by priests in Oaxaca. In Louisiana, my closest colleagues regard me as a therapist who works with the help of spirit, whether defined as the creative spirit or the holy spirit.

Not only do people carry within themselves all the necessary capacities for healing, growth, and making meaning but their mojo also sits inside them, waiting to be asked to spring into action.

I have walked side by side with many mojo doctors in healing traditions throughout the world and have learned that all masterful practitioners share the understanding that what matters most in helping people to change cannot be fully understood. It is a great mystery. A mojo doctor is someone who helps dispense mystery. There is know-how and wisdom in its handling, but its complexity is beyond all understanding. Mojo doctors simply serve the ways mystery is able to transform people.

What does it really mean to be called a mojo doctor? There is no easy answer to this awkward question. It certainly does mean something, but it is beyond our ability to adequately articulate. It has less to do with appearance than presence. You won't ever see me walking down the street wearing a loincloth or a Japanese robe, or carrying a spear or a wand of feathers. You also won't hear me shouting strange sounds in a séance. Well, you might hear me make some unexpected sounds, but it will blend into whatever is happening on the therapeutic stage where you happen to find me performing my shtick.

As you will see, we do not have to go to war with the experiences that trouble us. We can instead harness them and make them work for us in a positive way. Pulling this off requires some good mojo.

In my previous book, *The Bushman Way of Tracking God*, I told the story of how I accidentally became a holder of old practices that have been an accepted part of other cultures for thousands of years. I learned that so-called witch doctors, shamans, and mojo doctors of past and present were largely the psychotherapists, counselors, spiritual coaches, and practical consultants for their people. You went to them to sort out your life challenges and to get yourself back on track with a revitalized sense of purpose. They helped you fulfill your life mission and destiny.

In this regard, I am an old-time mojo doctor—one who knows how to handle witching and bewitching the spells that come on people. I learned this from elders all over the world. They taught me how to handle symptoms, problems, and suffering other than by medicating, punishing, or exorcising them. As you will see, we do not have to go to war with the experiences that trouble us. We can instead harness them and make them work for us in a positive way. Pulling this off requires some good mojo. I'll have plenty more to say about this.

My practice and teaching take place in some of the poorest places in America—the small towns near the Mississippi River Delta. There, I have the great pleasure of witnessing people's lives magically changing in the same ways as those in villages in the most remote corners of the Earth, and all through the experience of an extraordinarily inspired creative moment that touches us in a magical way. Mojo is still alive here, and I carry some of it in my belly and in my heart.

Mojo Opens Us Up to Transformation

It's important not to take mojo and witch doctoring too seriously. Please know that it does not have to be the least bit scary. At its best, it is simply old-fashioned heart medicine based upon the workings of creativity, laughter, and love. Strong mojo is fun and sometimes funny. I once was talking to a group at a dinner party and explained that a witch doctor was only strong and effective if she was kind and full of joy. One of the household residents, a bright fourteen-year-old, added her opinion: "Does that mean that a witch doctor is the opposite of a bitch doctor?" We all laughed, though she had made an excellent point.

The emotionally cold and overly rational delivery of help, whether as a medical intervention or a counselor's practical advice, may too easily become bitchy if it is conveyed too seriously, scientifically, or professionally, shutting down playful, creative interaction. On the other hand, soft, warm, humorous, and loving encounters open us to natural transformation and growth, bringing the best we have to creatively offer one another.

Mojo charms you to lighten up and open the door to the sweet spot of your heart, where you find the healing, meaning, and growth you desire. It's been said many times and in many ways that your heart holds all the treasure, talent, hope, joy, and guidance that you require. This is where you find your personal mojo—your cool essence, natural-born gifts, and vital life force. A mojo doctor helps you find the inspirational light and inner might that can waken and strengthen your life.

When someone treats another person without love, the medicine is weak because the absence of love too easily inspires fear, and brings on a darkness that blinds and shuts us down. We lose sight of our heart. The most effective mojo doctors exercise the strongest love: they empower relationship by embracing all sides, perspectives, and attitudes, even when it is contradictory. They help you find yourself by taking you on a journey to reclaim your origin—your beginning place in the heart of your heart.

Never forget that the greatest mystery is love. Its effect on people is as miraculous as watching a flower bloom for the first time. Love is a mojo that shines, opens, blossoms, and cross-pollinates. It is contagious and it spreads, sending a wildfire from heart to heart within families and across neighborhoods and communities. It delivers the beacon that helps you walk the line toward your unique destiny. When things get you down, whether they are rooted to economic, social, physical, or relational distress, know that you don't need a pill. You need some good mojo, a return to your truest inner source. Only it can lift you up, show you the way, and carry you across troubled waters.

An Invitation

This book is an invitation to a new form of personal healing. Conventional therapy and counseling have been rendered ineffective by their utter lack of mojo, and the time has come for us to invite real magic into our lives. Most of the overly simplistic, pseudoscientific superstitions of our time are derived from the professions of psychology and psychiatry. They too often limit what we hope to achieve; they lead us away from the unexplainable, awesome experiences that hold the power to transform us.

Rather than ignore the teachings that have been fine-tuned by other healing cultures for thousands of years, I am asking you to notice that you have more options and choices than you ever imagined. Whether you are suffering from pain or yearning for joy, know that mojo is the bridge that carries you to the other side of what you envision. Only it can inspire, mobilize, and actualize your most significant dreams. Say no to psychobabble and shout yes to mojo action. Venture toward the widespread heavenly gates of glorious transformation and run like crazy to get away from any shrunken door that takes you inside a psychotherapy clinic.

I hereby declare myself a rebel—a revolutionary who calls for the end of the mental health professions. I am taking my stand for mojo. I am a mojo doctor who dispenses magic. Step right up and let's dance with the gods! Let's open ourselves to letting the spirit move us. No diagnosis, no drugs, and no hospitalization. I'm here to help you find your mojo, dreams, inner gifts, love medicine, ultimate meaning, and destiny.

Explaining problems alone doesn't fix them; it just gives reason to continue the suffering. That's why mojo is preferable to psychological explanation. It asks you to do something unexpected and out of the box. It hands you a new creative way of being in your situation and draws upon multicultural, proven ways of mobilizing your own inner magic. You go to a mojo doctor to get a prescription for change and receive an experience that is not ordinary. Nothing less can deliver the outcome you seek.

If you are a therapist, you must find your own unique way to access mojo to be truly effective in your practice. Without it, you will only be recycling clichés and psychological recipes that lose their efficacy faster than the speed of sound. However, in spite of any professional training that turned your attention away from the very mojo you need, there is still hope. You are part of an ancient healing practice that is older than today's professional guilds. If you stop doing most of what you think you should be professionally doing, a space will be cleared for mojo. Ask for it, and it will come—but prepare a space so there is room for you to notice its arrival.

If you are seeking personal healing, know that the only thing that can help you is mojo. It lies within your deepest being and it is all around you—in your home, neighborhood, work, and play. You are lucky if you find a mojo doctor who can help you uncover your own magic and encourage you to not be distracted by all the voices that ask you to turn away from everyday enchantment and wonder. On the other hand, you don't really need anyone to make you any mojo; you already have it. Your job is to ask for it to come forth and be more engaged with your daily life. You, too, have to clear a space so there is room for it to show up. Quiet your own psychobabble and start acting with the expectation that real mojo can totally transform your life.

How to Use This Book

When nothing else works and people search for alternatives to solve their personal problems and suffering, guess who sometimes gets the call? I'm one of those eccentric characters that therapy clinics contact when they are stuck with a clinical case. Though I pose as a therapist, I arrive at the emergency scene as a secret mojo doctor. And I want to invite you inside my work, allowing you to experience real examples of how I work with patients and other therapists by using means that are largely invisible to others.

Although the names and personal facts of identity are altered, the stories I am going to share throughout this book actually took place in a clinic, therapy institute, consultation center, or clinical teaching classroom. My work is filmed (with clients' permission) to use their stories to help teach others how it is possible to find healing and growth in whatever troubled situations may arrive at a person's front door. I will include excerpts from the transcriptions of what was actually said in these sessions to help bring it back to life. I will also comment on what was going on behind the scenes, particularly as it concerns how mojo took part in the action.

My hope is that you will see that magical objects do not land in our world to simply entertain us as if they were part of a freak show at a gee-whiz spiritual carnival. They come to serve as a helping hand in our work with people who suffer. This is true for all mojo. If it's only used to send you into a spiritual high, it isn't really mojo. It's only a little brain squirt, not a whole universe big bang. Mojo is more than an entertaining libation. It is the transformative fuel that helps a therapist fly with a client. It inspires the magic flight that takes you to a creative spirit-filled sky where therapeutic sunshine, clouds, wind, lightning, and precipitation wait to bring forth change.

The Geography of This Book

In the chapters that follow, you will hear about the flying drum and other mojo that has returned to our time and place. More important, stories of how mojo has helped others grow in their daily lives will be shared. Then I will give you prescriptions for bringing the mojo into your life.

Each chapter is organized into these three parts: first, a story about the mojo, how I came to it and what the mojo is; second, a story about the mojo in action; and third, prescriptions for readers to bring the mojo into their life. Along the way I will invite you to step inside the inner workings of how we as human beings are as easily subject to being cured and realigned as we are to getting messed with and mixed up. Mojo, especially when mixed with good humor and a loving spirit, is an extraordinary, magical yeast that lifts our spirits to allow healing, learning, and transformation to take place naturally and effortlessly, sometimes as quickly as the snap of a finger.

My hope is that the flying drum, along with its mojo brothers and sisters, will enter your psyche and take you on a trip that goes all the way to the heart of your soul. There, your own mojo can be awakened to come out and play in your everyday.

The world is filled with mojo, and we need to find it in order to transform the problems and suffering that come our way. I will introduce testimonials about real mojo I have uncovered from all around the world—magical objects and practices that have an authenticated history of healing, transforming, and inspiring. This mojo is mysterious and inexplicable to the rational mind, but it nonetheless has great impact on the lives of those who come into contact with it.

**The world is filled with mojo, and we need to find it
in order to transform the problems and suffering
that come our way.**

When I was given the flying drum (a story that I will tell in chapter 1), I knew it would stimulate others to ask many questions about whether the drum actually flies in the same way a crow flies in the sky. Does it fly to our mind when a shaman does transformative work? Is it the shaman or mojo doctor who sets in motion a visionary flight? Is this a flight of the mind? Asked differently, is the mind drumming up a flight, or is the drum flying our mind? Similar questions rocked the academic world during the late 1960s and early 1970s, when anthropologist and writer Carlos Castañeda claimed he met a Yaqui shaman who could fly. While philosophical journals pondered the question, does Don Juan fly?, Joyce Carol Oates came closest to the complexity and mystery of the truth about flying shamans and flying drums—or anything else—with her words: "Everyone writes fiction to some extent, but most write it without having the slightest idea that they are doing so."

I have experienced ordinary things as extraordinary and extraordinary things as ordinary. And so have you from time to time. When our world flips back and forth between ordinary and extraordinary, reality and fantasy, fantasy–reality and reality–fantasy, among other turnings, we feel a movement that inspires a greater truth than that held by any particular settling point. Holding a drum that is purported to fly ignites this motion and sets our creative imagination on fire. It did the day I was introduced to the drum, and it continues every time I see a client who needs movement in his life.

The mojo presented here involves more than a mind-blowing encounter. It came into our world primarily to help those in need. Whether it is a flying drum, a dancing doll, a vanishing pot, a magical drawing, a samurai pillow, a mystery book, or an Amazonian feather wand, the mojo objects presented are shown making a house call to social service agencies, university clinics, and psychotherapy centers to help transform people's lives. We will take a peek at how the old ways of healing can infiltrate and direct the course of therapeutic help for everyday people. I have spent a career bridging the ancient healing traditions and the modern practice of therapy. You will see how a modern mojo doctor is able to bring movement and change to people whose lives are stuck in existential quicksand. But there's more.

The stories presented about mojo are themselves a kind of mojo and can be regarded as seeds of magic to be planted in your mind. The same is true for the reported cases about how a magical object has influenced healing and transformation. These stories and examples provide the preparatory ground for prescribing how you can bring mojo into your life and how it can navigate your everyday.

In addition, the prescriptions in each chapter are not token exercises but specific ways of cooking up some magic in your life. They are designed to be out of the reach of your habitual understanding and are sometimes purposefully designed to run counter to what you think is rational. This helps them get past your conscious know-it-all mind and slip into the deeper regions of your more creative unconscious, the source of your greatest talents and gifts. When you carry out a prescribed task, be unattached to any need for explanation. Giving up the need to know in order to do something unexpected provides a clearing for mojo's arrival. The power of these prescriptions is awakened when you actually carry them out and allow your imagination to spring forth.

Mojo is available to everyone, and it is found everywhere in the world, from ancient ruins to your own backyard. I invite you to take notice of how the world awaits your becoming more enchanted and entranced by it. You are embarking on a remarkable journey that introduces you to a treasure chest of magical experiences specially prepared to bring authentic mojo into your daily life.

1

DRUMS OF THUNDER

*A*fter decades of learning from traditional medicine people, witch doctors, healers, and spiritual teachers from all over the world, I finally woke up one day to realize that I had become one of them. I even imagined being teased by my grandfather, who might shout down from the heavens, "You're now a silly old mojo man."

The absurdity of all this hit me rather dramatically when I was living with the Bushmen of the Kalahari. Over a decade ago, I woke up in the middle of the night hearing the deep sound of a pride of lions near my tent. As I trembled with awe at that raw experience of the African wild, I surprisingly amused myself by silently commenting, "I need a break from *The Lion King*. It's time to go see another Broadway show. I really need a vacation." When I remembered that the Copenhagen Jazz Festival would soon be taking place, I headed out of the bush and went straight to Europe.

Within a week, I was no longer in a tent but checking into the Grand Hotel Copenhagen on Vesterbrogade, situated in the center of Copenhagen. Built in 1890, it is bordered by Tivoli Gardens and Central Station. I went there with the hope of having a real break from all matters spiritual and anything involving mojo. The very first morning, I went to the breakfast table with my appetite set on devouring a plate of sweet Danish pastries. That was the only ambition I had for the start of day, followed by full immersion in jazz until the nighttime, when there would be nothing to interfere with the lively pursuit of cheer accompanied by local beer.

After the second sweet roll at the breakfast table, I started to feel a bit dizzy. I stood and wondered whether I would faint. At first I hypothesized that I had received a sugar overdose, but I had not eaten that many danishes. I then recognized that I was going into a realm of experience that mojo doctors are familiar with. Something from the world of mystery was beckoning me to go on a spiritual hunt. I knew it, but I didn't want to believe it. I had come to play and be away from all that inexplicable madness. But a person has little choice or influence regarding when, where, and how mojo will take place and what it will bring. It just happens out of the clear blue.

And happen it did under a beautiful blue sky in Copenhagen at the opening of another jazz festival. I surrendered to that unrequested state of mind and allowed my body to be moved down a cobblestone street. I just started walking without consciously knowing where I was going, though I knew exactly where to aim. Down the street I walked like a zombie. I had no expression on my face other than a stoic sense of purpose.

After strolling for a while, I saw some old stone steps on the left side of the street leading to an old shop that was partly below the ground. I knew this was the source of the homing signal that had drawn me into the morning walkabout. I went down the stairs, knocked, and tried to open the door, but it was locked. I looked through the window and saw an older couple in the store. They were having quite a discussion, most likely about whether to open the door. The white-haired man came to the door and shouted something at me. I said I spoke English and that made things worse: his face turned red. He became even more visibly upset and began yelling something about my not being welcome. He didn't want anyone there that morning and wished I'd go away.

As he did this, his wife started talking back to him and came to the door. "I'm sorry. My husband is very irritable, and he doesn't like people. I try to keep him away from the shop, but today he insisted on coming in with me. Please come on in and pay no attention to him. You are welcome to look around."

I carefully peeked in to make sure the coast was clear. When I stepped into that old shop, it was difficult to discern what was around me. The lighting was quite dim, and the place was packed with so much stuff that at first I wasn't able to recognize any particular item. When things came into focus, I realized I was facing the most amazing collection of Inuit art I'd ever seen in my life. It mostly came from East Greenland, a region so isolated by big ice that until the late 1800s no outsiders knew there were any people living there.

I looked at the carvings and art and tried not to be distracted by the old man's curiosity about me. He finally came up and apologized for his rude greeting. He asked what I did for a living, and I decided to be blunt and tell him that I worked with mojo. Seriously, I said, "I do whatever the world of mystery tells me to do." I explained how I sometimes had visionary dreams and that I would follow them. The dreams were not the kind of psychological drama that could be subjected to interpretation. I heard phone numbers, saw geographical maps, and sometimes received instruction as to where I needed to travel. That's how I had been led to elders around the world who were masters of diverse cultural ways of working with mojo. I then said I came to Copenhagen to have a little break from all that.

I expected him to go off on another rant, but he listened carefully and slowly selected his words. "I know this sort of thing is true because it has often happened to me. Ever since I was a young man, I started having dreams that showed me a magical object. I was then given the address of where I could find it. At first I was skeptical, but then I decided I had nothing to lose. So I went to the address I had recently seen in a dream, knocked on the door, and asked the woman who answered if she knew anything about the object. To my surprise, she said she owned it and had just decided that she wanted to sell it."

The shop owner paused and leaned slightly forward to see how I was taking the story. I was delighted and could not help but show it because I had met a kindred spirit—another dreamer who was led to specified addresses in a visionary way. He went on, "You see, everything in this store was found that way. I created an amazing collection of East Greenland Inuit art and artifacts because I went looking for the objects that came to me when I was asleep."

I told him that his story was amazing but I could accept its truth. He was no longer the sour personality who didn't want to open the door a couple hours before. He now appeared thrilled to have found someone who understood and validated the secret of his life. I thought he would continue with his story, but he surprised me by suddenly ending the conversation.

He loudly announced, "Come back tomorrow morning. I want to show you something." He escorted me to the door, and it was then that I realized I was no longer dizzy. I did successfully manage to explore the jazz-filled streets of Copenhagen and relish the music, food, and beer, while wondering what the next morning's adventure would bring.

That night I had a vision. I dreamed that I met an Inuit man who said he was the son of Knud Rasmussen, the polar explorer and anthropologist who has been called the father of Eskimology. I didn't recall knowing about Rasmussen prior to that dream, but I researched him as soon as I could get to a library. In the dream, the man said that Rasmussen had fallen in love with an Inuit woman on one of his expeditions and that the Inuit man was their secret son. That was the vision. I had no idea what it meant.

The next morning, I met the old man at his shop, and he took me to his office in the back. On his desk was something that almost covered half the width of the desktop and was wrapped in an old, cream-colored cloth. Without saying a word, he unwrapped the item and picked it up. It was an old shaman's drum.

"This is the first drum ever collected from East Greenland. The first expedition there was conducted in 1886 by the explorer Gustav Holm. He was the first person outside of the Inuit to reach Anmagsalik in the ice-bound coastal waters of the East Greenland coast. There, his expedition met one of the greatest shamans of Inuit culture, whose name was Migssuarnianga."

He held up a full page from an old newspaper, the *Illustrated London News*, that had the headline "1886 Danish Expedition Coast Greenland Gustav Holm." I looked closely at the top left drawing, and there was a drum sitting next to a man I assumed was Migssuarnianga. The shopkeeper then showed me how the expedition account of the drum had been handwritten and placed inside the drum.

I would later learn that the shaman he was talking about had a magic drum that was reported to come to life during his ceremonies. As Gustav Holm described it in his diary, *Ethnological Sketch of the Angmagsalik Eskimo*: "The drum now started into motion, dancing first slowly, then with ever increasing speed, and mounted slowly up to the ceiling." Years after Holm's report, Migssuarnianga's son was interviewed on his deathbed by Rasmussen, who gave more specifics regarding what happened with Migssuarnianga's drum when it woke up during a ceremony. His account was published in Rasmussen's book *Myter og Sagn fra Grønland, I*:

The magic drum placed beside him had come alive and sounded as though a thousand spirits were beating on it.

When the drum touched his heel, it was as though the first white of dawn rose out of the night. He could see dimly in the dark. Later, when it touched his hip, the day itself came. Darkness did not exist for him in the night. His eyes cut through everything.

But when the evening finally came when the drum was led, as though by invisible hands, to stand trembling, with the drum skin singing, on his shoulder, the sun shone with all its light in front of his sight, and all the countries of the Earth were gathered in a circle in front of him. All distances and all remoteness ceased to exist.

Migssuarnianga had become all-knowing, and had gathered the whole world within himself.

I didn't learn these things about Migssuarnianga until after that second morning in the shop. I all but ran afterward to the National Museum of Denmark, where I was allowed to read the early expedition reports of Gustav Holm and Knud Rasmussen. As I tried to find out more historical information about the drum, I recalled over and over again the first moment my eyes gazed upon the sacred instrument. I had immediately felt its importance even before I knew that it had been the sacred mojo of one of the greatest shamans in all history.

That morning the old man at the shop handed me the drum and said, "This is your drum. It now belongs to you. The National Museum has wanted it for years, but the drum will suffocate if it lives with them. Please take it. I know you are now its custodian."

My heart nearly stopped, for I knew this drum might change the course of my life. I didn't know how, but it was one of those gut feelings that was stirred by authentic mojo. There was more on the table than the drum. A medicine bag with all its original medicine contents sat there. It also had belonged to Migssuarnianga. His beads of protection were there as well. Everything was handed over to me. Speechless, I held them for several moments until I could find a way to say my thanks.

That's the story of how I met the flying drum, collected in 1888 by Gustav Holm who inspired Rasmussen who, in turn, learned about its original owner from Migssuarnianga's son in his final moments. I went home with the drum and the accompanying medicine items and soon discovered that its mojo had come back to the world, but not as any hocus-pocus of New Age shamans and workshop trained healers. It came into the world of today's truest form of authentic shaman—the counselors, social workers, and therapists who are at the front line of addressing people's struggles and suffering.

On the day I received the flying drum, I introduced myself to the curator of Inuit culture at the National Museum. Still haunted by my dream, I asked him whether Rasmussen had fathered an Inuit boy. He replied, "How do you know about that?" I obviously did not tell him I had dreamed it, so I said I had simply heard a rumor. He subsequently gave me access to the museum archive that included Rasmussen's records and books, but he made no further comment on the subject of interest.

I found out that during his long expeditions to the Arctic, Rasmussen had fallen in love with a North American Inuit woman named Arn, whom people called his Eskimo wife. Yes, she gave birth to his son, sometime between 1921 and 1922. Rasmussen was at the birth, and he held his son and named him, though his notes never recorded it.

Rasmussen lived a double life, one with an Inuit wife and another with a Danish wife whose family was one of his financial backers. To protect himself from scandal, he falsely wrote that the child had another father. Rasmussen was a famous man whose expeditions had been compared to those of Lewis and Clark, and he did not want to risk his reputation for a long life of exile in the Arctic. He and Arn decided to give the child away to another couple who ended up raising him in Nome, Alaska. It is said that he, the man I dreamed about, lived as a hunter in the Arctic. The word is that he was alive when I had the dream. I wonder whether he was a shaman with a flying drum.

> **Mojo enables us to cross back and forth over the boundary between the ordinary and extraordinary, and in so doing, our dreams are made real while the everyday becomes enchanted.**

Rasmussen lived in two worlds just like the shamans he met. Though he believed he had to finally leave one world to return to his European home, the Inuit elders he became friends with lived their whole lives going back and forth between realities. They had the mojo that enabled them to venture far into unknown territory and then to return safely, over and over again. They did it with the help of mojo, whether it was in the form of a flying drum, a singing canoe, or a whistling wind. Mojo enables us to cross back and forth over the boundary between the ordinary and extraordinary, and in so doing, our dreams are made real while the everyday becomes enchanted.

I am not sure I fully understand why a vision told me about Rasmussen's secret or why I received the flying drum. What I know is that the mojo from the unexpected mystery that took place in Copenhagen has helped people who have come to see me in therapy; that is the fruit of its magic. It helps heal others and does so without anyone knowing a thing about its presence. Mojo is like that; it is not important to flaunt it about. Just use it and help others, doing so with an open, loving heart.

Magic Drumming

The flying drum from the Arctic lives in my soul. From time to time, it comes to life and brings an inspiration regarding how another person might be helped. It brings rhythms that lift my spirit, and it pours spontaneity into my encounters with others. It sometimes invites me to notice how another drum awaits the honor of bringing transformative magic into the life of someone needing an upbeat intervention.

At a university clinic in the South, a mother brought her seven-year-old son, David, to therapy because he was afraid of thunder. I don't mean that he simply called his mommy to his room when it thundered during a storm. Sometimes he went berserk whenever he heard thunder and was so uncontrollable that everyone around him was concerned. Most of the time thunder made him physically ill. He'd get nauseated and think he was going to throw up. The only thing that would help him was going to sleep next to his mother in her bed.

I was invited to see the family by the university clinic director. The room had a one-way mirror so other therapists could sit and watch the session in a room behind the mirror, which is typically the setup for a teaching clinic. A group of graduate students and faculty wanted to observe how I would handle the case. Mom, David, and Tom, his eleven-year-old brother, had been meeting with Susan, their assigned therapist, for several weeks before I was introduced to them.

I heard the family describe how their life revolved around watching the television news each morning and night to see what kind of storm might be on the horizon. If there was a forecast of rain, David would get all worked up, turn sad and even depressed, then experience severe stomach pains. Whenever Mom would ask David what was wrong during one of these episodes, he'd say, "I'm sad about Dad."

In the first moments of our meeting, I learned that all this began after a terrible tragedy took place in the family. David had been riding in a car with his dad and his grandparents. It was a stormy night, and the sky was filled with thunder and lightning. In that storm, the car skidded off the highway and crashed into a tree—his father and grandparents were killed. David was the only survivor. Ever since that time, David's life was organized by the weather. If he heard it was going to storm, he became symptomatic by getting either agitated or sad or sick. It always resulted in his cuddling up with his mom. Nothing else seemed to help.

As I heard this story, I felt the wind of the flying drum come into the room. That's how mojo sometimes works. With a slight wind, the drum arrived and whispered something into my ear. It is not something others usually hear or feel, but that is probably because they aren't paying attention. This time the flying drum said, "Look at the corner." I turned away from the family and looked at the corner. There sat some bongo drums along with some other toys. With that inspiration, I sprang into action, pointed to the drums, and asked David a question, "Do you like to play drums?"

David, who had been staring at the floor, looked up and replied with a matter-of-fact voice, "Yes."

I responded like an excited child to see if I could throw an ember of enthusiasm onto the idea. "Oh boy, let's talk about that." Expecting David to join me, it was his mom who immediately piped right in, "Yes, that's true. He likes to play the drums."

Knowing it was important to acknowledge all her good intentions and motherhood, I turned to her and spoke as a therapist. "By the way, Mom, I'd like to extend my congratulations to you. You're doing a great job with your son. You've got a good mom, don't you, David?"

"Uh-huh," he replied on cue.

"Why, thank you," Mom said with a smile that also indicated I could proceed with her full support.

"Your mom is great. She has steered you through many storms. Given the storms that have come up in this family's life, I'm sure it has been surprising to see what these storms can bring to each of you. But you also know that the sun does come out from time to time. You've had some good moments when you've learned some interesting things."

I then paused for a moment to prepare them for the direction I wanted to move them toward, the movement toward the drum. This is what the flying drum suggested. I was sure of it because I felt it in the special way that mojo doctors feel these things. I spoke slowly: "Now I'm wondering whether you have been discovering anything about drumming."

"Uh-huh," David answered without any delay.

"Do you have a drum at home?"

"I wish," he snapped back.

Wanting to reassure Mom that everything was fine and that I was not pointing out any problem, I threw in verbal praise that expressed what I felt about them. "I like the way you are with each other. I like the kind of happiness and joy you can express. That's a good thing—especially in a weird room like this with that dark mirror."

We all started laughing because the room was clinical and, like most clinical rooms, it looked and felt like one. The one-way mirror was dark as if it were a portal to another universe. On the other side was the unseen dark space where other beings were observing what takes place in the lives of a real-life family. In other words, it was not an everyday place for having a conversation about the intimate details of your personal life.

I returned to the direction of the drum. "So, no drum at home."

"All I got is a guitar."

"Do you think you might get lucky and get a drum?"

"Maybe."

I turned to his mom and asked, "Would that be a nice graduation present from therapy? What about getting a drum for David?"

David was so excited about the prospect of getting a drum that he couldn't be quiet. "It'd be nice to get a drum for Christmas."

I continued addressing Mom and the whole family. "It could also be a special present to help you remember the good times you had here. Do you know what a big drum really sounds like? It can make a big sound. Sometimes it sounds like thunder."

I paused before advancing the next idea that would take us into the world of mojo. Clearing my throat and with a slight change in vocal pitch, I announced, "I am reminded of something I should tell you about. There are places in the world where people play the drum as a way of trying to make it rain. Did you know that?"

Susan, their therapist joined in. "You've heard of rain dances, haven't you?"

I quickly picked up on her question. "Have you heard of a rain dance? People will dance with the hope of making it rain."

I picked up the bongos that had been sitting in the corner of the room and proceeded to play them quite energetically, going into what an astute observer would notice is a slight trance-like state. I was performing mojo, using the same rhythms I use when I am at an African ceremony, and conjuring the same vital force and presence of spirit that always pulses through my body. In front of their eyes, I altered how I was in the room. But I did so without saying what was happening. I was, for reasons that serve their comfort and trust, only pretending to mimic what the drumming for a rain dance might be like. But I called the mojo into our session.

This progress made the flying drum happy. In my mind's eye, I could see that it was flying and fully lit with a luminescent glow all around its oval shape. It made me wonder whether the moon was dancing in the room. The drumstick was hitting the rim of the drum, rather than the skin, as it did over a hundred years ago. This was no ordinary drumstick. It was made from a special wooden branch found by the first owner of the drum. The shaman, Migssuarnianga, carved the end of the stick to be the face of his spirit helper. He even drew a sketch on a piece of paper of what this spirit looked like to him. I have that image as well—it has the face of something that resembles a seal. It is alive when the drum flies. I have seen the spirit, and it was with us that moment.

At the moment when the flying drum takes over, my work is essentially done. I just have to keep my rational mind out of the way and remain a vessel so that the unexplainable mojo can do its job.

As I played the bongos in the room, my eyes closed so I could see the movement of the flying drum. It had fully come to life, and as it mysteriously played, it inspired me to play my drum. What the family heard was orchestrated by the drumming of the flying drum, but again, all of this was a secret. At the moment when the flying drum takes over, my work is essentially done. I just have to keep my rational mind out of the way and remain a vessel so that the unexplainable mojo can do its job. I handed the session over to the flying drum.

No one knew this. However, the therapist sitting with me said she felt something different in the room, but she called it energy. If Susan were religiously inspired, she might have said that spirit had entered the room, as many therapists I work with say. The observers from behind the one-way mirror also sensed this energetic shift but did not feel the impact as strongly as Susan did. I know this is true because I occasionally bring observing therapists into the room to feel the difference, and they sometimes see a luminescent glow. Whether felt, seen, or heard, something shifts in our experience when mojo enters the scene. The room comes to life. It turns into a holy ceremonial ground—a place for helping people transform the compost of their life into a revitalized garden. This alchemical gardening is initiated whenever a mojo doctor calls the mojo forth. I did so with the drumming, and the clinical atmosphere was sizzling.

It was as if mojo milk had been poured on some invisible Rice Krispies and everything was snapping, crackling, and popping. We could almost taste the changes that were taking place in front of us in the family. As the mojo took over the guidance of this particular session, the clients continued to be introduced to it with the metaphors that arose in the therapeutic hour. I spoke for the flying drum again.

"When people play the drums like that, they hope that it will wake up the thunder and start the rain. I know people who say that when it starts to thunder, it means that the sky is drumming. It's like there is a big drum in the sky.

"I think that whenever it starts to thunder, we could do something fun, and bring out our own drums and drum along with it. Sometimes we might simply start shouting at the sky and make all kinds of strange sounds. These sounds could be made every time it thunders. I bet you know how thunder startles you and makes you feel like electricity is coming into your body. That can make you want to shout. When that happens, you are easily able to shout, sing, dance, drum, and play with the drummers in the sky."

Susan pointed out that there were some electronic drums in the corner, and I asked her to bring them to us. She plugged them in as I asked David to show me how to play the drums. He played them with great fervor. Everyone in the room was taken by how enthusiastically he was drumming.

I asked his mom whether she had ever played the drums with him or if she always had been his audience. She asserted that she had never played a drum.

"OK, we're going to make that happen right now," I said and handed the bongos to her. "I want to hear the kind of sounds that can come forth when you let yourself go with this. Mom, come on, let it rip."

Mom started playing the bongos as David played the electric drums. As this spontaneously erupted into a jam session, Susan and I added our hand clapping. The flying drum was soaring.

After the performance wound down, I held up my hand indicating I wanted to make a special announcement. "Now I'm going to say something to you that might be taken as a sort of unusual idea. This is what I think: I think your home's ready for a drum. The more I think about it, I think your home's ready for two drums."

"Sure," Mom agreed without debate.

David was right there with us. "Yeah, that'd be nice."

I pointed out that they now needed a drum for Mom, David, and his brother Tom.

"So we need three drums right now, don't we? Here's two drums right here in the room. I know how we can create the third drum. You can take a bucket and hit on the bottom. I've been to Africa.

It's a faraway place where they play drums on anything from buckets to gas cans. So you all can make some drums if you'd like.

"I invite you, Mom, to get them a kind of reward for all the good things that have been going on here. I know you want to take this learning and bring it home with you so it will always be there. By the way, getting some drums and bringing them home is a way of taking home the good things that have happened here. Think of the times when all of you can play the drums together. You're going to be surprised if you get out the drums and just sort of go wild, and have a celebration with all that whooping and hollering."

After a pause to allow my words to settle in, I continued, "What I'd really like to see is this: the next time there's a thunderstorm or you think it might rain, get out your drums. When you hear the thunder, hit your drums. I want this whole family to play drums with the sky. Do you know something? I believe you will be the first family in the entire history of the world that will play drums with the sky. I don't know if anyone has done that before as a family. Whenever it starts to thunder, whenever there's drumming in the sky, you and your brother and your mom will all play with it, and you will make history."

David was absorbed in this discussion and suggested, "We could get several kinds of drums."

I responded to underscore the importance of his involvement. "Did you hear what he said?"

Susan commented, "He's working out how many drums he needs. Because everyone's going to need a drum."

David provided the answer. "We will need five drums. One drum for me and four more drums for my brothers and mom."

I felt the flying drum soaring around the room, touching everyone with its inspiration and awakening call. I allowed it to fill me with enthusiasm for what I as witnessing. I spoke again: "Mom, would you like your family to make history?"

"Sure, I'd love for that to happen."

"You might even want to make a video of this so you can watch yourselves doing it. Do it whenever you hear thunder. Of course, there are all kinds of thunder. There's the kind of thunder that is outside the house, and then there's thunder that is sometimes inside the house. When there's a lot of racket in the house, it may sound like thunder. For example, when the kids start arguing, you could say that sounds like thunder. That's another time you could get out your drums. Whenever there's any kind of thunder—any kind of thunder at all—the family can get together and hit the drums."

At that moment, David started playing the drums loudly with purpose and determination.

I readily affirmed his contribution. "That's right. Everyone plays the drum whenever there's thunder. You know, some people say that the angels live up in the clouds. Maybe it's the angels playing the drums whenever it thunders. How soon can you get the drums so you can play with the angels?"

Mom interrupted to say that she was definitely on board. "We can get some, can't we?"

I was happy to hear her take a stand. "Yes. And you can make them, can't you?

"Sure."

To celebrate what had happened and to offer more praise with words, I said, "It touches my heart in a good way to see the good relationships you have here and to hear the good news about all the wonderful things you people have done for each other."

David said, "Uh-huh," and Susan asked him to give me five. We slapped each other's hands as I said in my best hip voice, "All right, dude."

Now Tom, the other brother who had remained quiet, offered a request, "Can I get a drum?"

The flying drum whispered in my ear again. "Sure, we can turn things upside down and make a drum. See, there's a drum." I got the trashcan and turned it upside down, beating it as a drum before handing it to him.

He was pleased as he said, "Ah, there we go."

The flying drum was beating loudly in my ear. It wanted everyone to drum, and I knew it. Accordingly, I passed on its advice. "Before I leave, let's do something special. Here's what I'm going to ask you. Let's ask the people who are watching from behind the mirror (I pointed to the mirror) to do something with us. Let's ask them to drum. They're going to be the thunder in the sky, because the thing about thunder is you don't see it. But you hear it coming from somewhere in the distance. So let's pretend that behind this mirror is thunder.

Susan turned to the mirror and addressed it, "Are you guys ready to drum?"

"Let's hear it," I added. "Thunder, are you ready?"

A rumbling sound immediately came from behind the mirror.

"They're ready," I underscored. "Now let's wait for that thunder. It's just like it is before a storm. We are wondering when the thunder will be heard. When the thunder starts, we're going to play with it."

In a few moments, "thunder" sounded from behind the one-way mirror as the observing therapists pounded on the mirror and wall. The family beat on their drums until everyone started laughing at how much fun the experience was.

I marked the moment with enthusiasm. "Excellent, congratulations. You got that down, buddy. All right, that deserves another five. I now know that you're all going to do something very special. You're going to do something no other kid has ever done in his life. Do you know that? Your family is going to drum with the thunder.

It's going to drum with the sky. That's going to bring surprises in your life. It's going to give you all kinds of good feelings. OK?"

"OK," David replied.

I stood up and walked toward Mom. "Excellent, you're a good mom." I shook her hand.

"Thank you," she added. "It was nice to meet you."

"I should say thanks to the thunder that exists behind the mirror. You can't see them there, but behind that mirror are some good people who really care about you. But you could hear them make some thunder from time to time. There isn't any reason to think that they are not there for you. It's fun when you understand that.

"I bet the angels in the clouds and all the people in heaven are just like that. They all want to help you and reach out to you even though you can't see them. But they can make a big noise in the sky and remind you that they are there. Nothing pleases them more than when you play the drums with them.

"Whenever it thunders and I hear it, I'm going to think of you, wondering how your drumming makes the thunder happy. I know it will. Even though I'm leaving you now, I will always feel connected to you every time it thunders. I can't wait until the next storm."

The flying drum had left the room, so I knew the session was over. I finished my goodbyes and departed.

After I left, Mom said, "That's a fun thought, isn't it?"

"It's good," David commented.

Their therapist asked, "Do you like the drumming?"

David and Tom both said uh-huh while their mom smiled at what she had experienced.

"All right. Dr. Keeney says we are doing so well," Susan concluded. "He is amazed at what's happened. He's amazed at how cool David is."

David unexpectedly got up and walked over to the mirror. A rhythmic knock came from the other side.

"I bet that was Dr. Keeney," Susan commented. Their therapist was as excited as the family about their new reality. "I hope it storms soon, don't you?"

The older brother responded, "Me too!"

Susan continued, "So everyone can drum together. Was today fun? Was it really fun?"

David and Tom agreed, "Yeah!"

This family came to therapy with a young boy who was afraid of thunder. Of course he was. Thunder reminded him of a frightening moment in his life that led to sadness. His broken heart made him sick every time he was reminded of his great loss. You don't need a degree in psychology to figure that out. But what can we do about it? Explaining it doesn't necessarily help. It could possibly make things worse. After all, knowing why this causes pain only verifies the reason for the suffering to go on. Why take that chance? That's why I prefer mojo experience over psychological explanation.

The flying drum taught us that thunder is simply another kind of drum roll. When thunder is heard as percussion, it implies that there is a drummer behind the drumming. In our imagination, the drummer can be the angels, the gods, or even our ancestors in the heavenly sky. In this framing of the situation, we may be connected with thunder in a positive way. It connects us with an unseen drummer who might be someone we thought we lost.

Love is not bound by time; it is eternal mojo.

In this new experiential reality, thunder doesn't have to trigger the sadness of loss. It can remind us of something that can never go away—the feeling of love we will always have with the beloved.

Love is not bound by time; it is eternal mojo. For David, thunder can remind him of the heartbeat of a father and son's love that need never go away. His father is held in his imagination by the clouds and the sky. The rain can be a downpour of joyful tears, something to celebrate with drumming when it joins him with the unseen drummer of a thunderous sky.

Drumming is a good thing to bring into our lives. It sends a vibration of rhythm that helps us move along. When there is a rhythm, you can jump on it and catch a soul train to joy. Even the blues can pick you up when you are caught by its lament, carrying you away with its empowering beat.

The flying drum teaches us that one of the most powerful forms of mojo takes place whenever we create a beat from the rhythmic tides of our deepest emotions. Inspired rhythm invites us to move with its affirming pulse. Once we are taken by the beat, we don't have to get off the rhythm express. It can carry us past any burden and remove us from any stuck place. Not feeling well? Then make some mojo rhythm and hop on board. Its magic helps make you feel renewed, retuned, and sometimes reborn. It's one of the oldest ways of doctoring, and it has been around since the beginning of human culture. It's never too late to find your mojo rhythm. It sits there wondering why you have waited so long to search for it.

Prescriptions for Creating Your Own Flying Mojo Drum

I invite you to create your own flying drum. This is a special mojo drum that requires being made with your own hands, and it takes less than a minute to create. It is important that you do more than imagine this mojo exercise. Get up and actually do it! Mojo is not about thinking; it is about novel, out-of-the-box action.

Take a green pen and draw a circle on the palm of one of your hands—you decide which one. On the other palm draw a drumstick.

With drum and stick in each hand, proceed to clap your hands. Allow the green drum to momentarily land on your hand, but do not spend too much time wondering what this has to do with the flying drum from Greenland. What's important is this is simple: you have a mojo drum ready to make rhythms when you need it. Notice that when you clap, the drum is flying. There are many ways to play your drum. You can use a finger as a drumstick and go at it that way. You can also wave your hands about and get the drum to fly. Consider the many ways your drum can move and the ways in which you can bring on some impromptu beats and rhythms.

The drum and drumstick can be as small or as large as you choose. Like the Arctic drum of Migssuarnianga, it can have a handle—just draw it on your palm. It can be a simple oval shape of any color. It can be decorated with symbols or words. I personally like writing the words *Flying Mojo Drum* on my drum. You will need to remake the drum each time it fades away. Use your imagination to bring forth the drum and drumstick that are most pleasing, inspiring, or amusing to you.

To kick your mojo up a notch, I recommend that you hold an ice cube in the palm of your hand after you draw the drum. Hold onto that ice and imagine that this holding makes you experientially connected to the Arctic. Your drum can then become more related to the original flying drum from East Greenland. Say this incantation as you hold the ice, "East of the sun and west of the moon, my Arctic chilled drum will swoon like a loon." Sing that line and you'll have a mojo tune that lifts your spirit like a helium balloon.

For big mojo drumming, take a deep breath and at the height of your inhalation, draw an invisible, though felt, circle on your belly with your finger. Now exhale and imagine that this is your drum for addressing the deeper challenges. Either silently or out loud, voice a wordless chant of random, free-associative sounds. Call it mojo sound improvisation. While doing this, pat your belly drum with your hand to provide a magical beat. When you have finished a drumming session, take your hand and wipe your belly, releasing the drum. Do this every time you need to summon your deep mojo.

**Do more than turn lemons into lemonade;
turn thunder into a jam.**

Like David, use these drums whenever thunder comes into your life. Whether it descends from the sky above or arises from a commotion below, drum along with whatever racket and noise life presents. See each drumming performance as a jam session that reminds you that any loud disruption can be played with rather than fought, feared, or resisted. Learn to smile whenever life roars at your situation or a thundering voice comes at you. See every thunderclap as needing a mojo handclap.

Drumming with thunder excites all flying drums and makes them airborne. Here we learn the first lesson of mojo: Do more than turn lemons into lemonade; turn thunder into a jam. It's no surprise that Louisiana is more than the holder of rich traditions of mojo doctoring. It's also the birthplace of jazz and late-night jam sessions. Here, life is improvisation. As Louis Armstrong said, "What we play is life," and as George Gershwin added, "Life is a lot like jazz ... it's best when you improvise."

Step into a Louisiana state of mind and grab hold of your drum. Its mojo can turn the blues into a party and harness thunder for a march to joy. Without a rhythm and an improvised beat, you won't be able to pick up your feet. As stride pianist Fats Waller suggested, "You get that right tickin' rhythm, man, and it's on!"

A successful and fulfilling life is not about believing, saying, or doing the right thing. If you aren't moving with buoyant rhythm, your everyday will sink. The magical flow of exuberant living needs mojo to empower it, and one of its original sources comes from tapping a special rhythm born out of the unique particularities of a given moment. You don't have to be in the Arctic or in New Orleans to access the mojo of a flying drum. Everything you need is close at hand.

2

DANCING WITH
A MAGICAL DOLL

*T*he story of the magical object in this chapter holds extraordinarily strong mojo. It is arguably more mysterious than the flying drum. I still have a difficult time believing what happened to me, but it did take place, as several witnesses can testify. I am going to tell you about a doll, but not the kind of doll a child would own. This doll almost scared me to death. When you encounter especially potent mojo, it is that tangible.

Since the beginning of human culture, there have been reports of mojo that is exceptionally strong. Some of it is so potent that even hearing its name or reading a story about it is enough to bring about an influence. We can be powerfully charmed by mojo without meeting the object that is purported to hold it. As traditional practitioners know, an object in itself is not the mojo. The magic is found in how we dance with whatever experience it awakens in us.

The flying drum lifts off the ground and carries us with it because our imagination relates to it in a transformative way. Stories about mojo reach out to touch us with the possibility for a magical interaction. Anything heard, seen, tasted, smelled, felt, voiced, performed, or imagined about its magic has the ability to mobilize the powers of enchantment that are sleeping inside us.

Even those who readily dismiss mojo as mere superstition, fantasy, or literary invention are naturally curious about it. In a world that leans too heavily on technical expertise and scientific knowledge, we still enjoy entertaining the possibility that there are experiential mysteries that will never be understood. Independent of what anyone thinks, old mojo doctors conduct their business with the assumption that magic is hidden everywhere. As a member of this guild, I have seen many examples of how mojo is capable of shaking up a person's life in a completely unexpected way. This dramatic impact can happen at any moment whether or not you believe, prepare, or ask for it.

My adventure with this especially strong mojo began at a social reception hosted in Minneapolis by Mr. O. T. Thompson, the owner of a local art gallery that specialized in indigenous art and artifacts. That night, he asked me if I'd be willing to give a series of talks that his business would sponsor. The gig was to come tell my mojo stories in his gallery and, in exchange, he would let me select a piece of artwork—perhaps a carving, painting, or some aesthetic object not easy to categorize. I accepted, and we continued with these bartered exchanges up until his retirement.

One day in early December, several years after we first met, O. T. called me and asked if I could come by his shop. This was during the middle of a Minnesota blizzard, and heavy snow covered the entire state. His call sounded urgent, and I knew he needed to see me without further delay. I bundled up and decided to make the ice-ridden trek. There was no way I could have been prepared for what would take place on that cold, dark, and blustery winter afternoon.

"I have something you need to examine," he had said on the phone. "I'm not sure what it is, but I think you should get here as soon as possible. Can you come right now?" As I drove, I recalled how his voice indicated that he was seriously worried. That is why I had immediately canceled my meeting at the university in St. Paul, where I was teaching. I had never heard O. T. express this kind of anxiety, so my mind tried to imagine what sort of difficulty he was facing. I assumed it concerned shamanic matters, for why else would he bother to call a mojo doctor?

When I walked into his warehouse gallery, he quickly jumped up from his desk chair and nervously waved me toward the back room. He didn't even take the time to offer a social greeting. Without a doubt, this was a serious crisis waiting for me. The back of his shop was a workshop for making repairs to his antiquities, and that's also where he framed some of the paintings and put aside things to be mailed to clients. He was storing something strange there—the object that was the source of his concern.

As I entered the workroom, I felt an immediate change in the atmosphere. The room was quite a bit colder than the main gallery, and it felt eerie. Something odd was residing in there, and I could feel it. O. T. deliberately reached for a cardboard box that had been slid far underneath a table. He pulled it out, opened it up, and removed something that was wrapped in an old ragged quilt with a star design on it. This was something old, and it seemed to require being hidden from sight.

When he unwrapped the quilt, I thought it would be something completely unrecognizable; I did not expect to see an old wooden doll. It was a primitive carving, slightly over one foot tall, and had what appeared to be a few strands of human hair on its head. A single bell attached to a string belt around its waist, and a strong smell of earth and rotten wood surrounded it. The object gave me goose bumps when I approached it. It was definitely strong mojo, and I wondered whether it was dangerously strong. I took a deep breath and braced myself for whatever he would say about it.

"I received this from a Dakota Indian family in South Dakota. They said it belonged to their grandfather. I had a strange feeling about the doll, but I took it anyway. I was going to sell it, but something happened when I brought it in here and I don't want to talk about it. I actually don't want to say anything more about this doll. Please take it and find out what should be done with it. Please, take it, it's yours. Do whatever you think needs to be done with it, but do the right thing."

The doll clearly was a potent vessel for spirit work, but I did not know the purpose for which it had been made. I wanted to ask more about it, but I saw that O. T. was in distress and wanted to let it go. I'd never seen O. T. act like this; he was not a superstitious man but a successful businessman who loved art. I accepted the mysterious object, and watched as he wrapped it up carefully and put it back in the box. As I carried it away, I wondered what I had gotten myself into. "Another day in the life of a mojo doctor," I quietly mumbled to myself.

Upon arriving home, I decided to place it on an altar space that was located in my basement. I cautiously unwrapped the doll and gently stood it in front of some other mojo objects, like a specially decorated buffalo skull. You might say that I was introducing it to others of its kind. I also wanted my personal mojo to keep an eye on this thing. I didn't want it messing with me, for I knew what wild and irrationally disturbing things can happen when you hang out with magical objects. Tonight I was in no mood for any unsettling monkey business.

Suffice it to say that it didn't matter what precautions I took. So-called protection did not matter, for that evening I experienced something unexplainable and unforgettable. At around three o'clock in the morning, I had what I shall humbly regard as a waking vision. I looked out my window and saw an old, tall, thin man, dressed in a black suit, slowly walking down the sidewalk in front of the house. It reminded me of the priest walking to the house in the movie *The Exorcist*. I simply said, "Oh, shit."

The big shock came when I noticed that there was a small child, a girl, sitting on his left shoulder. Her legs were dangling across his chest, and neither she nor her elder guardian was smiling. Children don't sit on an adult's shoulders like that—unless it is some kind of carnival show—and they certainly don't walk around the neighborhood at that time of night. I knew I was in for an uninvited adventure. Both the old man and the young girl had a look on their face that was far too serious for me to be comfortable with. They looked like zombies, the walking dead. There was no spirited animation in their movement—it was too robotic. To say the least, I was very apprehensive about what would happen next. I unabashedly wished I had not picked up that doll and wondered if this is what had happened to my good-natured friend who owned the gallery.

To my horror, the outside strangers started walking up the concrete stairs that led to the front porch of my bungalow house. I leaned over to see what they were doing, and the situation became more disconcerting. The old man placed his hand on the doorknob. He didn't use a key because he didn't need one. He just turned the knob and the door opened even though I had locked it before going to bed. To say that I immediately panicked is an understatement. I ran to the phone to dial 911.

What happened next sent a chill down my spine. As I used to say as a kid, "It scared the bejesus out of me!" When I picked up the phone, my mind went blank. I could not remember the number to call in an emergency. This old man and young girl had somehow (so I thought at the moment) managed to induce a state of amnesia regarding the emergency number no one ever forgets. I started to yell, and it woke up my wife.

"What's wrong?" she asked with fear.

I knew she could not be protected from being upset because I was clearly scared—and for good reason. Something really scary was in our house.

I tried to downplay my concern, but to no avail. "I'm not sure, dear. I think I might have been having a nightmare." I was already wondering whether these intruders were from the world of spirit because who else opens a locked door without a key? I threw on a robe, and grabbed a small flashlight and the heavy, lead-filled wooden club that I kept under the bed for protection. Armed with serious wood and humble light, I went downstairs. Obviously, I was praying for help and protection as I took the walk of fear from the second floor to the ground level. I searched the premises, but no one was there. The front door was locked and no windows had been opened.

I decided to have a look in the basement—I knew that is where these uninvited visitors had headed. Where else would they go than to the mysterious doll that was spending the night in our humble abode? As I went toward the basement door, I suddenly stopped, frozen with terror. I heard a noise that I should not have heard. As I slowly crept several steps closer, I realized that I was hearing a single bell ring. That's right, the bell on that doll was ringing.

I waited many years before telling anyone about what happened next. It has been said that magic and miracles are a distraction from the highest truths. I agree. But ignoring them may also be a distraction from the necessary search. I am quite a few years older now than when all this took place and will tell you some of what happened, knowing that a lesson emerges in the midst of this most unusual encounter with mystery.

When you experience something that lies outside the boundary of what we commonly agree is reality, it dramatically blows your mind. You feel like something inside your head has been punctured; a hole seems drilled into the container that holds your abilities to perceive and know. The old man, the girl on his shoulders, and the doll did this to me. That night, I watched the old man bend over as the girl jumped off and then proceeded toward the doll. She gracefully stepped into the doll as if she were its spirit of animation, and this brought the doll to life. The girl literally dissolved into the wood and disappeared. I faced the doll and the old man and they appeared alive, but not completely in the sense that we regard one another as alive. Both were present, perceivable, and communicative like a neighbor might be, but they were also from another dimension—an experiential plane that was more real than what we regard as real. There are sleeping dreams, waking dreams, everyday wakefulness, and then this realm, which seems hyper-awake.

When I stepped into the mysterious reality that belonged to the doll and its elder custodian, my relationship to them transformed. They were no longer scary and strange. The doll became beautiful while they both uttered the most profound wisdom. Lyrical words were spoken as she danced in a seductive though innocent way. My attention focused on her charming engagement with me, as her words were the first I heard, pouring a teaching into my unconscious.

"Yes, dear one," the doll spoke. "You may open your heart to us and cast aside fear. If it is your time to die, you cannot stop it. But if it is your time to live, it will be so. Surrender to this moment so we may pour the hidden knowing into your deepest well. My father will be here to calm you as I excite your sensibilities."

She proceeded to dance in a mesmerizing fashion that made me long for her in a way I had never felt before. My longing only served to open a portal inside of me that begged for the wisdom of the old man. That's when he spoke calmly and surely, "We have come so that we might enter the depths of your oldest presence. We have come to bring you back to where you once began so you may know where you must return again and again. Once we are in—and rest assured we are—we will never leave. Our essence will remain inside you as the sacred husk of a seed that must travel on in your forthcoming days and nights. I will tell you what you know, but you will pretend to forget as the demands of your everyday ask you to feign an ignorance that is neither noble nor humble."

The old man continued as the doll danced in a sublime way. In that moment, I was flooded with the desire to love the doll with all my passion. As it peeled away any resistance within me, the old man continued with his talk. "Magic, my son, is all there is. Science is the great superstition. Logic is a lie while the complex illogical serves the greater truth. Every clown knows that the gods are fools and that fools are closest to the holy ones who have walked among us. Watch her dance and be taught by desire. Know that it is not a fulfiller but an opener. It readies the vessel for the elder ways, the earliest forms, and the ancient truths. Here, you find that beauty and longing will guide the way."

The doll turned to me and, without making a sound, asked me to dance with it. My body immediately gave birth to an elasticity that was impossible. I moved in extraordinary ways—as if I were part of an acrobatic troupe—and as I did, I let go of the remaining assumptions that held my reality together in a stable matrix. I became unglued. In this deconstruction of my everyday presence in the world, the doll danced me. You could say that it changed places with me and observed my motion, doing so with heightened emotion.

The old man suddenly stopped talking. With the doll, he sang. It was a simple song that left me wondering whether I should laugh or cry. Though sung in an unfamiliar language, my mind made an on-the-spot translation:

Into the dance we go, making some old mojo.
Here and there, shaped like a pear, cleansing the wear
*   and tear.*
Into the dance we go, bent like a willow tree.
She's sent by a fellow who walks like he's Jell-O,
Carrying a young wooden doll.
Yes, we weep and laugh to water the earth,
To bring out the mirth, marking time that's so dear.
Into the dance we go, dancing fear into foam,
Brewing beer, bringing near, secrets of darkened roam.
Dance, my friend, you are now the doll.
We shall sit back and enjoy your show,
knowing we will soon have to go.
Into the dance you go, into the dance you go,
Far away and very near, this is the dance we know.
Into the dance we go, making some new mojo.

This dancing and singing went on throughout the night. At its height, I never really knew who was doll, girl, elder, or myself. It was the world of magic, interpenetrating real and unreal, waking state and dreaming fate. There is more to say, but the rest must be sung and danced, because it is past the ability of words.

When it felt time to depart from my new friends, I said a prayer and made a little offering for the doll and old man, asking them to go back to sleep. The bell eventually stopped ringing, and I was able to make my way back to the master bedroom. Exhausted from the experience, I fell asleep.

I slept soundly until the phone rang several hours later. I answered, but there was no sound. No one said a word. I was used to this. It usually meant that a Native Indian medicine man, one of my mojo friends, was calling. Some of these guys have an economy of speech that can be unsettling to folks outside their culture. In my case, they liked to test me to see if I could intuit why they had called.

I closed my eyes and tried to imagine who it was. "Gary, is that you?" I asked, thinking it was the Wahpeton Lakota medicine man, Gary Holy Bull. I had written his life story and over the years had been to his healing ceremonies, including the ones called Yuwipi, in which objects were known to fly around the room. My spiritual antenna could beam into him, and I was fairly sure that's who was on the other end of the line.

"Ho," Gary replied. I knew he wouldn't tell me why he called. He never offered any clues. A silence went by. This time I was going to outwait him. He knew what I was up to, so he simply asked, "You have something to tell me?"

"Yes, I had a visitor last night."

Gary grunted again to let me know he understood. I went on to tell him what had happened with the doll and how it was with me in the basement. I started to tell him about the old man and the young girl who sat on his shoulder, but Gary surprised me by interrupting.

"Our people call these dolls tree dwellers. They are made of wood, and a spirit is placed into them. We use them to heal and help find lost objects. When one of these dolls comes to our community, we build it a little house or container to live in. We know that this one is looking for us because of what happened last night."

My mouth was wide open, not because of what Gary said, but because I had seldom heard him talk that long. He went on with his narration.

"Last night a little girl in our community had a dream that an old man came to her room. He was one of our ancestral spirits, holding the wisdom of the old ways. He asked her to come along with him. He leaned over and told her to sit on his shoulder. All this happened inside the vision. What happened in the physical plane is

34

that she got up and walked in her sleep. She walked out of her room, away from her house, and came to my place. I heard her trying to open my door.

"When I saw her, I knew she was inside a vision. I also knew, because my elders had taught me about these things, that she was brought to me for a reason. She would be the next custodian of one of these tree dwellers or spirit dolls. I asked where it was, and that is how I found out it was visiting you."

Without hesitation I told Gary that I would immediately bring it to him. I got up and drove straight to Sisseton, South Dakota, with the sole purpose of delivering a mojo doll I had danced with the night before. Before I handed it over, I already knew that a strong mojo object has an unexplainable way of leaving its mojo with you.

The doll did not leave me empty-handed. It downloaded its mojo into me. You might say that it gave me its twin, a mojo presence visible only to those with spiritual eyes. The first appearance of the doll was scary, but when I danced with it that night, I found it beautiful, discovering that the old man had come to dispense wisdom of the purest kind: the twin of fear is desire, and the twin of evil is good. I danced with fear and was given her twin sister and father—the desire and wisdom of ancient ways that had become lost when we thought the two lived apart.

> **The first appearance of the doll was scary, but when I danced with it that night, I found it beautiful, discovering that the old man had come to dispense wisdom of the purest kind: the twin of fear is desire, and the twin of evil is good.**

This gift became another resource for working with clients who come with problems and struggles. They are blinded by fear, not knowing that a twin is near. My job is to help them dance and sometimes fly in the magical space between dark and light. Such is the life of a mojo doctor.

I met Gary and delivered the missing doll. Then I went home with its invisible partner. However, this is only the beginning of the story.

A week went by and, during that time, I found out more about the mojo doll. Sometimes called a *canotida*, "tree dweller" or "little forest dweller," it is well known in both Dakota and Lakota mythology. When you only see what arouses fear, it can be a tricky and sometimes malevolent character. It is known for getting you lost in the woods, and it enjoys playing that trick on people. In my case, it got me lost with the phone: no matter how hard I tried, I couldn't remember 911!

A canotida usually first appears in a vision. If caught by a medicine man or woman, it can be converted into a spirit helper and then summoned to work for good purposes. Only those who experience the vision of the doll are able to catch it and can later use it in appropriate ceremonies. This is how I came to catch a mojo doll and be introduced to its counterpart, a link to ancient wisdom: through the desire that opens our hearts to receive wisdom held inside the dance of change.

During that period of my life, I always embarked on a special gift-bearing mission the week before each Christmas holiday. Specifically, I would visit Kate Gurnoe, the mother of Sam, one of my friends who was a traditional medicine man. She had sentimentally adopted me as a special son, and every year at the holiday season, we'd exchange gifts. She had a passion for carvings of turtles, so wherever I traveled in the world, I was always on the lookout for special turtle art. This year I had found one made in Japan. With seasonal joy and a celebrative mood, I went to her house, handed my gift to her, and as always, she acted surprised to see that I had given her a turtle.

She, in turn, gave me a story. Every year she gifted me with a story about her life. One year, she'd told me about her early childhood, when she was taken away from her family of origin on the reservation and placed in an orphanage. There she was punished for speaking her native language. She and her best friend were playing in the schoolyard one day when Kate found a tiny, round white stone buried in the dirt. They believed it was a pearl. Her friend stared at it with great desire, so Kate gave it to her and told her to carry it for the next forty years. After that, she said with a smile, her friend could give it back to her. Unfortunately, the two friends were separated after they finished school and did not see each other for forty years after graduation. When they finally reunited, Kate's friend reached into her purse and pulled out the stone. With joyful tears in her eyes, she handed it to Kate and said, "It's your turn to carry the pearl." That's the kind of story she would gift me with.

Mother Kate handed me a plate of oatmeal cookies and a glass of milk before she began her tale for this holiday season. "This year I am going to tell you a story that only my son and my deceased husband know about. It is one of the most remarkable stories of my life, and it holds great mystery. I will never be able to explain it to you, Brad, but this is what took place.

"Years ago, our local Indian community had a very strong medicine man. He made good medicine even in his old age, but sadly, he had a stroke and had to learn to talk all over again. My husband and I watched over him and helped him recover. After months of rehabilitation, he was finally able to take care of himself. Soon after that, we received word that he wanted us to come over and pay him a visit.

"We went that night to see him. He was sitting in a big easy chair, waiting for us. When he heard our footsteps on the porch, he directed us to let ourselves in. Before we could sit down on his worn-out green sofa covered with old blankets, he announced, 'I want to show you something. It's my way of expressing thanks for all that you did to help me during my sickness. Go to my bedroom and you'll see my drum and a bundle sitting next to it. Bring it all to me.'

"I fetched his drum and the big bundle sitting next to it. It was wrapped in an old piece of quilt. When I handed it to him, he unwrapped the worn fabric, and my eyes immediately locked onto the most magical object I had ever seen in my whole life. It was a wooden doll that was over a foot tall. It had some human hair on its scalp and a string around its waist that held a single silver bell. I cannot explain why, but I really wanted that doll. I felt an incredibly strong desire to own it. Something about that doll had a firm hold on me.

"That's when the old medicine man told me to carefully place the wooden doll in the center of his living room floor. He grabbed hold of his buffalo hide drum and began beating a rhythm that commanded spiritual authority. When he sang, a miracle took place: that wooden doll came to life. I mean to say that it slowly gathered itself and stood up on the floor like it was a tiny person. And that wasn't all it did. It proceeded to dance. I have never seen anyone dance like that—it was pure magic! It was so beautiful that it took my breath away. I couldn't take my eyes off of it as it danced, and it danced as long as the old man sang. All around the floor, it glided with a supernatural grace. Now I truly wanted it no matter what the cost. Yes, I did want it more than any object I had ever seen.

"When the old man stopped singing, the doll slowly lay down on the floor and went back to sleep. Once again, it was as stiff as a board. My husband and I were unable to say a single word or make any sound whatsoever; we were in complete shock. We respect the old medicine ways of our elders, and we knew we had witnessed something extremely rare and extraordinary.

"We also knew that watching the doll dance was itself a powerful medicine. We had been given a medicine that would feed our spirit for the rest of our days.

"We simply nodded our heads in appreciation, and got up and left. We did so without any conversation as we carefully drove all the way home; our questions were respectfully silent. We just absorbed the mystery of the moment and went home, embraced by the holy.

"Now I have told you this story. It's not simply a story but a medicine story. You are very fortunate, for you too have received its medicine. It is a powerful thing, and your life may never be the same."

Yes, my mouth was wide open with awe, for she had described the doll that had recently made a visit to me. I had no choice but to tell her what had happened at the local art gallery, and she was both surprised and not surprised. I asked her if she wanted to meet the doll again, for I knew by her description that it was the same object. She and her son said that its magic was way too strong for that to take place. She might not be able to stop wanting it again. She had already received its medicine, and it would always be with her as a special story.

Like Kate had done with the medicine man, I stood up, nodded my appreciation, gave her a hug, and went home. The dancing doll had given me mojo again. I was reminded of the desire I'd had for that doll. Past its scary side was a tender and pure open heart that desired to dance a celebration of life. Its magic was found in how we dance with it, an experience that transforms the flight response of fear into the ecstatic flight of joy. That dance is now a deep part of me, and there is no way I can ever explain how it made its entry into my life.

Over the years, I was to learn that the tree dweller, or little forest dweller, was found beyond the Dakotas. These dolls were found in other parts of the world, including Africa. For the geographical region in South Dakota near where I was then living in Minnesota, it was regarded as a kind of wood sprite or fairy that lived in a tree. One of its forms was that of a small man, and it was known for its ability to seduce you into following it into a dense thicket or impassable swamp where you'd lose your way. But if you caught up with him, he could grant you the mojo gifts of healing powers, clairvoyance, good luck in hunting, and the ability to prophesy. The Dakota word for it, *canotida*, literally means "god of the woods."

The tree dweller has other forms ranging from a little child to an elf, animal, or bird, especially an owl. When a shaman meets one in a vision, she can then make a wooden carving or draw an image of him. This is kept with the shaman's other medicine items and mojo paraphernalia.

Other American Indians, including Menominee, Potawatomi, Sauk, Fox, Delaware, Shawnee, Ojibwa, and Winnebago, used these dancing dolls, but there are very few accounts of them and what they are capable of doing. They are mentioned in two academic papers published in 1920 by the scholar Alanson Skinner, who presumably took the first photograph of a dancing mojo doll at that time. His research found that in the old days, some of the medicine men of the Wahpeton Lakota medicine lodge used the tree dwellers, but it was an extremely secret practice. Skinner concluded another report, in 1924, with an account of how they were used among the Potawatomi:

> At a doll bundle ceremony of this nature, each person who owns one of these charms brings it and stands it up with the rest in the west of the lodge. All are dressed in fine new clothes. Anciently, it is said, they danced magically with their owners, but nowadays no one has the power to do this any more.

I am witness to the fact that this mojo has returned. Like the flying drum, the dancing doll is back with us. Its mojo can be absorbed by all those whose hearts and minds are open to receiving its story. And you don't even have to come into contact with the doll in person, as I had. If dreamed, it can be captured and drawn upon to help you with the concerns of your life, including assisting others with special needs. Let me tell you how this doll showed up in the life of two young women who came to me asking for guidance.

Two Dolls Dancing Their Worries

A young married woman named Christine who works as a high school counselor volunteered to work with me in front of a training group that was learning how mojo can be used to help people transform their lives.

"I had a crazy love roll for lunch," Christine said as she opened our session.

"You had a what for lunch?" I had never heard of a love roll.

She pointed to a friend in the audience, another young woman, and said, "Shelley talked me into ordering one." While she explained that it was something offered at a local sushi restaurant, my attention drifted elsewhere. At that moment, the dancing mojo doll appeared in my mind and started laughing. It directed me to be ready to bring Shelley up to the stage as soon as there was an opening.

Mojo loves silliness, especially when it appears at serious discussions. The oldest healing cultures know that the worst way to invite the spirits is to be pious and overly serious. That's why so many churches and clinics feel like funeral homes. However, when there is teasing and laughter, the gods notice. Due to these two women's good sense of play and humor, mojo was already in the room at the beginning. My mojo doll came down to play because it looked like a good time was about to commence. I listened and wondered what was in store.

I played along, though I was uncertain where we were going. "Oh, really? Did it eat you, or did you eat it?"

Nothing excites a mojo doll more than reversing the roles of a relationship and playing with opposites. Tease someone about a doll becoming human, a human becoming a doll, or food eating the diner, and a spirited dance will get off to a good start.

"I ate it. It ate me. We kept going round and round," Christine quipped back.

I saw this as a possible metaphor for her life. "Wow. Is that the way your life is? Do you run in circles?"

"Yes! My life does run in circles, actually! Yeah, I can't sit still. I am spread out all over the place."

Mojo dolls help a conversation dance. They relish turning things inside out and spinning them round and round. Our words were already dancing and flying in circles. Since she was a counselor, I suddenly switched from being silly to being serious, to keep things unexpectedly turning. I asked, "How are you going to help the world?"

Christine frowned and then laughed. "I never thought I could help the world. I just sort of feel I'm here and do what comes up. Maybe that's helping, but I don't know. But I never planned to help the world." In my imagination, the mojo doll nodded its head and I could read its mind: Christine would soon be helping her friend, Shelley, in this session. I vowed to be patient and wait for the right moment. It was coming.

I told Christine that I thought she was modest, and she again giggled.

"I think you plant a lot of seeds, tend to a lot of gardens, and do so in very interesting ways, though sometimes quietly."

She agreed with my opinion and then volunteered that she is presently trying to turn around the entire school staff because they are too angry and sad about their lives. "I'm trying to shake it up at work," she added.

The mojo doll became my co-therapist. With its counsel by my side, I was reminded that its dancing shakes things up. Nothing like seeing a stiff wooden doll doing the hula or the twist or Lindy Hop to shake up your mind! This absurd image reminded me that religious shakers also danced in an ecstatic way that must have looked possessed and wild—as if the dancers were human dolls suddenly becoming animated by something magical and mysterious. I teased Christine, saying that the founder of the New England Shakers was a woman named Mother Ann Lee. Christine was surprised and commented that she didn't know that. I played further with this line, "Maybe you're the reincarnation of this mother."

"Maybe I am." She laughed.

The introduction of a shaking mother had spun the session completely into the hands of mojo. Now we could be taken anywhere. The theme continued as I added, "But I think she didn't smile and laugh as much as you. I think she was much too serious about it. So maybe this time around you're going to get it right. They called her mother. Do people call you mother?"

"No."

"Why not?"

"I've never thought of myself as a mother. I don't feel very motherly, and I've never had a maternal instinct."

I challenged her gently. "I think that somewhere in your body is a mother."

"Maybe," she softly answered. "I guess I must be because I take care of a lot of kids at school. I guess I just don't like the label."

"You just don't want to let everybody know," I quickly added, "because too many people would come to you for mothering."

"Yeah!" Christine rolled with laughter.

"It's because you're so good at it," I piped in. "You walk in a room and people sense there's something there that they're comfortable with. And they can say things they wouldn't feel comfortable saying with others. So you're the mom of the whole school."

Christine paused before concluding, "Yes, I am mom for the kids and for the teachers too. I am a mom." She shook my hand as confirmation of this agreement.

During our talk, I continued to notice how close Christine was with her friend Shelley. They pointed to each other and made frequent eye contact like sisters who are best friends. The mojo doll agreed that this was the time. It felt like the right moment for a shaking mother to dance with her friend and maybe shake her up in a transformative way. I invited Shelley to come up and join us. I then said to them, "It's interesting how in sync you both are with each other right now."

Shelley agreed, "We've been friends for a long time." I found out that they first met in college, where they both taught writing classes. Now they frequently exchanged emails and talked on the phone.

I asked them, "Are you both the exact same height?" I don't have to say how I thought of asking this. Mojo directs, and I follow.

Shelley answered, "I am five four and a half." Christine acknowledged that she is the exact same height. This is intriguing—it highlights a bit of mystery in their relationship. I was reminded of how the ethereal girl who visited my home years before had dissolved into a wooden doll. At the time I didn't know whether it was more accurate to say that the girl became the doll or the doll became the girl. Two things that once appeared different suddenly became the same. In this session, two friends were appearing more similar than different. Like the little girl and the dancing doll, these two women had the potential to bring more creative animation to one another.

"Isn't that interesting? Do you finish each other's sentences? Do you know what the other's going to say before she finishes the sentence?"

Christine acknowledged that this was true. "We can anticipate what we're thinking, and we find the same things to be funny."

I asked Shelley, "So what's your favorite thing about Christine?"

She didn't hesitate. "She's soft and strong at the same time. Her softness isn't a weakness in her, and her strength isn't a shield."

My mojo doll teased me, whispering, "It sounds like they are describing a new kind of doll!"

I then asked Shelley, "What do you hope for her more than anything?"

Shelley accepted the challenge and spoke freely. "Maybe a swim in the ocean this summer. The summers keep going by, and we don't wind up fully in the water. Only our toes feel the wetness. I'd like for us to jump in."

Christine agreed, "Jump in, yeah!"

My mojo doll knew what they wanted: more animation and spirit to get their lives moving in the free-flowing stream of life. It recognized its sisters—two dolls ready for spirited action. I stayed with what they had presented. "So let's assume you jumped in the ocean this summer. You swam somewhere. What would you like to have happen in the ocean that's never happened to you before? What if you both turned into mermaids?"

My mojo doll knew what they wanted: more animation and spirit to get their lives moving in the free-flowing stream of life.

Christine showed immediate delight and proclaimed, "That would be cool. Or we could be swallowed up by a whale and taken to different places before being spit out on the shore. We could experience it and pop back in the whale's belly before being swum to the next place. But we can't let the whale men get us. The Japanese are fishing for whales. I don't want to talk about that."

The dancing mojo doll noticed that Christine was afraid, so it wanted us to dance with that fear. I accordingly made the first step and said, "So you worry too much."

"Yes, I do. Sometimes I just—"

I interrupted once she had confirmed this, "So this is why you've really come here today. You worry too much. You worry that you might be harpooned."

Christine agreed, "Yes, I might be harpooned. I might make the wrong decision to take an adventure that gets me harpooned. Although that has not happened before, it's always in the back of my mind."

I turned to Shelley to ask her, "Does she show you this side? Does she show you that she sometimes worries too much?"

Shelley acknowledged that she does, but then Christine interrupted to say, "Shelley worries for me if I don't worry." I asked if Christine did the same for Shelley, and she did.

The mojo doll was delighted that they already danced their worries. We decided to follow this lead and suggest some new dance steps. "So you worry about each other. You have a worry exchange program." Everyone laughed about this absurd proposition. But to my surprise Shelley took no time to admit, "We were just talking about this!"

"Then you must do it in a more organized manner," I responded. "Because it's confirmation that the universe is saying this needs to be done." In other words, the mojo doll was asking for this. By handling the worries of others, it helps free people to move on with their lives.

Christine agreed, "Let's do it. This would be good."

I was ready to spotlight the importance of this move and turn on the dance hall music. In my mind, I was thinking that it was time for the mojo doll to present some sizzling choreography. "When you figure out how to do this worrying for another person, sell it! Create a big business. Tell people that you two will worry for them, but at a price."

Christine loved this idea. "That's great. It's perfect."

I kept the conversational ball rolling. "There's already house sitting and babysitting, so why not have worry sitting!"

Christine was on board. "Worry sitting! Give us your worries, and go and have a good time!"

"Absolutely! You can offer a twenty-four-hour plan, a weekend plan, or a life plan. Sell family coverage," I added.

"Yes," Christine said with her eyes on fire with a newborn sense of purpose. "Let's offer worry insurance! We've got you covered."

The mojo doll suddenly performed an extraordinary pirouette and reminded us that in Mexico, they have worry dolls. "Let's call the two of you the Worry Dolls." Need I mention that the mojo doll was dancing, leaping, and flying all over the room?

Shelley looked surprised. "That's pretty funny because right before Christine came up here, I was telling her that I was worried about something that had to do with dolls." If there was any doubt, now I knew why the mojo doll was my co-therapist in this session.

Christine stepped in to explain. "You see, Shelley has all these dolls, and she doesn't know what to do with them when she dies. They are a very special collection of dolls."

I couldn't help but exclaiming, "Perfect! Put them to work! You have some professional Worry Dolls looking for a gig!" We all laughed together.

I suggested that they create a website for their worry dolls so they could market their service. When Shelley commented that she had two hundred dolls, I again told her to get those dolls to work. Christine turned to look at Shelley and said, "I love it. We'll do it."

"I think you might," I added. "Do you want the money from this new business?"

They both said that the money is not important. They wanted the experience of doing it.

I responded, "Then you won't have to worry about it. This will be the one thing you don't have to worry about. Worry Dolls, Inc. What a story!"

I could see that Shelley was starting to worry. She said, "I'm feeling protective already."

I anticipated this reaction and was ready. "You're worried about the dolls."

"Yes," Shelley quickly responded. "I always have been worried about them."

I provided some advice. "Then you need to set aside some dolls that will worry about the other dolls."

Shelley got it. "That's perfect. That's really perfect. I feel better already."

Having previously heard that Shelley had produced documentary films, I added this challenge: "Why don't you create a documentary as if all of this already happened? Make it from the perspective of the future. This documentary would tell the story of what you did over the next five years. Show how it took five years for you to be an international sensation. Show the actual physical room where it all started. You might even be able to use some of the footage we took today. Where do you keep the dolls? Are they in your bedroom?"

"They used to be, but now they are displayed in the foyer. I had an apartment renovation, and they were the main part of it."

I had no idea that the dolls were actually a major organizing aspect of her life. Now I could say with authority, "This has been preordained. You didn't even know why these dolls had such a hold on you."

Shelley added, "I did try to get permission from the creator of the dolls to write a book about them. They are called Topo Gigio dolls. They're little mice dolls with ears. One of them was on *The Ed Sullivan Show* thirty times. That doll is known all around the world. I even went to Italy and met with the creator of Topo Gigio."

I underscored the drama that was unfolding. "Wow, you met with the dolls' god?"

Shelley said that she wanted to publish a book about the dolls. "I had created a book with my friend, and we wanted to get permission to actually publish it. This was twelve years ago."

I was stunned by the importance the dolls held in this woman's life. "This is unbelievable. Did you get permission?"

"Yes I did, and I lived in Italy to have access to archives and make it all happen. But my collection of these dolls was not the real character, so I got stuck."

I responded, "They are your dolls, and you've already seen how serious these dolls can be. You've seen how it involved a pilgrimage taking you to the god of the dolls. Some people might wonder why in the world you created the most special place in your home for these dolls. You have lived a life organized around these dolls. It would only make sense that you and the dolls are searching for the purpose of your lives, for a mission. You found each other, and now you know your destiny. This is extraordinary. I'm starting to believe it's true. You have mojo dolls. And you have a mojo mission. I think someone is saying that this is Mojo Topo."

I couldn't help but revel at the sweet absurd truth of this woman's relationship to her dolls and how it had generated a source of mojo she could tap into for helping others. The mojo doll I first met years ago had dissolved into the conversation of these women. I remembered again how the dream-like girl had merged with the wooden doll, and how it was experientially possible to transfer an essence, spirit, or emotional presence of one thing into another. Worry dolls—from the perspective of magical thinking—can easily absorb the worries of others. The dancing doll had taught me that this was natural.

"I'd really love to see a documentary about this," I added. Shelley pointed out that a movie was made about this kind of doll. I again suggested, "Can you make a documentary even if it is only ten minutes long?"

Christine asserted herself, "Yes, we can do that. Let's do it. We'll do it."

"Go ahead and create your future now and then broadcast it," I added. "I'd recommend a musical, but I think that has already been done. I believe it was called *Hello, Dolly!*"

We laughed, but the idea was still very much alive. Christine took charge. "We're doing it. It's done. Say no more. It's happening."

I paused and then spoke slowly to both of them. "The only question I have is whether or not the dolls you now have, the ones that have been in some ways protective of the reality that you've created and the whole world that you live in, whether they are best suited for being the protection dolls. Nobody ever sees them. These are the ones who are behind the scenes. Maybe there need to be new dolls that these other dolls protect. What do you think?"

Shelley said, "I'm not interested in other dolls. That's the problem. These are the guys. This is the whole troop."

"Amazing," I responded. "Will they ever go on tour?"

To my surprise Shelley told me, "They already put on shows. There's a show being planned for when I get home—my spring production. The dolls put on little musical numbers."

Christine filled in the details. "She brings them to my house, they perform and torment the dog, and then she takes them away."

I asked, "Do they all have names?"

"Yes, they do. They all have names. One is Dalai Stickers."

I responded, "Good, he can worry about things that are sticky." We all had a good laugh.

How could I not say, "Well, we've really opened and walked into something here, haven't we?"

Shelley laughed as she commented, "We actually flew into this."

I silently heard my dancing doll wanting to tell them something, so I delivered its pronouncement: "We've walked into another reality that you already have been enjoying. Yes?" They both nodded and giggled. "Now more of us are a part of it. You are going to tell the world about what you've created. I've never known anybody who had such an army of dolls. It's time to put those Worry Dolls to work." As a celebration of her wild creativity, I concluded, "I can't wait to see the documentary, and I can't wait to see what happens in the world."

We stood up as we recognized that our dancing conversation had come to a natural end and gave each other a group hug. There was a buzz of excitement in the air regarding their new creative project—the birth and delivery of this unique form of mojo doll. Their very announcement would start a transfusion of mojo into the lives of others.

Shelley and Christine are women of action, and they subsequently gave careful consideration to how they would be partners in the ways these dolls could be brought to life in service of others. With the help of mojo, they found a creative outlet for their worries. They learned how worry can help their dolls come to life and, in turn, brought new ways of uplifting their everyday. When we creatively bring life to something that appears inanimate or dead, we awaken a magic that enlivens us. To become alive, raise the dead! This is one of the great teachings of mojo. Suffice it to say that both women are well on their way to becoming mojo doctors. Be on the lookout for their creative work.

When we creatively bring life to something that appears inanimate or dead, we awaken a magic that enlivens us.

The next time you see a doll, please pause and think about whether it is a candidate for carrying some mojo. In your imagination, consider asking it whether it is in show business. Or ask it to take a worry you are having difficulty releasing. When worry shows its face, know that it has a twin that wants to come to life. Allow worry to walk into an inanimate doll. Doing so transforms worry, enlivens a twin doll, and changes you. Dolls can perform all kinds of services when your creative imagination invites them to come alive.

Prescriptions for Transforming Worry

The dancing doll from South Dakota isn't the only doll that holds a forest spirit. There are others. That, you most likely already know. What is less known is that sometimes a medicine person made magical dolls by methods other than carving. She could make a mask of the spirit's face and then wear it. This, in effect, transformed a human being into a doll. It works both ways: the doll can become human or a person can become a doll. The mojo comes from the moment of transformation—the crossing from one form to another. This is a big teaching, and nothing more needs to be said about it now. Recognize that this action can bring mojo into your life.

Make yourself a mojo mask that can help turn you into an angelic doll. I recommend a simple though uncommon way of producing a spiritually enlightened mask. Take a blank piece of white paper and consider it the foundation for a special mask of your highest self, showing you as a being of light. Cut out the shape of a halo and gently place it on top of your head. Believe that this is a unique, over-the-top mask that is perfect for presenting your radiant perfection.

Whenever you feel that something is worrying you, put on your angelic mojo mask and, for a moment, allow yourself to become a specialized worry doll.

Whenever you feel that something is worrying you, put on your angelic mojo mask and, for a moment, allow yourself to become a specialized worry doll. Being a doll does not have to inspire a weird experience. It should take you back to your childhood, when it was common to play with dolls, whether they were Raggedy Ann dolls, Barbie dolls, G. I. Joe dolls, or Mojo Topo dolls. As a child, I had a Sad Sack doll based on a cartoon character who was a soldier of the lowest rank and kept experiencing the absurdities of military life. Dolls are made to play with; they are designed to bring you into the world of imagination. Become less serious when you bring out a doll. When you are a doll, become more childlike. Children are more capable of play and free-flight fantasy.

Put on your angelic mask, and in your living doll state, take that worry of yours and write it out on a piece of paper. Name or describe the worry in one sentence. Make sure that the sentence fits on one straight line. For example, you could say, "I'm worried about my kids," or "I worry about my health," or "I worry that I worry too much." Do not write more than one line because that would be too much to ask of any child who enjoys playing with dolls. Now be prepared to do something childlike.

53

When you have written out your worry as a one-line sentence, see that line as the spine of a stick-figure drawing of a doll. Add a head to the top, arms to the side, and legs for the bottom. Hold this stick figure worry doll on your knee and give it a little spanking with your finger. After that, tickle it with the tiniest finger of your other hand. Now say, "Your worry has been spanked and tickled. Now you can dance with the other dolls." Now dance the paper doll by the power of your own hands. If you prefer, attach a string to the top of the doll and hold the string. Dance it with your breath, blowing on the paper to make it move. As it dances for you, imagine that you are releasing the unmovable grip the worry used to have on you. I personally use a stick doll given to me by a healer in the Kalahari.

You may have some dolls and choose to do what Shelley did. Select one or more of them to handle your worries, or those of your friends or family. Put those dolls to work, but make sure you show your appreciation by taking their job seriously. Give them a little pat on the back for praise and encouragement.

Learn to enjoy playing with your worries, knowing that mojo can take you through a remarkable journey of transformation.

From time to time, a worry may get lonely and want to come play with you again, but this time you will know what to do with it. Rather than allowing it to suffocate you with obsessive, adulthood seriousness, put on your heavenly mask, get out your doll, and play with it as a child. Learn to enjoy playing with your worries, knowing that mojo can take you through a remarkable journey of transformation.

When I was a child, my grandmother, Bess Gnann, used to play the piano and sing for her friends and family. I was convinced she could have been a star of stage and screen. One of her favorite songs was the 1911 ragtime love song "Oh, You Beautiful Doll." The song was featured in several movies, including *For Me and My Gal*, *The Eddie Cantor Story*, and *The Taming of the Shrew*. It also played a prominent role in some Looney Tunes cartoons such as *Hair-Raising Hare*. If you ever get scared and find your hair raising but don't have a doll or mask by your side, I recommend singing this song. As you sing it, think of all the mojo dolls that would like to dance with you, helping you to transform fear and worries into a song-and-dance routine:

> *Oh! you beautiful doll,*
> *You great big beautiful doll!*
> *Let me put my arms about you,*
> *I could never live without you;*
>
> *Oh! you beautiful doll,*
> *You great big beautiful doll!*
> *If you ever leave me how my heart will ache,*
> *I want to hug you, but I fear you'd break*
>
> *Oh, oh, oh, oh,*
> *Oh, you beautiful doll!*

Welcome to mojo showtime! It's in the dreamtime. Step right up and meet the living dolls that will charm you right out of whatever needs to be released. Cross the border and become a child again. In the Neverland of imaginative voyage, troubles never need to stay. There, magical play lives forever, just waiting to sprinkle fairy dust all over whatever you bring to it. Need more directions? Then put on your angelic mask and listen to Peter Pan: follow the "second star to the right, and straight on till morning." Take your worries and sadness and fly them all the way to the stars, where they will look as small as the tiniest speck of dust.

If you want, forget all of this hocus-pocus, mumbo jumbo, voodoo-hoodoo stuff. Instead, go get yourself a Tinker Bell doll. Or if that is too much, just find a single bell. Hold it when you sleep and expect to wake up with a surprise. No need for things to be scary when you can sleep with a fairy. Hook yourself up with a living doll and find that mojo play will always get you off the hook.

3

THE BLESSINGS OF
VANISHING OBJECTS

When I was twelve years old, my grandfather took me on a train trip. We boarded a shiny silver passenger car on the Atchison, Topeka, and Santa Fe Railway late one night at Union Station in Kansas City, Missouri, and rode the rails all the way to Santa Fe, New Mexico. In the dining car, we met a well-dressed young man with black-rimmed glasses who was a journalist from Amsterdam. He had been sent to New Mexico to interview a Pueblo potter and wanted to have an adventure getting to know the people of our country by traveling across the country by train. We became his traveling companions.

When we arrived at Santa Fe, he asked if we wanted to come along with him. I begged my grandfather to accept the invitation. I had never been to Indian country, and this was an opportunity to visit both a land and culture of enchantment. We got off the train, hired a car, and drove to San Ildefonso Pueblo. There I met an American Indian for the very first time. She was Maria Martinez, the most famous Pueblo artist of all time.

I bought the smallest black pot she had and paid twenty-five cents for it. I remember her explaining that the revered black color of her pottery was made by throwing cow manure across the fire near the end of the firing process. Its smoke turned the clay black—

it carbonized it. Now that's some mojo: cook your art with manure. Since that time, I have learned that people also may cook their lives toward greater beauty by throwing their mistakes, foolishness, and existential crap into the fire of everyday living. That's how to be alchemically transformed into beauty.

Ever since that visit to the New Mexico Pueblo, I have taken good care of that pot. It was one of my first pieces of mojo, and it carried an important lesson. It also made me feel close to my grandfather, who had his own mystical life as a country preacher. That pot still accompanies me on my travels through life, a ride that is sometimes smooth and at other times rough, but with glory as the destination. That's the way my grandfather would have said it.

Many years later, in my adulthood and after I had become initiated as a mojo doctor in several African tribes, I decided to tell some therapists about what I had learned about healing in faraway places. At a professional conference, I shared some of my traveling healing stories. Some folks were excited about the news, but others cautioned me about mentioning these unexplainable experiences. They said I could ruin my professional reputation. I was known as a scholar and had written academic articles and books, but now I was talking about mojo. You can imagine the gossip this managed to brew.

When I came home, I said a little prayer because I didn't know if it had been wise to expose my relationships with diverse cultural mojo traditions. Keep in mind that I had not revealed much, though it seemed like a big disclosure at the time. Simply being open to considering something that is outside the recognizable boundaries of commonly regarded experience was enough to stir controversy in some mental health circles.

My prayer was simple and brief: "I am not sure about telling others about mojo. Please let me know whether this is what I should do. Please give me a sign." As I sincerely spoke these words out loud in my living room, I held the little black pot I'd received as a boy and rubbed it as if it were a magical talisman. I had barely finished saying the last word of my prayer when an impossible thing took place. I hesitate to even report it. *The pot simply disappeared from my hand.* Yes, I am saying that it vanished, dematerialized, or was zapped by the universe.

I looked to see whether it had dropped to the floor. I examined my hands in case it had crumbled into a powder. The academically trained mind fights seeing any miracle. It will invent ridiculous hypotheses to account for the unexplainable. I wondered right there and then whether a professional magician was hiding in my house, secretly performing a magic trick. I really did think that, but then it slowly dawned on me: There was no way to explain away what had happened. The pot had vanished just like that.

I was so overtaken by the shock of this realization that I felt my knees giving way. As I started to collapse to the ground, I learned that when the laws of everyday materiality are suspended, it feels like an internal explosion. A hole is opened in your mind. Your world and all the assumptions associated with it collapse and leak out of your formerly well-organized filing cabinet. Mine certainly did, and I didn't know how to express my extreme surprise. I certainly trembled and made some wild noises. Shouts of joy and a momentary fear of losing my mind danced together in that revolutionary moment when my mind was overthrown by the impossible. Reality is not limited to what our science books claim it is. There is more to our experience than rational reality. "Real" is as real as a soap bubble.

With this crack-in-the-cosmic-egg experience, I felt my closed bubble of reality pop and disappear. I had been encapsulated inside a cocoon made of cultural assumptions and had burst free of its cozy interior. The temple holding my everyday knowledge was leveled by an irrational earthquake. When one pillar collapsed, the whole thing fell apart. I was in a philosophical free fall as my new questions became louder than what I had previously considered answers and had never challenged.

My mind became so open that it released one assumption after another regarding what realities are possible.

I prayed again, this time expressing appreciation for the sign that had been given me. But being a university-trained skeptic, I still managed to conjure some doubt, unable to hold onto what I had experienced. I asked again, "Please show me that this is real." Again, the unexpected tapped me. I felt someone place something in my hands, but there was no one else in the room. I looked, and there was the black pot again. This time I did fall to the floor. I was unable to control myself. "My god, my god," I shouted. "I had no idea, no idea whatsoever, how mysterious everything is." Suffice it to say that ever since that moment, I have never taken seriously anyone's claim for objectivity. If an object can disappear, then so can objectivity! My mind became so open that it released one assumption after another regarding what realities are possible. That's right: endless realities, not just one.

The vanishing pot was the start of an interesting month of disappearing acts. During that time, I witnessed five objects disappear and then reappear. I was certain that I was not having alterations of positive and negative hallucinations (seeing versus not seeing what is there). I reminded myself that I had never taken any mind-altering substances, and my work as a scholar was still being published and not regarded as irrational. Surely, I was just being shown some mojo.

After that pot did its thing, I made contact with a renowned Zulu spiritual elder in southern Africa, Vusamazulu Credo Mutwa, who was known as the pope of all witch doctors. I would later write his life story, though I had already been on many wild adventures with him before I called about this particular concern. Some people consider Credo Mutwa to be the highest sub-Saharan African shaman alive today. Others see him as a charlatan. Whatever the case, his credentials inspired His Holiness the Dalai Lama to meet him on a visit he made to South Africa in April 2000. Mutwa was asked to throw the divination bones. This Zulu tradition utilizes a collection of sacred, symbolic objects that are thrown on the ground in a ritualistic manner. The patterns that the spread-out objects make are interpreted by the diviner, doing so with the guidance of ancestral spirits. After throwing them, Mutwa made a gasp and pointed to the pile of assorted items spread about. The spirits saw a carved hand with a small sword laying in it, while right next to the hand was a miniature gun made from wood. "Your hand, Your Holy One, stops the sword," stated the High Sanusi, as Mutwa is sometimes respectfully called. The Dalai Lama carefully scanned the whole pile and then pointed out something else. There was a carved, wooden toy car resting on its roof. "I like technology, so what can that mean?" he asked half jokingly, to which Mutwa replied, "Oh, that's nothing to worry about. That car is simply making love to the sky." His Holiness and everyone witnessing the divination burst into laughter.

Credo Mutwa was one of my mojo consultants, as was his aunt who initiated him and lived to be almost one hundred years old. I told Mutwa what had happened with the pot. He made a prophecy: "There will be a total of five more objects coming into your world, disappearing, and then coming back again. When this happens, make a list of the objects. Make sure you list them in the order in which they come to you. When this happens, contact me again, and I will tell you what to do. But make sure that you accept this as a natural thing. Do not get too excited and do not get scared."

Sure enough, a total of five mysterious objects came, vanished, and came back again. A (carved) eagle head, pot, otter bag, pin, and (painted) tree arrived and disappeared in magical ways. I went to see Mutwa, and he was ready for my return. He said in a matter-of-fact manner, "Take the first letter of the name of each object and see what word it creates. What does it spell out? What five-letter word have you been given? This is your answer." That's all he said, and I did what he suggested. The letters spelled out a word I was unfamiliar with at the time: *epopt*.

I soon discovered that it is a Greek word that originally referred to an initiate in the Eleusinian Mysteries of ancient Greece, a cult of Demeter and Persephone that was centered at the town of Eleusina. The word later came to mean a seer, someone initiated in the secrets of any mystical system. Back in Greek times, an epopt was one who attained *epopteia*, the seventh and highest degree of initiation in the Eleusinian Mysteries, a time when the gods luminously shine through you, indicating that you are one with divinity in the ecstatic experience. In other words, becoming a heavy-duty mojo doctor.

Epopteia was also called the "holy light of the holy night." I went to Eleusina and stood in the ruins of the old ceremonial grounds. I was filled with broad wonder as I contemplated how so many mojo doctors had faced a mysterious luminosity and become familiar with its secrets as the light poured into them. The early Greek philosophers knew about this mysterious form of teaching and Plutarch even described it as "a strange and wonderful light" that comes to meet you. This was certainly the case for me when I first met the light that opened the door to becoming a mojo doctor. I found this experience to be present in mojo cultures all over the world. My previous book, *The Bushman Way of Tracking God*, provides further discussion about this luminous opening to the original mysteries.

The vanishing pot was not a magical act staged for mere entertainment. It was the arrival of a mystery teaching that things sometimes appear and disappear in ways that go past our understanding of what is possible and real. The subsequent arrival of an ensemble of these particular mojo objects brought another gift: a word—*epopt*—that pointed to the source of all magic. The holy light of the holy night is the time and space for the creation of mojo. From that place, anything can appear or disappear.

The vanishing pot was not a magical act staged for mere entertainment. It was the arrival of a mystery teaching that things sometimes appear and disappear in ways that go past our understanding of what is possible and real.

Mojo doctors do not need to read textbooks, earn diplomas, or pay for professional licenses. They don't even have to know how to read. The same is true for any gifted artist. It was certainly the case for Maria Martinez, who could not read a word, including the highway sign that named where she lived. However, her family and friends would quickly point out that "she sure sees everything." Maria Martinez had mojo in her blood, and it transferred to her art.

I found another maker of mojo art through my first academic position at a university in west Texas. There, I met Richard, a retired fireman who, over several decades, had collected enough antiques from across the country to fill a warehouse. I had helped his family with a therapy issue, and as a gift, he gave me books from his inventory. One of the "books" he gave me was not really a book, though it looked like a giant manuscript to him. It was a portfolio of the earliest color sketches of the first modern Pueblo painters. The most famous of these artists, Awa Tsireh, has works in major museums including the American Museum of Natural History, the

63

Smithsonian, and the Museum of Modern Art in New York City. I found his work distributed in the lost portfolio that had been stored for more than fifty years in a Texan barn.

His illustration of a magical hawk sits near me as I write. Awa Tsireh was the brother of Maria Martinez. He, like his sister, knew that art is mojo. As American artist John Sloan once said about his work, "When Awa Tsireh sits down to paint a leaping deer, he remembers not only the way the deer looks leaping over a log but feels himself leaping in the dance." He also felt the flight of the hawk that now sits next to me, and I have no doubt that he would have felt the flying drum when it lifted the spirits of those who sought its mojo. Art does not need someone to read it. It requires a heart bridge to cross so that it can be felt directly, free of interpretation and word-built understanding. An open heart that feels art, or receives its vibe, is able to download its mojo.

Mojo needs to keep circulating in the world.

What is important about the disappearing pot and other mojo art that has come and gone in my life is that it brought more heart and soul medicine to help people who seek healing and guidance. As a mojo doctor, I have been very lucky; Mojo comes to me without my asking, whether it is an ancient magical instrument, a sacred art, or an enchanted item from Mother Nature. I have given as much of it away as I have received. Mojo needs to keep circulating in the world. Again, we must remember that all these gifts come to help us serve others.

Cancer for Sale—No Longer Have Time or Space

The importance of circulating mojo is especially relevant for people who suffer and believe that they want to get rid of something troubling them, whether it is a psychological symptom, an undesired behavioral habit, or the presence of a serious illness. I was conducting a demonstration of mojo work when a woman from the audience interrupted my therapeutic conversation with another person. She shouted out, "Stop! Please stop. I need to talk. I cannot wait any longer. I am sick with cancer and need to work with you now." I looked into the audience and saw a middle-aged woman whose face was visibly worried and stressed by her condition. Her request was both sincere and desperate. I started talking to her as she sat in the audience.

I told her about my old Zulu friend. "You remind me of a story of Credo Mutwa, a crazy old Zulu man who once went to a medical doctor. The doctor examined him, ran some tests, and announced, 'This is a very serious condition that you have. I think that at this stage, you don't have long to live. You have advanced melanoma.'

"When Credo heard the doctor's diagnosis, he replied, 'Melanoma? That sounds like the name of a beautiful woman. I shall devote my life to building the largest statue I am possible of creating in honor of this grand, glorious, and beautiful woman.' Credo left the doctor's office and proceeded to build a large mechanical crane, gather some supplies, and make a giant concrete statue of Melanoma, his new goddess. You could say that Credo built himself a very big doll. He set the stage for a magical transformation. Devotion to his inanimate hunk of concrete helped turn it into a goddess.

"He gave his life to creating this work of art. He expressed his deepest feelings for the mythological woman whose love he now longed for. He gave his life to Melanoma. That was twenty years ago. It wouldn't have mattered if that was the final chapter in his life, would it? It wouldn't matter because Melanoma gave him life. Full life is experienced as an eternity even if it's only for a second of clock time." For Credo, his goddess took away his melanoma, doing so as he threw his heart and soul into bringing her alive. His cancer disappeared while his belief in the impossible reappeared.

"You see, the big secret is that most people are the walking dead. They are a zombie movie. But every once in a while, death knocks on someone's door or it gets to a friend, a child, or a loved one. Then, to our surprise, it paradoxically delivers a moment of life. In the face of death, we can awaken our relationship to existence. So if you are worried about a part within you, maybe you ought to find another kind of relationship with it."

The woman, who introduced herself as Karen, responded in a way I hadn't expected, "Right on. We've been hanging out a long time." She laughed and continued, "And my cancer and I are good friends."

The vanishing pot is my expert on things that come and go. It comes to me and suggests an interesting question. When I say that my mojo talks to me, you should realize that my mojo is now an inseparable part of me. It is me. When I talk about mojo, my mojo is talking. When it needs to voice a message, I talk. When the drum flies, my mind flies. As the doll comes to life, so do I. If a pot disappears, so can anything else. This woman was in trouble and my mojo came forth, ready for action. It spoke and I spoke at the same time: "I need to ask whether you live in an apartment or a house."

The vanishing pot is my expert on things that come and go.

"I have a house."

"Does it have one floor or two floors?"

"Two floors."

I was locked into following the tracks of where mojo was taking us and asked in an altered tone, "I'm speaking to your unconscious. What floor does that part that you worry about live on?"

"It lives in the basement," she said clearly.

I stayed on track with this inquiry. "The basement. Which corner? Or is it a corner? Or is it in the middle? Is it in a box? Is it wrapped up? Has it been forgotten?"

She almost giggled. "It's funny. I see two places. I see the bedroom, and I see the basement. In the basement I see it over in a corner where the laundry area is."

My mojo suggested I voice an odd question. "Is it wrapped in an old newspaper?"

Startled, she gathered herself and honestly remarked, "Well, as soon as you say that, I see that."

I felt the mojo pulsing in the room, so whatever words came up in my mind, I wouldn't interfere with their immediate delivery. "Is it a classified ad?"

Karen laughed. "Well, it could be. I'll go with that. I see the print. It's black print."

"What might it say?" I asked. "What might one word be in that print?"

She said, "*The.*"

I wanted to make sure I hadn't missed something. "The?"

Karen kept reading the fine print in her imagination. "I see more now. It says, The space.... *The space of time.* That's what I see."

"So these words are holding your house," I proposed, bringing a bit of confusion to our encounter.

She looked puzzled and asked for clarification. "What's holding...?"

I kept it ambiguous. "It's holding your house."

"What's holding my house?" Karen still wanted to know.

"It's holding your house," I said with a louder emphasis on the word *it.* I continued, "The space of time. The basement. It's your foundation in some way, huh? In some way, it's part of the foundation of where you live."

Karen saw what was underneath this discussion. "Yes."

Mojo was asking for the newspaper print to be repeated. "*The space of time.*"

This session was bringing forth magical words for her, just like the disappearing objects brought me a word that pointed to the heart of ancient mysteries. She, too, would be shown an illuminated path toward changing parts of her life.

**This session was bringing forth magical words for her,
just like the disappearing objects brought me a word that
pointed to the heart of ancient mysteries.**

"Perhaps you are looking at a classified ad. At least you've seen it as such. For a moment, this thing is wrapped in old print with words giving it a particular meaning. Maybe you should think of putting it in another room."

Karen frowned and voiced her disgust with her sickness. "It's kind of horrible. I don't really like it. It's kind of like a hard turd or something."

Thinking of Maria, the creator of my disappearing pot, I recalled how mojo likes to play with manure. When used correctly, it helps make pottery have a beautiful black shine. I accordingly responded with great interest. "Yeah? Well maybe you should give it a makeover." We both started laughing.

I continued. "What I was thinking of when you first spoke is that somehow it's good for you to move your furniture around in your house. When was the last time you changed your furniture— I mean, moved your furniture?"

Karen's circumstances fit the question. "Well, just a week ago, I brought a piano in. My father died recently, and my parent's home has just been sold, so there's been a lot of furniture moving. I have been selling and letting some things go. There's a whole family structure that's now gone. I brought the piano in. I was going to sell it, but I brought it to my home, and there're only certain ways the furniture will fit because it's a small house . . ."

At this point, I felt it was time to bring Karen to the stage. Prior to this, we had been talking back and forth across the audience. Now my mojo wanted to get things moving—from her location in the room to the furniture in her house.

"Would you mind sitting up here?"

Karen made her way to the front of the audience and sat next to me as we faced one another. As I started talking with her, I turned away from her and gazed at the place where she had been sitting the moment before. I pointed there and started a talk that brought what we just said to our present moment.

"You know the last time I was here, there was a woman sitting over there who reminded me of you. She had a similar complaint."

Karen thought I was not talking about her. "Hmmm."

"She was worried about her life, about something that had come into her life, into her body, and didn't know how to relate to it and was confused about the choices. She didn't know whether to see it as a disease that threatened her life or to see it differently. Many people made suggestions, and she was frustrated about how to sort through all of that. As best as I can remember, I asked her where she lived. Did she live in an apartment, or did she live in a house?"

Karen acknowledged, "Right."

"She said, 'A house.' I replied, 'Was it one story or two stories?' She answered, 'Two stories.' And I said, 'Where in that house did that surprise guest reside?'"

Karen started laughing as she realized what I was doing.

I continued with my reminiscence. "She then said, 'I think in the basement.' For some reason I asked, 'Is it wrapped in old newspaper?' She answered, 'Since you asked, I can see that.'"

Karen really laughed then.

"And then I asked her, 'Is it classified, a classified ad?' Members of the audience laughed when I said that. I wasn't sure why they laughed. I was confused by their laughter because I was exposing classified information."

Karen was taken by this metaphor. She visibly showed that she was facing a new insight into her situation.

I continued on, doing so while feeling the altered, enhanced state of consciousness that mojo inspires. I was letting things be said without following any textbook prescription for how to help another person. I was dispensing mojo, the creative flow of releasing whatever is cooked up in the moment, guided by the relational connection with another human being. In those moments, the relationship between us is in charge; it is something bigger and more mysterious than either one of us.

I proceeded in this mode of expression. "So I thought to myself, *I wondered what she would see, because she was so focused and serious about this matter.* I was sure she would take the next step and put a little effort into trying to bring her inner focus to help her see what was written on the newspaper. She saw the single word *the.*"

Karen was moved by this engagement as she shook her head in amazement and said, "Oh my God!"

"Then she said there were some other words. They were either *The space of time* or *The time of space.*"

I went on with this, "I thought to myself, well that covers it all: space and time, time and space. Add an *e* to the word *the*, and it becomes *thee*. Eternity."

"Yes," Karen agreed with this point.

The day before, Karen had asked me whether she could have a session with me. I brought this to our present moment as I continued, "I remembered that the day before, the woman had asked me, 'Could we have a chance to talk the next day?'"

Karen laughed and turned to the audience, saying, "Which I did."

What Karen and the audience did not know was that I had been awakened in the middle of the night by my mojo. It told me that I would speak to her later that day and that I should tell her that she should move her furniture around. This is how it works for all mojo doctors. Some of my teachers have often dreamed their clients before seeing them. They already knew what to say at the beginning of a session.

I then told the audience that I woke up in the night, knowing I would tell her something. "Being a very different kind of person, I no longer have any curiosity as to why I would dream such a thought. I just know that I will say it to you and that it is the right thing to say."

Karen accepted this explanation. "Of course."

"I just remembered to remember that thought for that space and time. So at this time and in this space, I think it might be interesting for you to know, like that woman (I looked to where she had been sitting) and this woman (I looked at her), there's always at least two floors."

Karen nodded her head in agreement as I spoke.

"Sometimes you can go up, and sometimes you can go down. But for all the things in your house, you do have some say about where they're going to reside."

"I do," she responded.

I felt the vanishing pot fully present in the room. The flying drum and the dancing doll had been summoned and were also present. A mojo gathering had come together in this time and place, and all of its players wanted to speak. The encounter continued.

"You can give them different names. Sometimes you can worry about them. Sometimes you can laugh about them. Sometimes you can even—"

I was stopped in my tracks because the mojo was showing me what the woman must do. It sent a current of energy down my back. I made a special announcement. "That's it! Oh, I just got a little ripple of excitement. This is what I think you must do: you should put a classified ad in the newspaper seeing if anybody would like to buy this part of you."

She immediately burst into laughter.

I wasn't through delivering the message. "The ad should say *My cancer's for sale*."

As she gasped and laughed from her belly, I shouted out, "Whoa, isn't that an interesting way to live!"

Someone in the audience shouted out, "Wonderful!"

I responded gently, "So you'll have to decide."

Karen responded in kind, "I'll have to decide."

The mojo then pulled the rug from underneath her. "You'll have to decide how big the ad will be."

She joined me. "And which paper it will go into."

Seeing she was on board, I amplified the challenge. "You just might consider a full-page ad."

Karen wasn't shy at all. "All right."

Then I got serious. "It depends on how important it is for you to get on with this."

Karen was serious. "Right."

The mojo was going to do its work. Led by the wisdom of the vanishing pot, she was going to be told how she could move things around and, in so doing, be shown how things could change and get smaller and smaller. "But of course, you know, if you see a full-page ad, you can always reduce it to being a small full-page ad that appears to be smaller even though it's actually a full-page ad in your mind. That's how it began."

"Right."

I was reminding her that she had more choices than she might have imagined. "These are important choices, but only you can navigate through that."

"Right."

"You can know whether it's going to be small or big—whether you'll describe what you're offering is small or big. And of course, whether it's small or big depends on what floor it's on and how it's staged to the world."

I paused because I saw that she was taking all of it in. I also saw that she was in her head, searching for a rational understanding. She was ready to ask a question, but she only got the first word out of her mouth: "So—"

I immediately cut her off. The mojo came forth and made her question disappear. I said, "Don't think."

Karen was startled by the interruption and started laughing.

I reminded her of the advertisement she was to create—*For sale: A part of me.*

Someone in the audience provided another way of advertising: "*Do you want a piece of me!*" This brought the house down with laughter.

I continued with other ideas. "Some might say: *Cancer looking for another home.*"

An audience member moved by the mojo said, "In another space."

I echoed the mojo talk: "Another space and another time."

This caught her off guard. At first she said, "That, I like." But then added, "I really don't want anybody buying it, you know?"

There's no way to reason with mojo once it gets started. It was flowing and was going to improvise and utilize whatever came up in the session. "OK. Is it going to be for free? Or are you giving it away?"

Now she rebelled, but with a smile. "No."

I went on. "Some ads say that a person has something and they are looking for somebody who'd like to take it."

"That's true. I just did that with my parents' furniture."

I quickly jumped in. "That's another idea. You could have a yard sale."

Karen nearly fell out of her chair laughing. Then she got serious. "OK, I can see that, but somebody picking it up bothers me. If I make a newspaper ad and put the cancer for sale along with some of the old knickknacks of my folks, someone will come around and ask, 'Oh, what's this? I'll buy it.' I don't want somebody taking that."

My mojo teased her. "Oh, so you prefer keeping it in your home."

"No! But I don't want somebody else taking it into their life."

"Then you'll have to change it so it's something that will be that which you will be happy to see them take."

She was looking for a way this could work. "OK."

"Why don't you say it's a pet cancer?" Everyone laughed at this intriguing absurdity. I went on. "Maybe you need to put it in a bird-cage. What kind of cage would you choose? Would it be a cage for hamsters or a cage for . . ."

Karen answered, "I saw a birdcage."

"What size?"

"I saw one of those old-fashioned birdcages."

I was pleasantly surprised because I saw the same thing in my imagination. The mojo was leading both of us. "Yeah, that's what I saw. Victorian?"

"Yes."

"That's what I saw too. Interesting. We're in the same space and time, aren't we?"

Karen confirmed our mutuality in the moment. "We're in the same space and time."

I started to ask her a question, but she had already considered it. I could only get the first words out. "Would it be—"

She already answered, "It might be hard to give away!"

"That's what I was thinking! Maybe you'll decide that this cancer should be your pet held in a cage that makes it beautiful. I don't know! Maybe you just need to move it around first. Put an ad in the paper saying you're thinking about giving it away and you'll entertain offers. Or maybe you should go halfway in between. Maybe you should rent your pet cancer. People could check it out for a couple of days."

Karen took a stand. "No! None of that! I know about teetering around with it. I know about how it can come and go. Yes. No. Yes. No. Here it's back. No, it's not. Oh, I'm healed. No, I'm not. Oh, I know about the vanishing and reappearing act."

My vanishing pot knew why it had been called here to help this woman. It carries mojo for such a concern. It continued to direct the movement of our transformative encounter.

I spoke for the vanishing pot. "You know about being inside a cage."

"Absolutely! Absolutely!" She started to weep. "I do, though it has brought me so many gifts. But I still can't get it out. I know the shadow of it. I know the shadow of how it has defined me. I know the shadow of how it has been my—"

I interrupted, "I know the word. It has been your master. You've been the pet. It's time to turn that around. Go get a cage of the right size for the right space so you'll see who's the master."

"I will do that."

"And put out an ad."

"I will do both."

"Great!"

Karen leaned over and indicated she had something else to share. "I previously asked for a dream in case we would meet and talk about my situation. I had two dreams. Do we have time for me to speak about those dreams?"

I started an answer. "Yes, it's always time—"

And she finished it, "And space." We both laughed.

"This is the space," I added.

Karen told her dream. "A number of months ago, I had a dream that I was in a room and there was a woman behind the desk. She had her magical objects in front of her. I couldn't see her face."

I interrupted, "This is what we've been talking about, you know."

"Yes. And there were boxes like bento boxes on the desk. I then saw an image of myself, and I said, 'That isn't for me anymore, but this image is. I can pass over to another image of myself.'"

Again, I said, "We've been talking about this today."

"Yes, exactly. In the next moment, a young woman from my high school who I haven't thought of in a long time suddenly appeared. The woman behind the desk said, 'Ah, she knows everything about benches, and she will find your bench for you. I'm going to make a ceremony for you. The tumor is over.' After that dream, I had a lot of difficulty. My father died, and he had always been working with me. Furthermore, the tumor that had been contained for about three years has grown. It has grown over the last few months, which has been upsetting in terms of what that might mean. I feel that the dream hasn't come to completion, and there's something in me that is not able to complete—"

The mojo demanded to have its say. "Well, of course! It's because you're out to lunch."

We both laughed as she got the joke. She added, "Yes, you mean my bento box." We remembered how a bento box is a Japanese lunch box filled with all kinds of savory surprises.

I switched to getting serious. "Then maybe you need a bench. It would be a nice place for that Victorian cage which holds all your old-fashioned ideas."

Karen was powerfully struck by what this meant. She literally rose from her chair, and her whole body trembled from head to toe. She exclaimed, "Oh! Love that!"

I saw her body trembling and praised it. I pointed to her body and shouted, "Oh yes! That's exactly what you should do on your bench. That is it!" I pointed to how she was shaking, and I demonstrably shook to add an emphasis to the importance of her ecstatic body expression. I continued, "Do this so you can move around all the furniture within you."

The audience shouted, "Yes! Yes!"

What was remarkable about Karen's dream is its relation to the ancient samurai healing practice that is part of the lineage of my mojo expertise—seiki jutsu. It refers to the art of moving the life force throughout your body, doing so for healing and well-being. When this takes place, you can see your body tremble, shake, and make automatic movements. Its practice takes place on a bench called a seiki bench. Karen's dream and her trembling body held all this wisdom. I enthusiastically praised these aspects of her report, including her reference to Japan with the mention of a bento box.

It had come to the moment when I needed to wrap up my conversation with Karen because all the mojo she needed had been delivered. I took a deep breath and delivered my conclusions.

"You know what to do. So go be it. In this time and space. For all space and all time, and any time and any space, first or second floor. Even in a basement. Inside and outside, do it for her." I pointed to where she had formerly been sitting in the audience. "She was like you in a time I remember not so long ago. Because that time is this time and all time."

Metaphorically speaking, on one floor, things appear, while on another floor they disappear. Each floor is a different place and time, a separate reality. We are free to move from floor to floor, shifting from one reality to another, doing so as we watch former things vanish while discovering other things come to life. On one floor, we're inside a cage; on another, we are free. In one space, it's another time. In another time, it's a different space. Mojo walks across the borders of different realities. In the interstitial tissue that connects multiple realities, drums fly, dolls dance, and pots disappear. Moving within and across these spaces charges our body to tremble with joy, while initiating movement and transformation inside every organ, cell, and molecule.

**Mojo walks across the borders of different realities.
In the interstitial tissue that connects multiple realities,
drums fly, dolls dance, and pots disappear.**

We stood and hugged one another. In our embrace, her body trembled again and indicated that she was on her way to living with some new mojo. Her *ideas* about her cancer were free to move in any direction and be as small or as large as she chose. The same was true for what the gods could do with her cancer.

It is never solely about the nature of the condition you have. It is about dancing with whatever life brings you even if it is a troubling cancer. Perhaps you have something that is a part of you that needs some spiritual movement. Now is the time and space for you to go up and down, in and out, as some things disappear and others reappear.

Prescriptions for Clearing the Slate

Here's a prescription for creating your own vanishing pot. Purchase an Etch A Sketch. When you get it, draw a tiny pot on it. (It doesn't have to be an elaborate rendering. Any simple sketch of a pot will do.) Hum or sing as you do this because mojo is always drawn to music. Once you have drawn it, put the Etch A Sketch away in a safe place so no one can bother it. That night, before you go to bed, take out the sketch and stare at the pot. Stare as if you could magically set the pot on fire. Envision yourself playing your flying drum—your ticket to the shifting realities of mojoland—as you allow your stare to be a trance flare. Keep singing as you do this. Then give it a good shaking and notice how the pot disappears.

A good shaking clears the slate. It not only empties whatever your vessel holds but it gets rid of the whole container. It makes you a disappearing pot.

Know that the same is true for you. If you allow yourself to be shaken by life, it can erase whatever stuck ideas, behaviors, feelings, attitudes, beliefs, mind-sets, love maladies, loneliness, difficulties, challenges, symptoms, and difficult conditions you presently embody. A good shaking clears the slate. It not only empties whatever your vessel holds but it gets rid of the whole container. It makes you a disappearing pot.

When you shake your Etch A Sketch, feel that you are shaking yourself. Start doing this every night before you enter your new dreams. Think of the words of Edward Everett Hale, an early writer for the *Atlantic Monthly* and former minister of the South Congregational (Unitarian) Church in Boston back in the late 1800s: "Sometimes your medicine bottle has on it, 'Shake well before using.' That is what God has to do with some of his people. He has to shake them well before they are ever usable."

When you wake up, draw another pot. Think about how it is new and has never been seen before. It arrives empty, ready to hold whatever the day brings. Imagine that every undesired thing that happens to you will go into the pot. At the end of the day, you will be able make the whole pot vanish, taking away all its contents. At the same time, realize that whatever authentic mojo came to you didn't disappear. It was absorbed into your heart and soul.

The drawn pot symbolizes your mind and the wordy stuff it holds onto. Your mind processes the ideas you hold about your experience, and sometimes it needs digestive help. What should take place is that you keep the nutritious parts of your experiences and let the rest go. Unfortunately, when we hold onto everything that enters our mind, we feel discomfort. That's when we get a mental tummy ache.

With this in mind, consider your Etch A Sketch to be a mental waste management system. Consider taking a Magic Marker and writing *Ty-D-Bol* on top of it. Or if you are more artistically inclined, draw a crescent moon. Wake up each morning and proceed to gobble up the forthcoming day, allow it to digest, and then shake and flush away the waste. This is powerful mojo. Getting rid of what you don't need is as important as getting what you do need. Maria, the potter from San Ildefonso, might go further and say that it can make good compost for fueling the fire that brings forth your inner beauty.

Consider anything that disappears from your mind to be part of God's sanitation program. Here, intake and elimination are equally important and inseparable. Your vanishing pot is part of a holy plumbing system that takes away the garbage that becomes toxic if you sit too long with it. To stay vitally alive, make sure you have a means of handling your psychological garbage.

If this mojo pot makes you too squeamish or you don't feel comfortable handling metaphorical sewage, then try out an alternative means of addressing whatever it is that needs to disappear. I recommend that you get yourself a magic wand. You can make one or purchase it from a magic shop. Every night before you go to bed, get out one of your hats. (It doesn't matter what kind it is. It is simply going to be used to hold the stuff you place in it.) With your hat in one hand, pretend that you are putting in all the experiences of the day that were not pleasant for you. Perhaps someone was mean to you or a project didn't work out. Maybe you felt tired or got into an impasse with a friend, colleague, or spouse. Whatever it is, imagine that you are dropping it in the hat.

Now pick up your magic wand and wave it over the hat three times. Hum a little overture music and then say out loud, "Alakazam, this stuff is damned! Take it away before I get in a jam!" Pretend that it all disappears just like it would in a good magic show. Know that the act of performing this scenario actually sets mojo in motion. You can't think these things away; you have to carry out a performance in which every part of your body is involved. This is how mojo works. It is not about gaining new understandings. It requires radical, out-of-the-box action—something that can shake things up. Wave your wand and watch the magic begin.

When you start a relationship with disappearing mojo, I recommend that you write yourself a postcard at least once a week. Address it to Merlin, Houdini, or Sylvini, but make it in care of your address. Tell your magician of choice that you are happy when he waves his wand. Tell him that every time you wave at someone, it reminds you of waving a magician's wand. Go on to say that you fully hope that someday, magic will happen whenever you simply wave your hand. It will happen because the wand will become part of your inner mojo. It will jump inside your imagination and be inseparable from any waving motion you make. This is how it always was and always will be. If you don't believe this, then wave that impoverished belief goodbye. When you believe it, welcome it with an enthusiastic mojo wave of greeting.

Maria Martinez and Awa Tsireh grew up in a Pueblo culture where material objects were not given much importance. They didn't even have a written language. Maria, arguably the most famous potter of our time, was financially poor, but she considered herself rich. I am not speaking of spiritual wealth because her culture did not divide their spirituality from the rest of their life. There was only being alive in the fullest sense of the word. If money came your way, it was shared with your relations because happy relations were the source of happiness. In the old wisdom ways, treasure disappeared as soon as it arrived. But it never really disappeared; it just showed up somewhere else. It moved around the circles of relationship.

What needs released most in our lives is the attachment to things we think we cannot live without. Those things need to travel. Whether it's money, cool cars, hot furnishings, big houses, or fancy wardrobes, if we think our happiness is dependent upon holding onto them, then we need a good shaking and flushing that a disappearing mojo potion can help bring about. In addition, if we are keeping score of how much stuff we are eliminating in order to feel important, then that logbook also needs to vanish. A meaningful life is not about collecting. It is about appearing and disappearing, flowing with the natural rhythms of easy come, easy go.

Neither the night nor the day holds on. They release themselves to being transformed into their opposite. The same should hold true for you. Receive in order to give. Die in order to live. Disappear in order to make a new stage entrance on life's traveling mojo show.

I have a medicine for you. It's some crazy wisdom mojo. It asks that you disappear into your imagination. While you are there, reinvent yourself. Come back the next day reincarnated, recycled, rebirthed. Do this every day. But never get it right. The worse thing that could happen is that you become what you really think you want to become. That could be the end.

Enlightenment does not mean "en-right-enment." It is a dynamic that includes successes and failures in a never-ending dance. Make sure you take notice of all the errors and mistakes you make each day. Say a special thanks to them, for they enable you to get another ticket to come back. Said differently, you need to spread some manure over the fire that is cooking you. It will help make you a more beautiful pot. Do so as if you were the potter who shapes the form you are becoming and unbecoming. Be the smallest pot a fire can cook.

I received a letter from Karen several months after our conversation. She wrote:

Hi Brad,

I wanted to give you an update.

I posted an ad in the *Toronto Star* entitled, "Cancer for Sale—No Longer Have Time or Space." I found the perfect birdcage in a drive by sale on the way to a cottage. I also sent the cancer a "Dear John" letter. I actually mailed it. I think it was sad but understood it was over. The furniture in my house is moved.

I went to the corner of my basement and found I had stored a painting there that I did not like because of an abstract shape in the corner of the painting. It was sitting where I said the cancer lived in my house. The painting is moved. Perhaps I will leave it somewhere fitting in the city.

The shift from fear to confidence around the cancer was dynamic from the time we worked together. Thank you.

I recently received a checkup from my surgeon. Although the tumor was still there, the horrific surgical side effects she had previously discussed with me as a 50-50 risk factor had changed to being negligible. She also let it slip out that I would live to be an old lady. This comment could not have been based in her reality of talking to a patient with recurring cancer, but it was mysteriously said anyway. I felt my life had shifted into a new dimension of reality.

My longing is to keep the shaking happening and to keep on going.

Shaking all over,
Karen

Several months later she sent another letter:

Greetings Brad,

I met with a friend yesterday who I have not seen in years. She told me she had heard of someone who had placed an ad in the paper to sell their cancer.

Living in a new way. I will be in touch again.

Big love and delight to you,
Karen

I remembered our first conversation. Near the end, Karen had mentioned a dream of meeting someone from her past, a woman she had gone to high school with who told her—in the dream—that she needed to start shaking her life up. Karen did meet someone from her past who brought her news about how she had been pleasantly shaken by some recent news. I like to think that this happened because Karen enrolled in a higher school, the place where mojo teaches, guides, and heals.

In this place, things levitate, and mysteriously appear and disappear. You may even find yourself or a part of yourself in the news—perhaps the classified ads if it needs to be a well-spread secret. The mojo inside you may have been forgotten, but don't worry. That just proves it is disappearing mojo ready for you to call it forth with the wave of your hand. Greet it as a friend of a lost pot formed by the hands of a great potter—a mojo doctor who never read a word in her life. Call for the magic when you need it and know that it is ready to do its job, whether or not you see it or are able to read all about it in the news.

4

MOJO WORDS

Can the right words evoke magic? As a mojo doctor, I can tell you emphatically YES. A single word can bring on sudden and profound transformation. Through spontaneity, words also free up the tension between opposite or extreme ideas, allowing them to be teased and played with, which leads to even greater transformation. Words are a favorite playground for mojo. Literary mojo, as I call mojo in the form of words or books, can yield powerful effects once you start strategically placing it in your life.

Most of our everyday suffering is handled by words, whether in the office of a therapist, counselor, clergy person, spiritual adviser, coach, hairdresser, bartender, or close friend. We frame our problems with words, and we consider how to treat them through more talk and writing. When we find a magical word like *epopt* or construe words to bring a surprise in our life, like placing an unexpected ad in a newspaper, we find that a word can be more than a representation of what we already know. It can serve as a door to an alternative reality.

I was visiting the home of a university dean in South Florida when I walked into his library and a book immediately fell to the floor. I had not come close to a single volume; it appeared to have fallen of its own accord. I walked over to pick it up, and my hosts asked what had flown off the shelf. It was a book titled *The Zohar*, a foundational literary work in the Jewish mystical tradition known as Kabbalah. The wife of my host let out a shout, "Oh my God!" She took the falling book to have significance, but I wasn't sure what it meant. I listened to them tell me a bit about the book's importance, but I never followed up with any more inquiry. That was the end of it. Or so I thought.

Nearly a decade later, I had a dream to go to Venice, Italy, but decided against it. Then I received word that a volunteer worker at the Renato Maestro Library and Archives in the Ghetto of Venice had made a discovery. The library and archive housed books, manuscripts, and periodicals that had historical importance to the Jewish community of Venice. There Dr. Gadi Luzzatto discovered some boxes in a closet that had not been previously noticed or catalogued. He thought it might be the original publication of *The Zohar*. I remembered how a lively edition of that book had fallen off a shelf in a Fort Lauderdale home. My mojo started to buzz. I immediately booked a flight to Venice and made arrangements to see the old manuscripts.

It was possible that what had been hidden for centuries in Venice was the earliest known printing of *The Zohar*, a multivolume work that I learned was the most important contribution to the study of Jewish mysticism. When I arrived, I saw firsthand that the books had all the signs of being the very first volumes off the press. They showed the stamp of approval from the Catholic Church signed by Luigi da Bologna in 1558. The law back then required that all books be subject to approval or face censorship by the Catholic Church. The first book off the press had to be inspected and signed by the appropriate official. More important than the stamp of approval, however, was that the margins of these particular volumes contained extensive handwritten notes penned by Jewish scholars of that period. They presumably had never been seen, translated, or studied since then.

I secured funding from a foundation to restore the books, making sure the sensitive work was supervised by the most important restoration agency in the area, Save Venice Inc. As this process began, I learned that *The Zohar* was originally published during a time of vehement controversy, and the first edition was published in Mantua, Italy. The restoration of these important classics and the study of previously unknown commentary was an important undertaking.

The Zohar discusses the nature of God, the universe, the soul, our relationship to darkness, and "the light of God." When I was in Venice, I had visions the night before I was shown the books. I was shown what is called luminal darkness, referring to a light so bright that it is only visible as darkness. When we refer to the light of the dark, we draw upon a paradoxical way of communicating: we attempt to do the impossible and speak the ineffable, saying what cannot be said in order to see what cannot be seen. The early Kabbalistic view of the oral Torah, I later found out, was regarded as a "white fire written on black fire." This phrase obviously has multiple layers of interpretation, starting with the simple idea that printing requires black ink on paper. But there is also deeper meaning.

In my vision, I was taught that mystical experience is a form of paradoxical blindness, a higher order of knowing that requires utilizing the opposite of whatever you want to encounter as the means of meeting it. You know through unknowing and see through unseeing. As Elliot Wolfson, professor of Hebrew and Judaic Studies at New York University, concludes in *Language, Eros, Being*, "blindness . . . is true insight." It should not be surprising that *The Zohar* is assumed to have been composed by Shimon bar Yochai, a second-century rabbi who, during the time of the Roman persecution, hid for thirteen years in the darkness of a cave. There, he found the light of the dark and claimed that he was inspired by the Prophet Elijah to write *The Zohar*.

Elijah was a man who had his hands in life and death, darkness and light. He was known to have raised the dead, brought fire down from the sky, and ascended into heaven in a whirlwind. In Serbia and Bulgaria, he is regarded as the source of thunder during a storm. They call him Elijah the Thunderer. It seems fitting to say that the prophetic words of *The Zohar* were rumored to cause a book to fall off a shelf, stir winds of controversy, shake up lives with riddles as startling as a thunderclap, and bring new life to old beliefs.

When warm and cool air meet, wind is born. When opposites are brought together, something moves and comes to life. When darkness and lightness face one another, a wind of truth stirs us to go past the limitations of dualistic thinking that try to keep them apart. According to some scholars, *The Zohar* brings forth this idea, radically suggesting that even the divine is rooted in and sustained by the demonic. William Blake's sketch of God in his *Illustrations of the Book of Job* makes the same point when he shows a bearded face of a wise old man with feet that are the devil's hooves.

**When opposites are brought together,
something moves and comes to life.**

The Zohar teaches that ultimate perfection is containing the left in the right and seeing the light in darkness rather than separating the opposing realms. As *The Zohar* puts it: "Come and see: Light and dark were as one, light on the right, darkness on the left. What did the blessed Holy One do? He combined them and from them created the heavens." Floating at the midpoint of a polarity requires that we both hold on and let go. The mystical traditions occupy themselves with the journey to this center of the universe, a place where neither left nor right is victorious. In this vortex, where the whole is held by the presence and participation of all imaginable opposites, we find so-called magical action. Mojo lives at the center of creation. It lets go of everything so that it can be kept alive, holding the space for freedom of breath.

This mystical teaching came to me in the night while dreaming in Venice. I met *The Zohar* in the dark of dream before physically seeing it in daylight. I was shown scenes that depicted the marriage of good and evil. They were not the kind of teaching you might expect. For instance, in a dream, I experienced myself driving a car along a road stretching across endless miles of a wheat field. I picked up a hitchhiker, a young man who was quiet and appeared friendly. We drove along without saying a single word until I slowed down because I saw a huge black gate in the middle of the road up ahead. It was an entrance to a park filled with children at play. Wherever I looked, I saw wheat everywhere. We were in the middle of an endless wheat field, and at its center, children were playing.

The young man spoke for the first time. "Please stop the car and I'll open the gate. We need to pass through here to get to the opposite side." I couldn't think of any reason to disagree, so I followed his suggestion and drove the car into the park.

Halfway through the park, at its exact midpoint, the hitchhiker said, "Please stop. I have something I must do." I stopped the car, and he wasted no time hopping out. He reached to grab his suitcase from the back seat and set it on the ground. He opened it, and I was horrified. *The suitcase held an ax.* When he held the ax, his facial expression was transformed; he had the crazed look of a madman. I saw without any doubt that he was possessed by dark evil. Worse, he was preparing to harm the children. I got out of the car and went after him. The deepest part of my being knew that I must pray for courage in order to exorcise the young man.

I took a deep breath and placed both my hands on his chest, with my right hand directly over his heart. I was paying no attention to the ax. I spoke authoritatively and with great volume as I stared directly into his eyes. I saw flaming beads that radiated hot anger. What I said, I cannot repeat again. Words were given to me, and I uttered them with unambiguous delivery.

A powerful current of electricity immediately rushed into me. It traveled throughout my body, moving from my feet to my belly. When it came to the middle part of me, my belly button, the energy began to swell and pulse like a powerful piston. It then shot heightened energy straight up my spine and out of my head. The current was then a whirlwind capable of lifting me to the sky. It was gathering and throwing forth the internal fire. It was so strong that it sucked out all my insides and tossed them to the heavens.

To my relief, I felt totally cleansed. I had forgotten about the young man until I noticed that he was now glowing with health. He had been returned to light. I learned that as you cleanse others, so you cleanse yourself. As you stare at darkness, the light is brought forth. As the fire rages, the wind comes. I stood there, in the middle of that wheat field playground, with no insides. I was left with only skin and no internal matter. To my surprise, my skin wasn't human. It was the skin of a fish. I looked like the remains of a sole left on a dinner plate when the meal is finished.

I woke up still feeling the life force surging through my body. A voice spoke: "The light will always be with the dark. But you can choose the dark wisely. As others have done before, you can be with those who suffer naturally, whether from injustice, poverty, or severe illness. Be with those and the dark will provide a good marriage with your light. If you do not choose your dark carefully, it will seek its own form, which may be the unbearable evil fire of hell itself."

I sat in bed wondering why I had received this vision and those words. I was dazed and blazing with a spiritual fire. In several hours, the sun came up in Venice and I made my way to the Jewish archive. There, I was shown and allowed to hold the old volumes of *The Zohar*. I opened one and randomly pointed to a passage, asking the rabbi to translate. He said that the words I selected were about the relationship of light and dark. I remembered my vision.

The Hebrew word *klippah* (plural *klippot*) means "shell" or "husk," as in the husk of wheat. One of the major ideas of Kabbalah concerns the covering of the vessel in which light is encapsulated. Creative movement, the life force itself, is found in the relationship between the container and the contained. Though opinions and interpretations vary extensively, we can say that any act of separation draws a boundary that becomes the shell. Whether this boundary is our skin, the skin of a drum, the bark of a tree, a doll, a mask, any representation of a living thing, the clay of a potter, or a word, these things are dead unless a spark is lit inside them. Evil, according to *The Zohar*, is something dead—a shell or husk without light. Interestingly, prior to the dream, I did not know that *The Zohar* teaches that the fruit Eve gave Adam was wheat. My dream took place in a wheat field where the wheat kernels had to be removed from their shells. This happened in order for light to shine, all taking place in the exact middle of the field and the middle of the human body.

Lurianic Kabbala, the contemporary form of Kabbala started by Rabbi Isaac Luria in the sixteenth century, is concerned with helping restore creation so that the light trapped inside all shells can be freed. You might say that this mystical undertaking is a mission to free the kernel of light from its husk, to paradoxically separate it so that all other opposites no longer need to be separated. Stated more practically, we can pull the light out of our shell in order to heal the separations that destroy creation, including the difference between the feminine and masculine, good and evil, and light and dark. We must lift the light or "raise the sparks" in order to restore the dancing opposites.

The world created by words and texts, as told by various stories about our origin, established a babbling tower of nonsense that encapsulated the light. However, we can restore the pre-fragmented universe by entering the darkness that embodies the brightest light. Holy letters, holy words, and holy texts hold sparks, but their shell obscures their ability to be seen. If we remove the shell, the light is too bright. We must do the impossible in order to see the light of darkness. We must stare into the cave of infinite darkness and patiently await the appearance of its opposite—the light that is born out of the dark.

I have spent a lifetime receiving holy books that hold light. These books and the words within them are mojo, and *The Zohar* is a remarkable example. Over the years, several books have fallen off shelves as I walked by them. This has happened in university libraries, public bookstores, antique stores, and home bookshelves. I found that the mojo that comes in books, words, or letters can be used to help others. It helps awaken more mojo, and this, in turn, contributes to our participating in the greater alchemical dances of transformation.

In another time and place, I dreamed of going to an old bookshop. I recognized it as the first store specializing in rare books that I ever visited when I was a child. It was located in downtown Kansas City, Missouri. An old man with white hair was sitting on a bench in front of the store. He said, "We've been expecting you. Go on in." I entered the store and noticed rare books everywhere. As I was looking around, an older woman came out of a back room and asked me if I needed any help finding anything. Without hesitation,

I replied, "I am looking for the books written by Swedenborg." She started looking through some books, and while she did this, I saw a book catalog on the glass counter in front of me. I opened it and found a section titled "Esoteric Christianity." It had three pages of listings, and all the titles were written in Latin. Before the woman could return, my mother came into the store announcing, "It's time to go. They are getting ready to close the shop," just like she used to do when I was kid hanging out in a bookshop.

I woke up and prayed for another dream so I could learn more about those esoteric books. I fell asleep again and dreamed that I was sitting at a round table. I was in a very old European house. I looked over my right shoulder, and to my surprise, I watched a round loaf of bread come through the middle of the door. It slowly but gracefully floated across the room, and then it gently landed on a plate in front of me. I woke up even more confused.

The following week, I did some research on Emanuel Swedenborg. I discovered that he was a renowned Swedish scholar and scientist who advanced the science of metallurgy, the physics and chemistry of metals. In his fifties, he had a life-changing vision of the mystical Christ. As an aside, this happened at exactly the age I am as I write this book. The experience was so transformative that Swedenborg retired from science and started writing books about his spiritual visions. In short, he became a mojo man. All of his mystical books were published in Latin, and his followers referred to his work as esoteric Christianity. I ordered his book *Journal of Dreams* from a rare-books specialist, and when it arrived, I opened it and found the following account of a dream he had on October 12, 1743:

> I saw also in vision that fine bread on a plate was presented to me; which was a sign that the Lord himself will instruct me since I have now come first into the condition that I know nothing, and

all preconceived judgments are taken away from me; which is where learning commences . . .

Wheat was delivered by Eve to Adam. Later the bread, the body of Jesus, was served to humanity. Ever since that time, mystics have been served the grain that holds the light. When I opened Swedenborg's diary, I understood I had been served bread from a long lineage of mystical wheat fields. Later, I found that the same thing happened to W. B. Yeats. As he wrote, "Then one day I opened *The Spiritual Diary* of Swedenborg, which I had not taken down for twenty years, and found all there, even certain thoughts I had not set on paper because they had seemed fantastic from the lack of some traditional foundation."

I visited the home in Sweden where Swedenborg had his visions. It was the place I had seen in my dream. Later, in London, I visited the Swedenborg House, where books about him are published. There I introduced myself to Editor Stephen McNeilly and told him why I was there. I mentioned that I dreamed the books of Swedenborg. He became quite excited, like the shop owner I had previously met in Copenhagen, as he replied, "I believe you. The first time I learned about Swedenborg was when I dreamed one of his books. That's why I work here today."

There is a world of mojo dreaming where we find magical nourishment. I invite you to get in the mojo bread line and prepare to receive a magical word, mantra, or book. There are mysteries involving the word all over the world. These words are bread that want to serve you. *The Zohar* mentions angel bread, the bread of powerful beings that is a holy manna. God tells Moses in Exodus that he will deliver "a bread from heaven." The path of the holy bread runs straight down the trunk of the holy tree of life. It is the mojo that awakens us, and it is as alive today as it was for the mystics of past times.

Magical Mojo Wordplay

In the case that follows, a highly respected psychiatrist, Dr. Michael Mayfield, came to me bored with his clinical practice and wanting an infusion of creative mojo. He said he was tired of saying the same old therapy clichés and plodding through worn-out, habituated routines. In this regard, he is no different than everyone else. It is easy to get into a rut and become an automaton when every day is essentially a rerun of the previous one. Though the details may vary, the general patterns for getting through the day remain the same. We get locked into the boxes of our own making and forget that we don't have to live in a mundane square. Therapists and clients both face the trap of getting stuck doing the same thing over and over again, doing so at the cost of feeling more alive and resourceful to themselves and others.

We prepared ourselves to use words freely in order to release any overly bound words. Here the bread of mystery and surprise is served whenever a spark is seen in the darkness of therapeutic encounter. In other words, at this roundabout conversational table, clichés are doctored with mojo, enabling them to be more than empty husks; they will become stuffed with illuminated kernels of deeply held feelings. I have transcribed the words so not a single important crumb will be missed.

Dr. Mayfield, or Mike, as he asked me to call him, is a well-known teacher and mentor to other therapists. He is a medical doctor trained in family medicine and psychiatry who also teaches at a medical school. Over the years, he has diligently pursued learning a variety of alternative medical practices and is known for his creativity. He wanted to take his therapy game to the next level. I began by inviting him to stretch beyond his professional boundaries. "Let's not be constricted by all those habits of psychotherapy and expectation regarding what a conversation should be."

Mike immediately performed a clichéd therapy line, doing so as a parody of his profession: "How are you feeling about that?" We both laughed.

I knew that Mike is highly skilled with words and that this session would involve the presence of word mojo inspired by the magical books that have shown me how language participates in the construction of our experiential realities. I immediately got to work. "I think that's a question you've asked many times in your life." Mike, expecting me to be clever with him, threw back his head and laughed. I continued, "How much of your life does that take? How much of your life do you put into that question?" I was accepting his invitation to challenge status quo talk in therapy.

"I don't know, but I do know that one of my patients went into a mode where she was mocking me. She played the part of the therapist and asked me, 'Oh, how are you?' She was aggressive, and I recognized that she was mocking me when she said, 'How are you feeling?'"

"What holds you back from being all that you want to be?"

Mike acknowledged that this was why he was sitting with me. "Now we're focusing on the problem."

"Are you willing to go for this? Or maybe you're too willing."

Mike was surprised that I had suggested he is too willing. He started to ask for clarification. "Too ..."

I finished it for him. "Too willing to be open to becoming all you wish you could be. I mean, look at you. You have a T-shirt that says *Practice random acts of awesome*. You're wearing mojo." I was referring to his indigenous-made necklace. "Look at your bare feet. You're a barefoot doctor." Mike was laughing. "That's pretty open. Do people say that you're the most open shrink in town?"

"Some might, yeah."

"Have you rightfully earned that reputation?"

Mike was being honest. "Yes, in some ways. But there are these habits of the therapeutic voice like, 'How are you feeling?' and, 'Tell me more about your problems,' and, 'Oh, I have a brilliant insight about your problem to define it even more precisely.' As you were saying yesterday in your public talk, that doesn't necessarily help."

I joined him. "Do those well-rehearsed therapeutic lines put you to sleep? Does it disappoint you when those things come out of your mouth?"

Mike specified how he related to the moments when he was going through the motions in a session rather than being creatively alive. He also cited a case when he was an effective therapist. I brought him back to the original clichéd line that he started the session with. "But you started today with that question. You articulated it as a kind of comedic expression, but at the same time, you know that it is the bedrock phrase of your profession. I would like your imagination to consider how you might ask that same question with those same words in a different way. 'How do you feel about that?' Say this in a way like you've never said it before."

It is not the words that are the problem; it's lighting up the words, giving them some mojo. I was asking him to light a match and make his lines light up. I did so while remembering the wisdom of the ancient mojo books: as the dark holds a light, a cliché most assuredly holds a creative inspiration.

**It is not the words that are the problem;
it's lighting up the words, giving them some mojo.**

Mike had an idea. "Like in a strong Italian accent?"
"I don't know. What would that sound like?"
Mike tried an Italian accent. "How are you *feeling* about that?"
We laughed at his theatrical performance.

"I like that!" I did like it. Mike was an excellent actor and could deliver a good line when so inclined.

Seeing he had a receptive audience, he further responded with a more exaggerated Italian accent. "How are you *feeling* about that?"

I noticed that his slightly absurd rendering of the line was interesting and authoritative in a unique way, so I commented on the life he brought to the line. "I think that is all you have to say to be an interesting therapist. It would move me."

Mike interrupted to provide more comic relief. "To head for the door?"

He was playing with his words, and this opened the door for the creative winds to blow on his speech and anoint them with mojo. I praised the direction he was going. "I like it. I'd like to hear it again, but change the word feeling in some way. Maybe you could mispronounce it, but do so in an Italian accent."

Literary mojo plays with many different levels and kinds of opposites. Here, a perfectly executed cliché can be countered by an imperfectly expressed version, thereby creating an oppositional tension that may spring forth a release from clichéd discourse altogether. It is less likely for things to move forward if we suggest, "Stop being so cliché; be more creative." That request is similar to the paradox to be spontaneous: you can't force spontaneity or creativity. Starting with a more accessible creative opposite is a more achievable first step that gets things rolling. In this case, I simply asked him to mess up his clichéd line.

He replied, "So maybe mispronounce the word *feeling.*"

"Yes!" I applauded. "How would that come across?"

With a rehearsed Italian accent, he tried to amplify his performance. "How are you *feeeling* about that?"

I provided commentary. "It sounds like it has three *e*'s.'"

"Yeah, sort of a skip—a little bit of syncopation."

We were playing with words, and this attracted the attention of my literary mojo. As we loosen the grip that speaking habits have on us, unexpected words more easily arise. My mojo reminded me that the Kabbalistic theory of creation proposes that the letters of the Hebrew alphabet created the world. From this perspective, different combinations of letters and words awaken mojo. In other words, it doesn't matter what you say. It's how you say it—whether it has mojo or not. I asked the mojo to influence us in this kind of way, "You could add an *l* and drop one of the *e*'s, making it *felling*."

We went back and forth as I kept it rolling. "*Falling, fibbing.*"

"I like *falling*."

"*Fiving*."

"*Fe, fi, fo, fumming*."

I took it further and got serious about this absurd direction. "I think you could invent a whole therapy based upon the most clichéd line used by therapists. But use it with an Italian accident . . ." I stopped in the middle of my sentence. "Isn't that interesting? Did you notice how I said *accident* instead of *accent*?" Of course it was no accident. It was mojo slipping in an unexpected word. I received it as an important contribution. I was mindful of the fact that Kabbalists zoom into the many layers of word meaning. They knew that how a word is spelled or spoken has powerful consequences. They were early word mojo doctors.

At the same time and without a script, we simultaneously said, "Italian accident." We couldn't help but laugh about that accident!

I continued, "Well, I was thinking *Accidental Tourist*, but in your case it could be accidental therapist. I'm actually quite serious. I think we've stumbled, we've tripped . . ."

With a now familiar accent, Mike asked, "How are you *falling* about that?"

I flowed with the word and gave it a push so we could move forward. "Because we're falling into something."

I was ready to invite him to infuse his practice with this same kind of creative play, doing so to allow literary mojo to mess with the words. A seasoned mojo doctor knows that creatively playing around with serious concerns is often the surest way to reveal the deepest meanings and truths. This is not an idea that escaped other wisdom traditions. In his book *Man at Play*, Jesuit scholar Hugo Rahner calls for a *theologia ludens*, an interpretation of theology as play. Similarly, Catholic priest and academic Romano Guardini proposed that worship should be "a kind of holy play in which the soul, with utter abandonment, learns how to waste time for the sake of God." In his book *Beyond Theology: The Art of Godsmanship*, the British philosopher Alan Watts cited Saint Thomas, who wrote that divine wisdom is comparable to playing: "I was with him forming all things: and was delighted every day; playing before him at all times: playing in the world."

Mojo calls for transformative healing and existential change that creatively plays with words with no readily apparent purpose. Why be so foolish when a person asks for help with serious challenges and suffering? We do so because mojo wordplay leads us to the most important purpose: purposelessness is the highest purpose because it effortlessly throws you into the creative flow—the mainline source of life-changing insight and transformation. The truest mojo makes light of all things including mojo. As Blaise Pascal put it in *Pensees*, "True morality makes light of morality . . . to make light of philosophy is to be a true philosopher." To be a serious mojo doctor requires playing around with all serious talk.

Creative, absurd wordplay is a valid practice because it leads you to the core of the serious stuff, opens any blocks, and spontaneously arranges a transformative moment. Here, an accidental phrase turns out not to be accidental. It does not drive you away from the underlying issue whether it is related to early childhood family relations or your most cherished beliefs. Playing takes you right to the heart of all development issues and even to the divine home of spiritual truth. I was playing with Mike to help him face whatever was seriously organizing his life.

"I think you have the imagination, craziness, and creativity to dare to consider a whole therapy that is an accidental therapy, conducted by an accidental Italian who plays with words beginning with *f*. Here the change, the surprise, the variation that arises in a session revolves around which of those words you're using in a sentence." I invited him to take this creative license to his daily practice. "Let's think about how your office will have to be redecorated. Certainly a map of Italy needs to be on the wall. Maybe a sign on your desk would say *The F Father*. Not *The Godfather*. You're the *f* before the *g*. You play with *f*'s.'"

Mike was intrigued with the direction of office redecoration because of recent events at his job. "That's wild because I was talking about decorating my office this morning. Yesterday, which was April first, was the anniversary of when I first opened my clinical office. Of all days!"

I was not going to miss the importance of this revelation, "Of course, it's an F-Day. Happy Fool's Day!" I reached out and shook his hand. From the highest level of wisdom know-how, the most serious presence will be seen as derived from the most foolish. We are in the domain of paradoxical opposites. As we found earlier, fear can be turned into desire by playing around with a doll. In this session, playing foolishly with words sets in motion the possibility of bringing therapy to life. Creative wisdom is called to the stage by any twin jester.

In a particularly dramatic deliverance, Mike took this word to his practice. "How . . . how do you *fool* about that?"

**In this session, playing foolishly with words sets in motion
the possibility of bringing therapy to life.**

"That's exactly right. That's wonderful.

"You're filled with these words that begin with *f.* You are a *fun* guy. You are a *funny* accidental therapist. I think that's your resource. You (I pointed to his T-shirt quotation) practice random acts of awesome, which is an invitation to your foolish heart. Everything is awesome to you if it's in the domain of the holy *fool.*"

Mike nodded in agreement as he said, "It's the highest holy day of the year, April first."

I challenged him to own being more of a therapeutic fool. "Excellent. That should be the day you celebrate the beginning of your new practice. You could send an announcement to every client in celebration of your new practice ..."

Mike interrupted to say, "I have an *f* story." He wanted to show me that all this fit with his best therapeutic moments. His mojo was awakened with this kind of creative expression.

"I'm sure you have many."

"A patient with Lou Gehrig's disease was in my office. His wife had to talk for him because he couldn't talk anymore. She said, 'You know, he was the nicest boss. People still talk about what a nice boss he was.' I asked him, 'Were there any times when you really wanted to flip people off but you just couldn't or didn't?' The patient nodded in vigorous agreement while making affirmative noises. So I said, 'Practice this at home' and put up my middle finger. I taught him how to give others the bird."

Being nice all the time can get you into as much of a rut as being a constant grouch, particularly during those times when it does not express what you authentically feel. Mike knew how frustrated the man must have been without the ability to communicate with language. He also realized that he had no previously developed skill for expressing his upset. He playfully taught the man to give the bird, which in his limited communicative circumstance came in handy when he needed to do more than make a noise. It also allowed him to become a more interesting character and no doubt brought moments of amusement to those who would never have expected him to show such a display, which in itself helped relieve his frustration.

> **Clichés were vanishing and being transformed into moments of creative inspiration. New twists and turns on words were flying as surely as a magical drum.**

Clearly Mike's and my playful interactions recognized the mojo he already carried within him. He just had to learn to use it more often. I looked at him and said, "It all fits."

Thinking about his story about this patient, I said, "Look at how you're drawn to *fingers*. Of all the parts of the body you could choose to talk about, you chose the *f* part. That's extraordinary. These *f*'s are just coming down on you. They are raining on you. No matter what story you tell me, it all comes back to your being an accidental Italian therapist who uses words that begin with *f*."

The literary mojo had a hold on our conversation. Whatever he brought up in our talk was contributing to the presence of *f*. At this point, the letter had become pure mojo. It was like a magical word that pulled more and more *f*'s into the conversation. Clichés were vanishing and being transformed into moments of creative inspiration. New twists and turns on words were flying as surely as a magical drum.

Mike remembered something interesting about his life. "You know, in school I never got an F. I think I was just saving them up."

My mojo immediately recognized the importance of what he said. Here the opposite points the way to what is most desired. I saw that this *foolish* discussion was getting to the heart of what was most serious for him. I assumed that inside the husk of his nonsense was a deeply meaningful light waiting to make its appearance. Perhaps his success depended upon the right kind of failure—receiving a well-deserved F. I was moved to say loudly and clearly, "That's your problem, right there. You have always wanted to have an F. Yes, you've been waiting to get your F. You have the habit of perfection. The boy who had to be a nice doctor but really just wanted to give the finger. Look at how magical the universe is for you. It's as if clients were sent to you with fingers and the inability to say things that begin with *f* just to help you find that which you never were able to experience in its fullest form. All these clients have been little angels sent by the devil to sort of say, 'We've heard your prayers. We know that you want an F. I think you need to wear a shirt that has an *f* on it, an F-shirt. Not a T-shirt, an F-shirt."

Mike was intrigued by the mojo that had moved in our conversation. He sat with a look of wonder. We went back to the Kabbalistic inspiration that drove my mojo to tinker with letters and words to bring forth an incantation of creation and liberating progression.

I threw him another word: "*frivolity.*"

He threw another one back: "*freedom*"?

"*Freedom* is deep-fried *fun.*"

"*Fat.*"

"*Fat* and juicy *fun* is *free.*"

"*Fearless.*"

I challenged Mike to have more mojo wordplay in his therapy and life. Creativity, the fearless fat freedom of liberating tasty fun, is not simply frivolous. It is the highest purpose and most serious work of a mojo doctor. I put the question to him straight, with no chaser: "Will you seriously do it? Or is this just another amusement. Would you *feel* like you were a *failure* if you actually took this seriously and succeeded at it? Perhaps you need to mess up the stuff that's blocking you from getting the F that you've been searching for. Yes?"

Mike replied, "There's a book I almost brought you today but I *forgot*. The author writes about succeeding at *failure*."

Here I experience an epiphany realizing that the word *failure* becomes mojo when it is the right kind of failure. Mike was presumably hunting for a successful failure that could result in freeing him in a transformative way. The book he mentioned gave me this clue. I would encourage him to continue looking for the liberating mojo that was hiding inside a transformative failure. In other words, the darkness he needed to enter concerned failure. There, the right kind of failure would be his luminous darkness.

I remembered *The Zohar* and the many magical books that have literally fallen into my life, carrying an important message about the play of opposites. I seized the moment and immediately interrupted to utilize what he'd just said. "That's you. That's your calling. That's your mission. You want that success. You want it, don't you?"

"Yeah."

"You're starving for it because it's *fertile* ground."

Mike continued, "The author wrote this line: 'When failure is my goal, I cannot fail.'"

This quote, which I believe comes from Andrew Boyd, made my mojo start buzzing. I pronounced, "You want what you can't get because if you got it, you'd lose it. You should go for the F anyway. I don't know what it would take for you to go all the way and make a serious commitment to all the things you now *flirt* with. That would be different. Do you like to *flirt* with all the *f*'s?"

"It makes me *flit* a bit."

"Yep. You're a *flit* or a *flip*. You're a *flip-flopper*. That's easy for you. It keeps things ambiguous as to whether it's an F or an A. When are you going to make a commitment to go past the *flirtation* and become a card-carrying member of those who behold and uphold the mighty *f*?

Mike was giggling. "Why not *foday*?"

I shrugged my shoulders, indicating my doubt. "I think it's easier for you to say it than it is for you to immediately act as if your life depends on it."

"Hmmm."

"I know you want it. But I know the hold that your mind has on allowing you to flirt but not go too far."

Our conversation had allowed word mojo to play with any opposite that could be conjured. Now I started flipping the whole session: switching from play to seriousness. In other words, after encouraging him to be flippant with words, being flippant was then challenged as mere flirtation. Play was invited to dance with its opposite, serious side. Light banter brought us to heavy seriousness, with the hope that a deeper light would be revealed.

> **Now I started flipping the whole session: switching from play to seriousness. In other words, after encouraging him to be flippant with words, being flippant was then challenged as mere flirtation. Play was invited to dance with its opposite, serious side. Light banter brought us to heavy seriousness, with the hope that a deeper light would be revealed.**

Mike laughed and signaled that he knew what I was talking about.

"Because your mind wants to stay in control, it's made an agreement with you. It will let you *fool* around as long as it doesn't go too *far*. If you go too far, you might not come back. *F* might get in charge . . . instead of *m*."

Mike looked puzzled, "*M*?"

"Your *mind*. If you reverse it, that would be interesting. That would be what you're looking for. Let *f* be in charge."

Mike was with me. "That might be what I *find*."

"Yes. What would it take for you to know that you've made a serious pledge to be the accidental Italian, the accidental therapist, the accidental *F*? What would it take for you to know that you made that pledge and that it's more than a flirtation?"

He was serious now. "I don't know, honestly."

"What if you sent a letter to your clients saying, *You can now call me Doctor F*?"

"Oh, that would be going too *far*. It might be confusing."

"Is that a bad thing?"

Mike continued, "What comes out of my mouth to patients when they're confused is, 'Great, you're about to learn something.'"

I addressed the implication of what he was saying. "You are saying it would be confusing to you."

"Yeah, I guess."

"You've not been joining them in the confusion? It's been a halfway thing?"

"Yes."

I elaborated my point. "You've enjoyed confusing them but have not let the whole thing come back and confuse you. If you signed off as Doctor F, it would confuse both them and you. It's a little scary?"

"Yeah."

"Because then you'd be a little out of control."

"Uh-huh."

I added, "Do you know what would happen? You would find what you're looking for. Your mind would say, 'I give you an F for that. Maybe it is too much to say Doctor F. Perhaps you should just say, 'There're a lot of *f* words we should talk about.' That would be something that people would expect a psychiatrist to say. First they'll think the obvious, but then they'll think it might mean *fear*. Or it might mean *fun*. It might mean what is lost is now *found*."

"That, I can do," Mike asserted.

I agreed, "That, you can do. So let's supersaturate the accidental therapist office, the accidental setting of the Italian boot, with imagery and sound. You need to find the kind of music that would fit. How about opera?"

"Yes."

"You can get a soundtrack from *The Godfather*. Because now you're a fella."

He liked this idea. "A good *fella*."

As he spoke, I was thinking about the unique forms of magic that words are capable of bringing. They are another kind of fairy dust. I saw the images of all the mojo books that have fallen into my hands over the years, from *The Zohar* to Swedenborg's diaries, Charles Henry's *Cercle Chromatique*, e. e. cummings' original *CIOPW*, a galley proof of Thomas Wolfe's Nobel Prize–winning novel, a letter from President Truman that was folded inside a cowboy book, and ancient letters and symbolic items, among other things. As I saw and felt the literary mojo in my own life, a dose of inspiration poured into me. I realized that Dr. F needed a mojo book. I allowed the mojo to direct how I should advise his procuring one.

"I suggest that you go to a bookstore—it could be a used bookstore—and buy yourself a dictionary. Tear out all the pages and entries except for those under *f* and call it your *fictionary*."

Mike nodded in agreement and with enthusiasm for this task, adding, "Because for people to find what they're looking for, they have to invent some *fiction*."

"Yes, and you can start at random. Have them open this dictionary to find a word. You can suggest, 'We're going to talk about words that start with *f*.' Then consult your dictionary. Hand them the *fictionary* and say, 'Open it up at random.'"

I then pointed to the words on Mike's T-shirt and read it, but with a slight alteration, "'Practice random acts of finding your *f*'s.' You can then, as you suggested, create a *fiction* with them, a conversation about a word. A fiction you never imagined construing because it isn't guided by preconceived clichés, boring notions, or any tired understanding from the practice of psychotherapy. It is inspired by an *f*. If you ever get stuck, open up your dictionary and get a word."

Mike liked this idea.

There is an Old Germanic word, *lekjaz*, meaning "an enchanter who speaks magic words." In the worlds of Jewish mysticism and Germanic fairy tales, a single magic word can make all the difference. The mojo of an effective transformative incantation involves using the right word at the right time. It must be improvisationally born of the moment, not a mindless, memorized formula. Magical words are by their very nature a surprise—words that accidentally evoke mojo.

"I guarantee you that if you commit yourself wholeheartedly to being this kind of accident, you will practice random acts of awesome. These accidents will lead you everywhere, and that blank canvas in your room will be endless: There's no end to what your brush and paints can throw on it, and there's no end to it because this is the world of fiction. This is the world where accidents can make a difference. Every time you say something that pleases you, pleases the client, and they thank you for it, maybe you should say, 'That's why I'm an *accident*.' It's a different way of giving yourself an F, for it really had nothing to do with you. Maybe you should keep track of how many accidents you can be a part of in every session. Keep a scorecard. You might say at the end of the hour, 'For this session, I had three accidents.'"

Mike totally surprised me with an unexpected comment. "Does that mean I have to wet my pants?"

The mojo that was circulating in the room sent a direct response, and I passed it on, "What an interesting question. It does mean that you have to jump in the water. You can't stand on the bank and watch it go by. You can't be afraid to know whether you can swim in all of this. Yes, you have to wet not only your pants but also your T-shirt. Why? It's way too dry. It hasn't come to life. It hasn't been watered. It hasn't blossomed. It's just dry soil. Look at it. It's brown like soil." I said this as I saw that his T-shirt was brown. "The words expressed on your T-shirt have been planted in the soil, but they haven't been watered. Until they are watered, they aren't going to come forth. The heart of your T-shirt's truth is going to stay hidden inside but isn't going to come forth and bring what's possible in the deepest part of you. The accidents it can bring need to be awakened."

Swedenborg's Hebrew teacher is thought to have been a Kabbalist. The latter's "world to come" is Swedenborg's "the new church" and what Jesus called "the kingdom of heaven." All presumably refer to the absorption experience in a here-and-now present where mojo awakens the multi-presence of simultaneous oppositions. In this session, we brought forth as many differences, oppositions, and extremes without preferring one side at the exclusion of the other. We did so playfully but not merely as irrelevant flirtation; we did so as a more serious dance of the divine tensions of contradictory meanings.

In this session, we brought forth as many differences, oppositions, and extremes without preferring one side at the exclusion of the other. We did so playfully but not merely as irrelevant flirtation; we did so as a more serious dance of the divine tensions of contradictory meanings.

Mike jumped in. "So what you're saying is that I need to enter into a wet T-shirt contest so this will stick to me (he points to his T-shirt) and show people what I have underneath."

My mojo surged through me as I spoke without missing a beat. "See, now you're *fooling* again. You're avoiding jumping into the water. That's how you avoid it. You *flirt*. What happens when somebody says, 'Do you really think you might fall in love with me?' Your *flirtation* jumps right on top, and you don't take it seriously. I love the way you do that. It's entertaining. It sweeps us all away. But you don't get swept away along with it. That's the thing."

Mike was listening carefully. "Hmmm."

"You sweep everybody else away. I'm inviting you to jump in so that you're not on the bank observing the cleverness, the funniness, the randomness, the awesomeness of that which you have the talent to express. I'm asking you to jump in and be part of it."

"I will do it," Mike announced.

"Well, you'll think about it. I think you will try aspects of it, make considerations, and reflect on it. You might even dream of it. In fact, I would highly recommend that you go collect the most interesting letter *f* you can find; maybe it should be made. You could commission an artist. Ask the artist, 'Can I commission you to make me an *f*? I only want that letter.' Then place that *f* underneath your pillow."

I recalled how Moses Cordovero, one of the early Kabbalistic teachers, believed that words could bring something to life. Like a magical incantation, some words have mojo that helps bring forth magical outcomes. Sleeping on a letter is a transformative practice I use with clients; it attempts to birth life into a letter, paradoxically doing so by using a letter to inspire the dreaming of the birth of life.

My mojo inspired me to invite him to completely submerge himself in the deep parts of his imagination, where his mojo lives. "You will discover that placing a symbolic seed under your pillow is showing the deepest part of your unconsciousness that you are doing more than thinking about your life. You've gone into the world, found a seed, and placed it in the soil, and now you're going to water it. In the garden of your dreams, I expect something will come forth. Maybe you'll see a new *father*. It's another *f* word. A new *father* who guides you in ways not present before, though these ways have been longed for. A new *father* who provides what you have feared missing for all of your life. I don't know what your dreams will bring or what kind of *f*'s you'll receive in dreams, but if you get an *f* in a dream, you should say, 'Thank you for that *fream*.' That would be a good thing, huh?"

We both started laughing as he agreed.

I continued with encouragement. "I think if anybody can pull this off, it is you. I don't know that I've met anyone else who can do this, but I believe you can. I believe it's important to begin here as if your life depended upon it. Flirting is not going all the way. It's not getting the awesome; it's just the random. It's the yellow light (as I said this, I pointed to the yellow letters on his T-shirt) that pauses before the brightest light (I now pointed to the word *awesome* on his T-shirt, which was in white letters)."

Wrapping up, I said, "How *fascinating* our time has been. It took place because you asked a simple question, 'How are you *feeling* about that?' A question you thought you should run away from. All your life, that's been the question you wanted to run away from, only to find yourself brought back to its home. That's the place for you to begin. That's the accident that's been waiting to happen in your life."

Mike's facial appearance had changed, and he looked quite serious. It was obvious that he had something important to say. "You know, my father and my mother, but especially my *father*, would never ask me how I'm *feeling*."

I was not surprised by what he said because I knew from experience that play and foolishness often uncover the vitally important experiences and feelings behind a problem. I underscored that everything we had said now held greater meaning. "So this makes deep sense."

"Yes."

"Now you know exactly how important all this is," I reaffirmed as he nodded his head in agreement. "You must do it as if more than your life depends on it."

He finished this thought. "I must do it for others, too. Yes."

"Otherwise you'll miss the opportunity to *father* those who come to you."

Mike saw that all of our wordplay had awakened the mojo that got down to his core experiences: his father, who did not ask him about his feelings, and his unique fear of failure. Fooling around did that, and it also made him feel free. He again said, "Yes."

It was time for us to conclude our transformative conversation. I shifted my body, making the signal that we had come to an end. "The time has come for you to go on your way. Now you must enter your world with a whole new *fictionary* armed with accidents that free—go past flirtation—but utilize flirtation. The difference in you is profound: you will forever jump in the water along with your clients."

"Yes."

I reached out to shake his hand. As I did this, my mojo whispered a joke into my ear, reminding me that this was a psychiatrist whose profession historically began with psychoanalysis. I was reminded of Freud's idea that sex is underneath all human expression. I accordingly was inspired to leave Dr. F with these final words, spoken as the climax: "You might even have a wet dream."

We laughed heartily, hugged one another, and went on our way.

Mike came back later that day and unveiled a special T-shirt he had designed and had made since we'd spoken. It had a large *Dr. F* in gold letters on the front, and the back spelled out, *There's a lot of F going on.* A month later, I received a letter from him. In it, he said:

I am so pleased to tell you that I have (un)successfully applied to fulltime student status at F University. I had my first day of classes yesterday. I saw a marijuana-addicted patient who reported three days of not using it in order to feel motivated, engaged, and energetic. I gave her a series of four prescriptions dated yesterday, today, tomorrow, and the day after tomorrow. I then said, 3, 2, 1, and LIFT OFF! She doesn't believe that we landed on the moon, but she can now find herself in space . . .

Then there was the isolated Slavic opiate addict who, while absentmindedly scratching her hand, started to extend her middle finger. I noticed it and helped her point it toward her ancestors, thereby closing the gap between her lonely self and those who came before her.

Oh yes, there was a depressed computer mechanic who told a story of helping a poor, English-speaking electrical engineer from Eastern Europe get hired years ago just because he happened to notice his talent. When he finished his story, I told him about how my mother, in 1968, was an Eastern European immigrant with marginal English skills. Someone at a company hired her to fix and design circuit boards because someone noticed her and believed in her.

I am noticing a lot more these days.

Thank you for your tutelage.

This session with Mike shows that literary mojo provides a powerful means of transformation if you want to shake up your work life, a relationship, or anything that feels stagnant or stuck. Without knowing the specifics of where you are going, literary mojo simply takes you somewhere that is creative. It also gets you near relevant critical experiences that underlie your presence in the world, and it allows them to be altered in a gentle and playful way. Rather than crawl through a laborious rational analysis, mojo words grab hold of your imagination and tickle you to move in more creative directions of encounter. It does so with the spontaneity and freedom inherent in play. Instead of struggling with any battle of opposites, we allow differences to tease and please, becoming a muse for transformative movement. Literary mojo does not serve the overly serious and sometimes paralyzing work of getting to a big theoretical understanding of our life. Its purpose is to help lighten us up and make us more available to be moved by play. Here, the light of darkness is sought in playing with serious matters, teasing the intimidating, and fooling around with the burdensome.

Without knowing the specifics of where you are going, literary mojo simply takes you somewhere that is creative. It also gets you near relevant critical experiences that underlie your presence in the world, and it allows them to be altered in a gentle and playful way.

Prescriptions for Finding Word Magic

You, too, can find some word magic to bring creative sparks and the playful tension of opposites into your life. I invite you to go on a hunt to find mojo letters, words, and books. You can get started by bringing home a book that carries the only word mojo you will ever need. Like Dr. F, go buy yourself a dictionary. It doesn't matter whether it is old or new, small or large. When you have it, proceed to tear out every page except the page that has the word *magic*. On that page, cover all the other words. Only leave one word in the book: *magic*. Carry this book to work and then bring it back home. Make sure this dictionary spends some time in every place where you hang out, including both work and play.

Open this book whenever you think you need a boost or have forgotten what life is all about. Before opening the book, make sure you envision yourself enthusiastically drumming your flying drum, which transitions you into the world of mojo. A song gives mojo an extra boost, too. After you have grown accustomed to having this word mojo in your everyday life, decide who you will show it to. Ask if you can open up a special book. Tell them you have collected a most unusual volume—a dictionary that has only one word in it. When the time is right, open it so your mojo can be seen. Make sure you have a good feeling in your heart when you do this. If you are asked why you did this, simply say that you enjoy carrying magic in your life. Answer every question in a way that accentuates the theme of enchantment. If someone suggests you are crazy, smile and respond, "Magic does make you crazy, and I love that about it."

The luminal darkness of *The Zohar*, the paradoxical light in darkness, is related to the illogical clarity in a creative muddle and the contrary wisdom articulated in saying something relevantly foolish. Anything you do that inspires playing with opposites is a sure way to wake up mojo. Magic often requires that you voice seemingly crazy words and statements in order to announce what otherwise would be unheard. To enter the world of literary mojo, you need radically different ways of handling words. Here are some more directions and misdirections.

Be a missionary who only carries one word into the world. If you like, call yourself Doctor M, Professor M, Mr. M, Madame M, Ambassador M, Senator M, President M, or M Master. Find many ways to play with your *m* word and your Magic Dictionary. Maybe you will want to make custom dictionaries for others that carry messages of magic. Maybe they have more words about magic in their editions. Perhaps they have a rare, handwritten commentary in the margins, just like the ancient mystical books I found in Venice. That's your call.

Imagine a mojo encyclopedia. I'm sure you can find a cheap encyclopedia at a yard sale and then have fun cutting it up. Think about how a smile can be brought to someone who finds an encyclopedia filled with magic words. She might even have a good laugh.

Speaking of which, that's another idea for a dictionary. For this one, have only the word *laughter* in it. Or get bilingual and have a two-word dictionary: *love* and *laughter*, the two big *l* words. If you're on a roll, make it a trinity and add the word *light*. *Light*, *love*, and *laughter*; that's enough ideas to write a whole new religion! Maybe you would like to present it in one volume of an old encyclopedia, the one titled *L*.

What about a dictionary with one word for every letter? Open it up, and there you find twenty-six words: *awesome, bodacious, creative*, and so forth. (By the way, my *z* word would be *zap*.) Finally, consider gifting others with a membership to your newly created Letter of the Month Club. Every month you can email a different mojo word to them.

Finally, as always, sleep with your mojo. Place your letter or word on your bedside table, under your pillow, beneath the bed, or suspend it from the ceiling above you. Make sure it is inside the space where you sleep. Consider it a husky spark that can bring light inside your cocoon. Ask it to help you see the light of darkness. You might want to set it on a special plate—a plate you would use to serve a freshly baked loaf of bread. Pause to wonder whether Swedenborg ate his bread on a circular plate. Notice that a circular plate is like other things that spin in order to wake us up and deliver the mojo manna.

Before retiring each night, add an uncommon prayer to your final words of the day. Say to the vast luminal darkness of the night, "I want to be a *mojo mama* who delivers *mojo manna*." Don't say amen but pause to consider that the most important words in that prayer both begin with the letter *m*. End your prayer by saying, "M&M." Better yet, don't say a thing; just have an M&M candy sitting on the dish that holds your letter or word. Call it M&M bread. If you don't eat it, then lick it, or smell it, or at least rub it gently before going to sleep.

This is how you learn to make mojo out of an M&M or any letter, word, or book. See words as candy for children who seek the impossible light. Regard yourself as a magical cook who has been waiting a lifetime to read the words: *that which is least serious is the yeast for making mojo bread.* Feast on those words until you realize (please pause to take a deep breath) *that you must swallow an opposite in order to taste the luminal darkness of an invisible alphabet whose words never stop playing as they make crop circles and plant a most delicate wheat germ that serves the contradictions that enter the center of what you most deeply require as you move your shell game around the endless mire and set things on fire.*

In other words, make yourself comfortable, and have a nice slice of mojo toast. You won't believe the number of fascinating jams that can be spread all over it. Through such foolish talk, you can spread the word that it is possible to find the most serious meaning of absurdity sitting right next to the brightest light of absolute nonsense. This is why we are able to give magical consideration to any odd statement and then regard it as an incantation for mojo play. For example, "While a lark sings underneath the bark, a light shines above the flight." The meaning of this may surface tonight if you ask for a dream that is magically right.

Now it is possible to say what couldn't be said before: *Fly a drum to dance with the moon. Why? Because the dark needs to give birth to the disappearing and reappearing light of day so we may convey the words that bring life to objects that object to becoming fields of study rather than fields of wheat. Do so to fill your empty husk with the luminous presence of others, revealing the shaft of light that engenders magical flight. Shine, baby, shine! Turn everything off so you can get turned on by the gods who speak to cause a leak in the box that makes you square. Find your charm by doing the least verbal harm, following wordplay that weds magic to the everyday.*

My mojo is asking you to do just one more thing, a ridiculous task that offers another paradoxical entry into illuminated nonsense. Go buy yourself a loaf of Wonder Bread. Its nutrition will not come from what is inside the package. Instead, it will be delivered by what is written on the outside of the package. Cut out the plastic logo that says Wonder Bread, tape this over your heart, and spend the next twenty-four hours with it resting there. Make sure it spends the night with you. Allow the presence of this word to inspire a new sense of wonder as you contemplate how a dream about bread can bring mojo into your life. As others have dreamed being served a loaf of bread, so can you.

It happens to all who are inspired by what moved Swedenborg and W. B. Yeats—the stream that whets mystics and poets. It happened to me, and if it could happen to me, it can happen to you.

5

ENCHANTING A RELATIONSHIP BRINGS US LIFE

*N*early twenty years ago, I had a mojo dream that placed me in a visionary rainforest. I saw myself taking a walk with an indigenous shaman underneath a green canopy of beautiful trees that included the yerba mate, a tree that is known for its medicinal properties. Wearing a band of yellow feathers around his head and some black beads draped over his shoulder, he was helping me look for a particular stick in the shape of a Y. Near the end of the dream, we found the stick, and I shaved the bark off of it. I wondered what the dream meant but went back to sleep.

A second dream followed. This time, I was returning from the subtropical rainforest with the same shaman, but we were not looking for a stick. We were gathering feathers of a certain size and color. We collected the specified number from a wooden altar that was inside an open-air hut with a ceremonial wooden canoe nearby. There, he blessed the feathers and handed them to me. As before, I didn't know what the dreams were about or what purpose the gathered materials could serve. I fell asleep one more time.

Finally, a third dream came and showed me how to combine the feathers and stick. I had to make holes in the top forked sides of the Y and insert the feathers in a certain way. The object became a wand—most definitely a mojo wand because it was revealed in a vision. I still had no clue what to do with the sacred object, but I assumed that the dream arrival of the mojo wand was a forecast that an adventure would soon commence.

Within a week, I received a phone call from Asuncion, Paraguay, inviting me to be the keynote speaker and teacher for the opening of the first family therapy center in their country. I accepted and asked if they could arrange for me to find someone who might know any indigenous shamans in the semitropical rainforests outside the city. After searching for how to arrange a meeting with the Guarani Indians, their first custodians of the rainforest, they were told that the elders did not want to have any visitors. Paraguay had recently gained its independence from a long-standing dictatorship, and the Guarani now had more say about their affairs. They were free to choose who could visit them on their native land.

I went to Paraguay anyway to teach their family therapists. At that time in my career, I did not tell anyone that I used mojo in my practice. I referred instead to abstract theoretical ideas about cybernetics, systemic patterns of interaction, and circular causality to explain how I worked with clients. While those scholarly orientations provided accurate portrayals of what was going on, they did not reveal the unseen know-how that underlies how to wake up a transformative process when helping people change. The same is true for all theories of psychology, psychiatry, and family therapy. They describe and explain but do not activate the magic that brings forth transformation.

During those days, I wasn't ready to say that mojo was used by everyone who was therapeutically effective, whether they knew it or not, because I would be regarded as embarrassingly superstitious or as a dispenser of New Age nonsense. I was mostly quiet even though I had been sanctioned by numerous cultural traditions to teach these ideas. I created theories that hid the mojo while managing to point people in the right direction. More accurately, my theories were a different kind of mojo for therapists, helping free them from other lifeless ideas and embalmed practices. Like treating a client, I did the same to my colleagues whether they were my students at a university, supervised trainees in a clinical training program, or professional workshop attendees. In teaching, supervision, and practice, I remained a mojo doctor disguised as an innovative or creative therapist. I had arrived in Paraguay to harvest mojo, but I first had to teach therapists about the possibilities in clinical work without telling them too much about what I was really doing.

I arrived at the capital city of Paraguay and was given a warm and friendly reception. On the first day, my hosts, Fernando and Teresa, arranged a meeting with an ecologist, Oscar, who was helping the Indians reclaim their land. He was one of the few outsiders they trusted. When we walked into his office, it was obvious that he was filled with nervous energy. He could not wait to tell us what had happened that morning. He said that a young Guarani boy had walked all week from the rainforest to the city. His father was an important shaman and had sent him to carry a message, saying, "Someone has come from faraway to see my father. He is ready to meet him."

Wanting to do the right thing, Oscar forwarded this message to the political leaders of the Guarani and told them about my arrival. It was not possible for me to visit their land unless I received their permission. The next night, I was taken to a place in the woods just outside the city of Asuncion. The men who took me were three political leaders of the Guarani people. One of them, Ava Guyrapa Yvoty, was their president. He also had a Spanish name, Antonio Portillo, previously given to him by those outside his culture. He was all business and took this matter very seriously. On our way to the camp, he didn't smile or laugh. I wondered whether I had made a mistake setting all of this in motion, but I knew that mojo adventures sometimes have no easily recognized rhyme or reason.

Before we got out of the truck, Ava Yvoty and the two officials with him asked me to tell them the purpose of my visit. I began by telling them a greeting that had been given to me by my friend and spiritual compadre Sam Gurnoe, the son of Kate Gurnoe, my adopted mother who knew all about mojo, especially dancing dolls. Sam, a medicine man, had previously advised me to pass on some words from my North American indigenous relatives. "Should you meet the people down there, tell them you speak for us and that we stand with them in their struggle to preserve the old ways." Now that I was in a situation where his advice made sense, I passed on the greeting.

I could see that they were happy to hear this. I went on to tell them about my dreams and that I was being obedient, following wherever they led. They talked privately to one another for a few minutes and then their leader said, "Come with me."

I was taken to a wood building with a large open room, away from the other structures and activities. Inside were twelve men who soon gathered in a circle. They were all dressed in shamanic regalia. Covered with feathers, beads, bracelets, and necklaces, they held medicine rattles made of gourds. One man had what appeared to be a small wooden carving of a gun, which I assumed carried spiritual bullets. They placed me in the middle of the circle and asked me to show them my heart. My mind did not know what to say, but my mojo, which had been inspired by the three dreams that had brought me to this place, whispered that I should sing. I needed to release a song from the heart of my hearts, not the kind of singing that is recorded in a music studio or sung on a Broadway stage. I am referring to the spirited song of a shaman.

I closed my eyes, asked my mojo to pour through me, and started to sing. I felt what I had experienced years ago when Sam

Gurnoe sat me on a wilderness cliff to fast. That's when an eagle flew up and gazed into my eyes, sending a song into my heart. I reached for the remembrance and connection to that feeling, made the mojo hookup, and the sounds began to pour out of me without effort right there in the middle of a dozen Guarani shamans. I allowed my heart to have its voice in this ancient way of sharing relationship, not only with other cultures but with all that holds life. My eyes remained closed and my body shook as the music came forth.

When I finished, I looked and saw that every man had tears in his eyes, including their president. "This is a very special moment," Ava Yvoty spoke. "I must personally take you to our communities so you can see how we pray. There you can talk to the shamans and holy fathers. They will tell you about your dreams."

I was returned to the city, where I finished my teaching over the next couple of days. Meanwhile, Fernando and Teresa made arrangements to drive me to the home of the Guarani. We began our journey with Ava Yvoty as our guide. He took us far outside the city and into the rainforest. We first went to the village of Comunidad Acaraymi. If you have seen the Roland Joffé film *The Mission*, you have observed the geographical place where I was taken. Starring Robert De Niro and Jeremy Irons, it is the story of eighteenth-century Spanish Jesuits who try to protect a remote South American Indian tribe in danger of falling under the rule of pro-slavery Portugal. The tribe was the Guarani, the same people I was visiting.

The village we pulled into was approximately fifteen kilometers from Iguassu Falls, one of the most spectacular waterfalls in the world. It is one of the geophysical hearts of Earth, steadfastly pumping vital fluid into its South American river veins. Its 275 cascades make me wonder whether they represent all the countries in the world. They form a mile-and-a-half crescent where thunderous torrents of water wildly plunge over steep cliffs. This is a place for spectacular rainbows. In their misty display of color, the earth and the sky mate to remind us of the mysteries of life's interrelated nature.

**Mojo works this way: it awakens the magic in our life.
It brings a vibrant presence to every step, and it casts a
spell of enchantment over our adventures, filling us
with great wonder for the natural world and all
that takes place upon its stage.**

Iguassu Falls is in the midst of a rich, tropical rainforest filled with plants, birds, and a wide diversity of creatures including jaguars and mountain lions. In this wilderness of vegetation are its ancient dwellers, custodians, and priests—the Guarani Indians. This is where they still pray in the old way. When I arrived, the missionaries had not completely disrupted their shamanic practices nor severely affected their relationship with nature. As I walked on their land, I could not help but hear the music by Ennio Morricone that was the film score for *The Mission*; this journey felt like being inside a movie. Mojo works this way: it awakens the magic in our life. It brings a vibrant presence to every step, and it casts a spell of enchantment over our adventures, filling us with great wonder for the natural world and all that takes place upon its stage.

In the village of Comunidad Acaraymi lived a holy man named Tupa Nevangayu. I immediately recognized him as I walked toward where he was sitting. His photograph was on the cover of the academic book *El Precio de la Sangre*, written by the anthropologist Miguel Chase-Sardi, who had studied this community. A week before, I had met Professor Chase-Sardi and asked him about the wand I was curious about, though I did not tell him I had dreamed it. He had not seen such an object but referred me to another anthropologist, a woman who was an expert on Guarani religious items. When I described it to her, she emphatically declared, "I have never seen such a thing. It does not exist!"

While at the university, I looked at my interpreter and thought of the first day of my arrival in the city. I went to a special gallery where Guarani crafts were displayed and sold, and I spoke to the owner, who asked me to come sit with him in his back office. There, on a wall shelf behind his desk, sat the object I had dreamed. Although the feathers were of a different color, the shape of the stick and the number of feathers were identical. He said an elderly shaman had brought it to him a week ago with instructions to place it on that shelf and not sell it. This is why I was not influenced by any anthropologist's declaration that the mojo didn't exist; I had already seen it.

Tupa Nevangayu now greeted me in his village and took me to their spiritual gathering place. It was a large, thatch-roofed structure with open sides. On one side was an altar in front of a long wooden canoe, similar to what I had seen in my dreams. There were many sacred feathers of all colors and an assortment of mojo items sitting on the altar. He, like the previous elders, asked me to show my heart, so I sang my song with great gusto.

As I was finishing, I saw that he was holding an assortment of large feathers and waving them over my body. He blew over my heart and said, "You know how to pray. I have seen your heart, and you are carrying holy things. This is why we call you a holy man. We don't say this because you are a perfect person but because your visions are holy. It's your job. You are a messenger who must say things to the world."

He told me more about the purpose of my life and added, "You are at home and safe with the Indian peoples of the world. They recognize who you are. You need to be careful around white people. I will give you protection and put you under the watch of our spiritual forces." He then handed me the bracelet that he wore around his own wrist. It was covered with feathers. His father's mother had made it for him when he became a shaman. "It offers protection and helps me walk across spiritual waters and fires. When I lead my people through a river, I wear this. Now you must do the same. Wear it when you teach your people. Tell them about these sacred things. Take them across the rivers they need to cross. Bring them to a better place."

I am wearing this bracelet now as I recall how Tupa Nevangayu taught me many things about Guarani's old healing way. He said the spirits wanted this knowledge passed on so it could help other people. The Guarani healers and spiritual teachers were not like the fictional shamans invented for bestselling New Age books; they were more like the folks that went to my grandfather's church. They loved God, made sincere prayers, and sang sacred music. The Guarani shamans' love for God was so great that it opened their hearts to receive holy songs in dream. That was what brought them spiritual gifts. With a song, they were able to be a channel for deep wisdom and could deliver mojo words to their people. They even have a word for mojo talk, *ayvu*. They call it delivering the "word souls." Inspired by what I was taught, I wrote these words:

> *It is said that we are the strong shamans.*
> *We are the* Ka'aguygua,
> *The "People of the Forest."*
>
> *The forest is not simply a place where we live.*
> *We are the forest.*
> *It is our life.*

Our greatest gift is voicing the spirit of the forest:
Sounding the word souls, the deep forest mojo.

Someone dreamed that more and more people are talking about
*   shamans:*
Saying we ascend and descend into the Vision, saying we have
*   helpers of spirit,*
*   saying we have power, saying that the rattle and all of these*
*   things are*
*   independent of any God.*
They are saying all kinds of things, but they have no
*   word souls.*

KNOW THIS:
We, among the strongest who see spirit and experience its power,
We are called to speak our simple truth:
A shaman is someone who prays to God.
Prayer is the instrument and the link.
All other paths only pretend and deceive.
It is prayer, prayer, and more prayer.
This is what gives flight, brings sight, and administers light.

You will know a shaman by the sound of his prayer.
They carry the word souls.
No song, no shaman.
Songs of prayer come from a serving heart.
They cleanse, forgive, and rekindle hope.

There is no other way of the shaman than true prayer and song.
It is the way we know God.
It is the way we become the forest.

The old shaman gave me a Guarani soul name, Tupa Nemboa-guerovy, which means "one who receives the Guarani songs." He told me that we would always be related and that the spirits of the forest would protect me as long as I followed visionary guidance. He then added, "You must go on to the next village. There you will find the man you have dreamed." He had prepared me for the next stop in our journey. We left the next morning for the village of Comunidad Fortuna. There, I found Ava Tape Miri, the shaman others called "the priest of the forest."

When we arrived, I encountered the face I had seen in my dream. Though revered by other shamans, he told me his soul name simply meant "Little Seagull Man." I also learned that he was the one who had sent his son to Asuncion to deliver the message that he knew someone was coming to see him. We greeted, and he quickly gathered the community for dancing and praying. His ceremonial ground was the exact one I had seen in my dream. Before I even presented the reason I had come, he announced, "I will explain your dreams at sunrise. Tonight we must celebrate with the spirits."

We danced until we collapsed from exhaustion. I slept on the ground in front of the altar and canoe. I fell into a dream. This time I saw Ava Tape sitting in front of the fire. I was staring into his eyes in the dream when he made a loud grunting sound. It woke me up. When I sat up, I saw that Ava Tape was actually sitting in front of the fire exactly as I had seen him in my dream. He shouted out with laughter, "I too can dream you. I will always be available to you anywhere you are in the world. You only have to call out my name."

When the sun came up the next morning, Ava Tape was true to his promise. He explained that I had dreamed something very holy to their culture. "All Guarani shamans, our holy ones, dream of a special wand covered with feathers. We use it for healing and protection. When you have this dream, someone must go into the forest and find it for you. Since you dreamed me, it is my responsibility to gather these things, and show you how to put the wand together and use it. He then took me for a walk in the woods among the tall trees, and he knew right where to find the stick. After that, we returned to his altar, where the feathers were waiting for us. He had already prepared for my visit.

Holding a Guarani mojo wand helps you deliver the transformative words for therapy. It is therapy mojo that can be used to help heal family relations, including your own.

Ava Tape taught me how to use the magic wand and explained how it is used for a variety of things, including healing and protection of one's family. Every Guarani shaman has a wand, though the design is unique—according to what is shown in the visionary experience. When the wand is held in your hand, a prayer and song may be spoken. This opens the channel for the word souls to flow. In other words, holding a Guarani mojo wand helps you deliver the transformative words for therapy. Broadly speaking, it is therapy mojo that can be used to help heal family relations, including your own.

Ava Tape also baptized and anointed me with another Guarani soul name, Ava Tupa Rayvi, which means "gentle rain from God." He gave me more mojo instruments, including a *mbo'y*, a necklace worn as a protection against bad spiritual influences, and a *ubaraka mri*, the medicine rattle that communicates with God. The seeds inside it are respected as ambassadors for the Guarani shamans and sons of the community. When it is shaken, the whole community prays. The seeds are also the symbolic eggs of creation, while the handle is like a penis attached to the ball of the rattle—the female. Its shaking movement is a sign that the creative process is alive in the moment.

I was shown how to create an *akangua'a*, the shaman's head-band, or corona, that symbolizes the light of God and the wisdom inspired by mojo. It is the source of a shaman's power, and holds mostly yellow and gold feathers. I was taught that the Great God wears the first corona and that all other coronas are part of Its lineage. The *takuapa*, the feather bracelet given to me by Tupa Nevangayu, would help keep another person's illness and negative influences from passing into me when others are doctored. It would also help me to make important crossings. Finally, another feather wand was held over my mouth as I uttered the word souls. It is called a *mita karai jeypyi*, and its job was to protect me when I voiced my mojo.

Over the years, I visited these shamans several times. They brought me into their mysterious world of unique mojo, and I had numerous unexplainable experiences with the mojo they gave me. Once, I took my wand to a ceremony in New York City, and as I held it, a feather came off and flew right out an open window. I lost the feather. To my shock, when I went home, which was over a thousand miles away in another city and state, the feather was sitting in my front yard. Mojo can perform some strange behavior, perhaps to remind us that it is a mystery way beyond our comprehension.

When you hold a mojo wand, rod, stick, or cane, anything can happen. Even Moses handled a mojo staff that brought water out of a stone and parted the Red Sea. Like the Guarani paraphernalia, this form of mojo seems especially good at helping you get across troubled waters. Think of how birth is announced when a mother's water breaks. Mojo doctors always use water. They may sprinkle,

immerse, baptize, drink, spit, throw, or pour it on you. This breaking of your spiritual water calls forth the new.

Water, the most abundant molecule on the Earth's surface, is a
core component of most spiritual beliefs and practices. It is symbolic
of baptism, spiritual rebirth, and renewal. As the primordial soup
out of which life emerged, it is the first universe out of which each
of us was born. Water is the symbol of the Great Mother or the universal womb of creation. The spirits of water, however, express a dual
nature. Water spirits have both life-giving and destructive sides. Similarly, water can be found to be still or a tidal wave of radical change.
Its fluidity is the medium of change. It is no accident that Moses
used his staff to divide water, enabling transformative movement in
the middle of a parted sea.

The ancient Egyptian sign for a staff means "zest for life," referring to the universal life force. It indicates the presence of mojo.
Whether made of wood, metal, stone, ivory, or crystal, these hard,
phallic-like objects symbolize the awakening of any experience, springing a tired situation to one that becomes energetically
ready to provide a crossing, bridge, or entry into the dynamics
of creation.

A Guarani wand is capable of helping mojo walk into any situation that needs its lively help. The mojo given to me from the
rainforest, first in the dream realm and then in the physical realm,
sits in my office. There, it offers protection and helps me get ready
to see my clients. As an experiment, I once tinkered with it in a
way that was probably not wise. I decided to test its power by
seeing whether it could set up a situation where I would meet some
people at a certain time and place without their knowing anything
about it. I chose a couple I had no relationship with other than
having met them once. I held the wand and visualized meeting
them at noon in a specified location on the Avenue of the Americas

in New York City. I went there and almost fainted when right at noon, they showed up at that spot. They were surprised to see me, but their reaction was nothing like my internal response.

A Guarani wand is capable of helping mojo walk into any situation that needs its lively help.

If this reported experience is too unbelievable for you, I can ask my mojo what can be said about the scenario to liberate any uncomfortable residue. I suspect that it would suggest that I tricked myself into thinking that I made the event take place. But in fact, all the wand did was tell me what was already going to happen and then let me think that I was proposing it. It showed me the future rather than creating what would take place. It simply arranged for me to be at the right place at the right time. Now do you feel better? This is how mojo can take any experience, including the ones it creates, and help us relate to it in a better way.

Transformation with an Improvised Mojo Wand

I once had a clinical case that required some help from my mojo wand. It was a session where a father and his son, Sam, came to discuss the challenges of their recent reunion. The son, now a teenager, had not seen his father for most of his life. They were separated due to an unfriendly divorce when the boy was a preschool child. The father moved away and spent years heartbroken due to the loss of his only son. Now the father hoped to mend the bond that was previously broken. They had recently gone on a trip to the country and were delighted to have spotted an eagle there. That experience gave the father a glimmer of hope for their future relationship. However, the son had gotten into trouble for anger issues at school, and his mom asked his father, who now lived in the same town, to bring him to therapy. They were clearly two family members in need of a healing connection, which mojo wands are meant for.

At first, I only listened to them talk about their situation with their therapist, observing from behind a one-way mirror at a university clinic. When asked to describe his relationship with Sam, the father said it was "a little standoffish," so he didn't try to "crowd him." The father was clearly suffering: "I just want to be with him and do things with him. I have that mind-set of wanting to catch up for the ten years that I wasn't around him. I want to be his dad and his best friend, but I'm not trying to rush him. All I've had for the last ten years is a phone call. We are starting at ground zero. I feel like a stranger."

Sam nonchalantly said that "things are all right" since they had been reunited that month. When their therapist asked them what they wanted to work on in the session, Sam responded, "Whatever floats your boat, dude." His father then answered, "I'd like Sam to get a better understanding of me. I just feel like a stranger."

The therapist backed up and asked Sam about "the anger that everybody is talking about" and whether "everyone is overreacting."

Sam responded, "They ain't overreacting, I promise you. I would not lie to you. I don't lie anymore. I gave up lying because it resulted in my getting grounded. That's why I ditched it. Plus, I wouldn't lie to you; you're cool."

The therapist brought up what happened with the previous week's session, when his mother had been with him. "You know, your mom talked about your screaming at the house. Tell me more about 'the lava bed of anger within you,' as she called it."

Sam explained that he was frustrated by all the running around he had to do. He said someone always wanted him to go some-where—school, church, a restaurant, a friend's house, and on and on. He would rather have played his video games.

I entered the room and met Sam and his father. "I just heard a little bit of your conversation, and what impressed me was something that Sam said. It's something you don't hear young men say very often. He said, 'I don't lie anymore.' That's awesome. It shows that you're at least trying. It's important to have a principle in your life. I was also struck by the idea that there must be a lot of emotion underneath you guys because you had a separation that wasn't something you chose. It's an emptiness that is held in a space where something is always going to be bubbling. You might mess with it and not want it to come forth in a certain kind of way, but then it comes out in a different kind of way. I want to ask you, Dad—and I say it as a father who understands this special father–son bond—do you know that when Sam grows up, you will still feel this bond? It will always be there with your kid."

The father answered with conviction, "Yep."

I turned to Sam, with words for him, "Dad will always be stupid, you know. You'll find this out for yourself when you get older and have a kid. Sons will always have a part of them that thinks that Dad is dumb; that's the way it works. I want to ask you a question that is a big question. God forbid, what if something happened—and we certainly don't want this to happen—what if you never saw your father again? What if this is the last time you will ever see him? I wonder what you would want him to hear from you. What would you want to say to him? Because you never know; things happen. That's one thing I've learned in my elder years: just when you think things are always going to be a particular way, something happens. But you've already learned that lesson. You already know that you can't always assume that people are going to be there forever. But what if something unexpected happened and you never ever saw your father again? What would you like to tell him?"

Sam did not expect this question. He had lived ten years without his father and was in the unexpected position of being with him after wondering whether he'd ever see him. Now I presented the possibility that anything could still happen, including the same fate repeating itself. Like the magical pot that appeared and disappeared, we never know how long anything will stay with us, but even when it disappears, we can't be sure it is forever. This uncertainty brought the session to a critical here-and-now moment. Mojo thrives when we get that kind of full presence; this is why crises bring us a gift. They throw us into a moment where we are less distracted and thereby more in tune with the whole experience of feeling alive. Facing the possibility of death or disappearance, life is more present. With this reminder in the room, inspired talk (what the Guarani call "word souls") was ready to arrive.

Sam sincerely responded, "I would want to tell him that I honestly love him."

"Tell him that now."

Sam turned to his father and said, "I do honestly love you, Dad. I am right here."

Dad's eyes got teary as he commented, "I believe you."

I praised them for enacting what they had held back for all these years because the right situation had not invited them to do so. I looked at Sam, who was fully absorbed in this encounter, and asked him to consider when he might have entered the same dream as that of his father, the deep world of mojo: "Have you ever had a dream or woken up in the middle of the night over the past years and wished you could say that kind of thing to him. Did you ever feel that?"

Sam said, "Yeah."

I continued, "It always touches your heart, doesn't it?" I looked at his dad and asked, "Did you hear what he just said?"

Dad gently responded, "Uh-huh."

I was showing them how they had maintained a bond with each other even when they were apart. Similar to how my dream brought me to the Guarani Indians, their bond took place in the home of mojo—the world of dreaming. "He's dreamed about you and dreamed about saying that to you. I know he woke up weeping, too. I bet you had the same experience, Dad."

Dad agreed.

It was feeling very emotional in the room, and both had moist eyes. I took it a step further, "Why don't you give each other a hug? It's a good thing for men to hug."

Sam flew out of his chair and gave his dad a big hug.

I said, "We take life for granted, and we forget to say those kinds of things when we feel it. You each have been dreaming each other. Do you know what that means? It means you were never separate from one another." These were the same words I remember hearing from Little Seagull Man when he said that he and his relations are always with me as I dream them and they dream me.

I turned to their therapist and announced, "They were never separate. Their hearts were right next to each other. No matter how far away they were, they were dreaming, longing, and feeling each other. Their feelings may have been realized more intensely than those young boys who lived with their dads all the time. Those boys often take their relationship for granted. But these two were separate, so they couldn't take their relationship for granted. Their situation woke up a feeling inside of them that not all dads and their sons allow themselves to feel."

I turned to Sam and his dad and said, "What you showed me today tells me that you didn't take your love for granted. You felt it, and now when you are physically together, it must be sort of weird because you were so close when you were apart."

Dad agreed.

I continued to build this perspective, the one where mojo resides. "This is like another reality. You already shared tenderness for one another in your private moments and in your dreams. But now you are facing one another. I'm happy you brought your feelings here today and honestly expressed them, because you just never know what might happen."

Dad was right there with me. "Man, that is right on the money."

"Life is a mystery," my mojo inspired me to say. I am thinking of how this father and son would benefit from meeting my Guarani Indian friends and finding their old ways of healing and protecting their relationship. More words came to me. "We'll never fully understand the reasons why you weren't able to live physically side by side. But we do know that it is a great mystery that life gave you that heartfelt connection. Fathers and sons usually put a shell around their hearts, and some fathers and sons live their whole lives without experiencing what you just said to one another. It's hard to believe, but it's true. I've seen old men who were sad because they'd never said that to their father."

In the deepest part of my imagination, I was holding onto my feather wand, asking that the word souls come forth. I provided a way to tell them that this would now take place.

"I'm feeling something in my heart, and I am going to allow some words to come forth for both of you. You're both very lucky. Every human being is like a volcano with all kinds of emotions inside. Unfortunately, we usually put a cap on them and bottle them all up. Then we pretend that we don't have any emotions. But this wasn't so for you guys even when you were separated. You'd go to sleep, and *whoosh*—all that love and longing and missing would just come out. That's amazing because it means you're both going to be open and tender, not only to each other but to all of your life. I assume that it's such a powerful experience that when it comes up, it almost overcomes you. It's almost too much to handle sometimes. It hurts to love and long for your father that much. It hurts to love and long for your son that much. You almost wish that it would stay inside the volcano. Do you understand what I'm saying?"

Sam immediately asserted his agreement, "Yes, sir."

Father nodded his head and agreed, too.

> **My job as a mojo doctor was to show them the amazing connection they already had, a mojo relationship born from their own unique light of darkness.**

"You two have been opened by life. Not all men have been opened. A lot of men have so much armor around their heart that it's uncertain to others whether they really feel anything. But I know something about you two: you both have felt emotions as powefully and as deeply as is possible for a human being to experience. It's so interesting to find both a father and a son who have been opened."

These men had lived in the darkness of being away from one another. Yet in that void, there was a light for each of them—a heartfelt relationship that lit a fire of longing and loving. My job as a mojo doctor was to show them the amazing connection they already had, a mojo relationship born from their own unique light of darkness.

My mojo wanted to say even more about their lives: "I am not even sure why I'm saying this, but I feel that maybe you were chosen to be opened in this powerful way. Do you know what I mean?"

Both Sam and his dad nodded in agreement.

"This makes you different and special, but it comes with some interesting side effects. It means other kinds of emotions can flow out much more easily, too. So Sam, when you get annoyed, all that emotion knows how to shoot right up."

I turned to Dad and explained what had been going on with Sam's anger bursts in a way that confirmed what we had been talking about. "When he feels that he's been wronged or misunderstood, that things aren't rational, or when he's been put in a position that he shouldn't be in, his volcanic fire gets stirred and spews forth. But for him, it probably feels natural to shoot a whole lot of fire. A young man who has been opened to have the flow of gentle love also finds that the flow of angry fire comes easily, too; one doesn't come without the other. You see, he's going to feel strongly about everything."

I said these things as I remembered all the ways mojo had taught me to utilize the truth of opposites in all situations and concerns. What is true for one side is true for the opposite side, though perhaps for an opposite reason. Mojo always plays with polarities, making them teasing allies rather than warring opponents. For this father and son, distance bred closeness, unspoken emotion begat heartfelt expression, and heated anger easily hid a natural flow of gentle love.

Dad understood what I was saying. "Yes, that's right."

I turned to him and asked if the same was true for Dad. "I bet you have felt the anger, too, about how life has wronged you and about how things didn't work out the way you wanted. At times, it may feel like a crazy rage. You just want to lift your car off the ground and throw it across the road."

Dad agreed wholeheartedly as he exclaimed, "Yep!"

"So you both have those two things opened. You have felt the flow of love and the flow of anger. I'm wondering what other things have flowed from you. Have you also been able to find the deep, wild, crazy, ridiculous laughter that is within you? Do you guys know if you've had that one flow?"

They both smiled and nodded their heads with affirmation.

Sam said, "Oh yeah, we do."

I asked them, "Do you ever start laughing so hard that you can't stop laughing?"

Sam laughed and added, "There was one of them today. He cracked me up."

I was pleased to see this opening. "That's awesome. That's very impressive."

Dad got his two cents in. "I have laughed so hard that I cry."

I underscored the importance of this expression. "Wow! You guys are triply opened."

Dad proudly acknowledged this emotional truth.

"I thought that maybe you were so serious from the other heavy kind of openings that you might have missed this light one, but you got this one, too. That's great. So when you get together, do you ever bring this silliness into the world? I ask because the world doesn't give a whole lot of space for being stupid, silly, ridiculous, and a little crazy. You know what I mean? Everybody is too serious. Everything at school is too serious."

I paused because my mojo wanted them to initiate something new in their life—a lighthearted way of sweeping them off the ground into a flight of ecstatic delight. After a deep breath, I leaned forward and offered this advice: "Since you guys are already opened, you don't need to do the stuff that most fathers and sons need to do. You don't need to mess around with seeing whether you can open your hearts and express your love because you've been doing that for all these years. You both made that clear. You also know how to shoot some volcanic fire if the circumstances elicit it. I'm sure you'll learn how to manage all that. A lot of dads have to take their kids out and teach them how to take care of themselves. It seems Sam already has that opened, though it's a little clumsy right now. It will smooth itself out.

"I think you need to spend more time exploring how to be two funny guys together: two wild and crazy guys. I don't know exactly what that means. Maybe it means checking out a movie that is most likely to tickle you. Or maybe you become merry tricksters. Dad, were you ever a guy who pulled practical jokes and stunts?"

Sam piped in, "I do that all the time."

Dad said, "I have done some stunts. I had a good teacher. That was my father."

At this point, I turned to their therapist and gave some direction. "I think you should have a little talk with them about how they can turn themselves into rascals and unique characters. Ask them to find some ways to tickle themselves when they are together. Please talk about it while I take a little break. I'll watch you from behind the one-way mirror."

"OK, you guys are awesome. I'll be right back."

I left the room because my mojo called me out to cook up something special for them. I wasn't sure what I would put together, but I felt that I had to gather some mojo. I went back to the observing room and snooped around to see what I could find. After I left, Dad took a deep breath and exclaimed, "Wow! That was heavy. It was deep."

Sam responded, "It made an impact. It's very hard to make an impact on me."

They discussed whether they could do something wild and crazy, but to the therapist's surprise, Sam offered a caution. "Well, we don't want to do anything too crazy." That was my cue to re-enter.

"You two are way too serious."

Dad was with me. "I know."

"You know you don't need to be that serious anymore. Seriously. You already know everything you need to know: Your son loves you. He woke up in the middle of the night and felt the love so intensely that he would sob, and you felt the same. You guys have a bond that's going to last forever. We've heard you both say it and express it today. I don't think you ever need to talk about it again. From this moment on, remind yourself of this fact: you know what some fathers never know, and you know it in a way that some fathers would give anything to experience. They would give away all the money they ever earned to experience what your son has expressed and felt for you. Do you get that?"

Dad realized this. "Yes, I do."

"Will you accept it?"

"Yes."

"Let's just say adios to having to worry about it."

"OK," Dad punctuated our discussion.

When I had been behind the mirror, I took the objects that were sitting on a desk—a red tapered candle, a foam cup, some transparent tape, and two lollipops. I allowed my mojo to inspire me to throw everything together in an unusual way. I wasn't sure why I assembled it in the way I did. I didn't think about what I was doing; I just did it. Now that I was in the room, I held up the lollipop and announced, "Here's a lollipop. I want to see more lollipop in your life."

At this point, I presented what I had thrown together for them. It was the red candle positioned parallel to the floor with the white foam cup hanging from the candle's middle by strips of tape. The cup was half filled with water. "I want to see you guys be a little crazy with me now. Why in the world would a therapist give you something like this? You know it's a red candle and it has a wick. It hasn't yet been lit, but it could be, and then we'd have a fire. This candle has a cup attached to it with a little water, and it's held by sticky tape that may hold or not hold. Now that's crazy, isn't it? When you walked in today, you didn't expect that, did you?"

The father and son were both stunned by the absurd presentation of a red candle that held a suspended cup of water. I went on with my talk. "You are probably asking, what in the world are we going to do with that? I'm going to hand this thing to you now." I told Sam to hold one end of the candle and Dad to hold the other. At that moment, a father and son were holding both ends of a candle. They kept it level because a half-full cup of water was hanging from the middle of the candle.

As I looked at them, I saw that I had made them a mojo wand—a unique stick made of wax that had to be held in a certain way so the attached water wouldn't spill. When held by two people, they had to cooperate and coordinate its position. Its form encouraged the very act that mojo wands are especially useful for: connection. I felt the vibe of my own mojo wand in the room. It had something to say: "I want you two to take a pledge. You two will declare to the world that you are going to be a father and son unlike anything anyone has ever seen. Do you agree?"

They agreed.

"You will dedicate yourself to promoting silliness in every possible opportunity that comes your way."

They both nodded.

"You, Dad, will devote yourself to making Sam laugh so hard that it will hurt. Yes?"

Dad said, "Yes."

"And you, Sam, will devote yourself to making Dad laugh so hard it will hurt."

Sam liked this and eagerly said, "Yes!"

"Somehow, this is going to make another opening not only within each of you but with others you two meet in the world. This will surprise you. You might even wake up one night from dreaming that you've been laughing so hard that you fell out of the bed and are rolling on the floor. That would be something! Wouldn't that be something?"

They both liked this idea and expressed it with smiles. They were still holding onto the candle's ends, keeping the cup of water in place. Absurd laughter had been imagined and prescribed as they held a wand. In this way, magic would become associated with the lighthearted play of two people whose hearts had been heavy for too many years.

"OK, are you up for it?"

Dad exclaimed, "Yes!" Sam was nodding enthusiastically.

"Why continue looking for what you've always had? Why get angry over that which you can already handle? You know how to handle everything; you have what you need and what you want. You, Dad, have what he wants. You, Sam, have what Dad wants. It's all come down on you like a shower of blessings. You have everything; you just haven't gotten this in your mind. Do you know what I'm saying?"

"Yes," they both communicated.

"You two are amazing. I want to jump up and down, and be a cheerleader and say, 'Go out there and show the world what is possible!'"

Dad shouted out, "Yes!"

"Show them what a dad and son can do besides all the talk you might hear in a psychotherapy clinic. Forget all that. Don't pay attention to any of this nonsense. You guys have enough therapy; you've got each other. You hold each other's hearts. You've got each other in terms of knowing how to take care of what matters most. You know how to work yourself up if you need protection. When you don't need to do that, you don't need to do that. What is important now is for you to learn to be funnier."

I pointed to the water that was suspended under the red candle. "Maybe that's not water. Maybe it's nitroglycerin. Wouldn't that be something?"

Dad interrupted to say, "We wouldn't want to light the candle then. Or maybe we do want to light the candle and see what happens."

Sam objected. "That's crazy; we don't want to light it."

I spoke, "Very interesting. Maybe it's holy water, and if you put your finger in it, you'll be blessed for life. Maybe you'll be blessed in a way that will shock both of you. You might find that you won't be able to stop laughing. Perhaps you better not do that."

I paused because the object they were holding had become mojo. You could feel a different atmosphere in the room. A ceremonial moment had arisen, and we all could feel it. I was inspired for them to be touched by the mojo in a transformative way. It was ready to explode in a wonderful shower of closeness and love. I said slowly and clearly, "I am going to ask you each to touch the water now. It's important. Touch the water."

Dad carefully stuck his finger into the water. Then he looked at Sam and leaned his head forward to gesture that it was Sam's turn.

Sam said, "Who, me?"

Dad answered his son, "Yes."

Sam slowly stuck his finger into the water.

I spontaneously chanted, "Walk on water, walk on water. Yes, holy water, yes." My mojo flowed through me and brought those word souls into the holy space.

Dad suggested, "I say light the candle."

I laughed and said, "Hey, look where the wick is pointing. Look whose end has the wick." It was near Sam.

Sam said to his Dad, "I know you have a lighter."

His dad pulled out a lighter and lit the candlewick. The moment was pure magic. A father had lit the end of the candle near his son. It became a fire that promised a new light to their life.

I underscored what was taking place in the room. Whenever I sincerely believe that something unique is happening, I acknowledge and celebrate it. Doing this enables magic to be more intensely felt in the moment in which it is recognized. "I am going to propose that no one in the history of the world has ever done what the two of you are doing right now. I will bet everything that a father and son have never held a hot candle with a wick pointed toward a son who was sitting there ready to be lit."

I reached over and gave the cup a little push. It started swinging back and forth. I continued, "These men have baptized the tips of their fingers and walked upon this water. Now they are sitting here wondering what in the world this is doing to them, but of course, it doesn't have to mean a thing. It can just be an unexpected moment that is the beginning of more unexpected moments. I can just see them twenty years from now—maybe they will be at a ballgame or at home watching a movie—and they will say, 'Remember the time we held that candle and swinging cup?'"

Both father and son started laughing and said, "Yeah!"

While their loving bond may have been invisible to others, it was always burning with life. They were connected by a relational wand that conjured longed-for dreams of tender expression.

My mojo was directing the ritual to go further. "Let's cover up what is happening here. I think we can make this even more mysterious if we set it up so nobody can really see what is going on between the two of you." I then took some tissues and covered both of their hands as they held the candle and cup. "Now no one can ever see that you are holding each other's hands, side by side with the help of a lit stick that bridges the distance. Like before, this connection you have is so intense that it is red hot. It shows your hearts are wide open."

Dad and Sam nodded their heads and agreed. They were symbolically enacting their relationship. While their loving bond may have been invisible to others, it was always burning with life. They were connected by a relational wand that conjured longed-for dreams of tender expression.

"I see what has happened to you," I said in a hypnotic tone, as if viewing their life in a prophetic way. "Every once in a while, a fire in their world would overcome them and fill their cup with tears." I pointed to the water in the cup. "Sometimes this fire became hot and angry so that someone needed to take a little water and ..." At that moment I slapped the cup so it spilled some water. "Bam! Just like that, it helps that little fire get extinguished."

Dad understood as he nodded, smiled, and concluded, "That makes a lot of sense."

I responded, "Weird, isn't it?"

Dad again responded, "That does make a lot of sense."

"Here are two men with an invisible relationship that they can feel and hold onto. These two people have taken a special pledge today: they have promised they are going to do something together that is weird and funny. They might even go into their backyard and sing a song to a squirrel."

Everyone started laughing, but the burning red candle and cup of water were still in their hands.

"Do you two have pet names for each other?"

Dad said they didn't, but Sam offered, "I have a nickname from everyone at school. It is Weenie."

I pointed to the stick they were holding. "There it is, there it is. It's a red hot dog."

As we laughed, Sam asked, "If I'm the weenie, what is Dad?"

Dad answered for him, "I'm the bun. We're the weenie and the bun."

The room was full of laughter, and my mojo could not have been happier. "I love that! You guys, Weenie and Bun, make one interesting hot dog! You should choose a song as your anthem."

Sam said, "Yeah, that's cool."

"You should not hold anything back. Do as many things as you can that will be spectacular for the world. You might even write a book someday about your new partnership. It could happen."

Sam peeked under the Kleenex to look at the cup of water. He looked quite surprised.

I asked, "Whoa, Sam. Is anything happening under there?

Sam answered as if he had seen a miracle. "The water is a different color!"

"Wow! It changed color!" I repeated what Sam had said, knowing that mojo was doing its work.

Dad lifted the Kleenex and said, "Let me look."

I responded, "The mind is an interesting thing."

Sam looked at his Dad and asked, "Don't you think it has changed color?"

Dad shook his head with uncertainty.

Sam was convinced that it changed color. "I do, man!"

I gave them each a lollipop to put in their mouth. Now I could say, "Look at these guys with those sticks coming out of their mouths. What in the world are they holding? These two guys are funny!"

Someone knocked on the door. It was the clinic director, who wanted to take a Polaroid photograph of the father and son holding the lit red candle with the attached water that may have changed color, doing so while they had lollipops in their mouths.

"Yes," I responded. "We want to record this historic moment."

Dad pulled off the tissue so it could be seen. He said, "This doesn't need to be covered."

I answered, "Yes, that's right." I then looked at Sam and said, "You know your dad just took that cover off. Do you know what that means? It means that you two are being unveiled. You are now set free in the world as partners ready to have some crazy wild adventures."

After their photograph was taken, I made an announcement to the world. "Someday, I will pick up a newspaper and see a photograph that looks like this one, or I will see the news on television and find that they have become wild and crazy adventurers. They will take vacations together and enjoy surprise visits to roadside diners. They will do all this just so they can tell other fathers and sons that they need to lighten up. The headline will say, *Weenie and Bun Take Their Hot Dog Stunts Across America.*"

I paused before handing them the photograph. "I want you to take this with you as a reminder that you have always been holding onto each other and it's been a heart-to-heart connection. No matter how much heat life gives you, there is always a cup of water underneath to do what it needs to do."

I stood up to shake their hands. "You guys are amazing."

Sam was sincere when he replied, "It has been interesting to meet you."

"It was really nice to meet you, Sam."

Sam continued, "I am glad that I got chosen."

"I feel it, too, Sam. You will have a remarkable life because nothing like this happens unless it is meant to happen."

I shook his dad's hand, and he responded, "I am so glad I got to meet you."

"It is awesome, isn't it?" And I looked directly into the father's eyes as I spoke.

"Oh yes, it is!"

The emotion was so strong in the room that everyone hugged one another.

"Hey guys, the world needs us. They need to see this because the world has gotten too heavy. Everyone needs to lighten up. Go show them how. Have a great life. I expect it."

Sam and his dad experienced transformation as they held onto an improvised mojo staff that helped them cross some troubled waters. They found that they already had what they thought was missing—their love and caring for one another. What they needed more of was simple fun. Though being silly was already a part of their everyday, it needed to be given more importance. Did the water change color? The answer is found in a more mysterious question: did their relationship change? In the beginning, an adolescent sat with a man who felt like a stranger. At the end, they were two buddies, Weenie and Bun, ready to find their own adventure.

When the Guarani Indians experienced the invasion of the Spanish many years ago, it was a horrible intrusion of violence and destruction. The Catholic Church also wreaked havoc when it tried to destroy the old spiritual practices of the Guarani mojo doctors. Several years after I visited their villages, Protestant missionaries continued the invasion. They promised housing and money to anyone who would denounce the shamans and join their church. In all these turbulent invasions upon the natural order of things, men and women lost their sons and daughters. Heartbreaking separations took place, and mourning repeated itself every night in one household after another. All they had was mojo to keep their heartstrings connected. Whether separation from loved ones is an abusive act of physical, psychological, social, or legal power—as in the case of the Guarani Indians—or because of unfortunate family circumstances—as in Sam and his father's case—mojo is a powerful force for rescuing those connections and bringing them back to life.

Prescriptions for Mending Connections

Nothing hurts us more than when our loved ones are hurt or separated from us. Every family crisis can benefit from some good mojo, and every family should have a wand of protection. Keep in mind that even if you don't have a typically defined family structure, you have a network of people that serve's as your familial support system, even if it's located in your memory or imagination.

Every family crisis can benefit from some good mojo, and every family should have a wand of protection.

With this consideration of your relational nexus, the web of life that holds your important relations, I recommend that you go find yourself a stick. Go to the woods and find a tiny, thin branch that is around six to eight inches long. When you get it, play your flying drum, take a deep breath, sing or hum a song, and make a wish, asking that your closest relations be renewed and protected. Then break the stick in half. With some yellow thread or yarn, tie the two halves back together. Make it one again. The Greater Mind, which is bigger than any of us, understands that everyone has a break in his emotional heart that awaits being sewn together by the yellow cord of the sun's healing light.

Proceed to wave the wand over a cup of water. Remember that water is the first universe from which you came. Water is the mother of invention, the antidote to tired convention. When creativity dries up, get out some water and make things wet again. As you respectfully address your cup of water, imagine that all ancestral spirits are watching you, including those of the Amazon. Hear them whisper in your ear, "This is good." They are blessing your action and fully understand that you care enough about those you love to actually make a wand, even if it is completely irrational to do so. Remember to think of how Weenie and Bun held onto a stick that united them forever.

Place your mojo stick in a special place where it is safe. I recommend attaching it to the back of your television set. Whenever you watch television, know that it is watching over you; it has your back and your front covered. It is mojo that can bring a relationship back to life, and this takes place whenever you bring together whatever has been pulled asunder. The symbolic act of tying together things that have been previously broken triggers a powerful force within your creative imagination. It awakens the other actions necessary to bring light and joy to whatever is now on the mend.

Years ago, I went through a very difficult divorce in which I feared losing contact with my son. That's when I received the instructions for the mojo I am giving you now. I went into the woods and found a small branch, broke it, and then tied it with some yellow cord from a Tibetan rainmaker. After waving it over water and saying prayers that asked that our relationship be protected, I felt a peace come over me. My son remained a vital part of my life and became one of my best friends, and we continue to be very close today. I still have the magical stick that was broken but then tied together again.

I had the pleasure of bringing the two grandfather shamans from Paraguay to my hometown. I arranged that they live at a Catholic university and conduct a special ceremony. By a lake on that campus, they poured water onto hundreds of people who came asking to be baptized in the Guarani way. A step was taken toward mending a centuries-old injured relationship. The Church that once broke the heart of the Guarani people was now hosting their healing, even without their priests knowing what was taking place.

This is how mojo works. Whether done in light or darkness, day or evening, seen or unseen, find the wand that starts the process of bringing back together whatever has been broken in your life, home, community, or culture. Tie a broken stick together in a special, heartfelt way. Shine the light of hope over the wand and pass it over some water that may include your tears. In this way, you will bring mojo into the relations that bring us life.

This is how mojo works. Whether done in light or darkness, day or evening, seen or unseen, find the wand that starts the process of bringing back together whatever has been broken in your life, home, community, or culture.

I'll never forget the time that Little Seagull Man in Paraguay became seized by his mojo. He stopped what he was doing and got on the ground, crawling on all fours. He growled and appeared to be experiencing himself as a jaguar. Without warning, he threw me to the ground and pounced on top of me. I was stunned and did not know what to do. At that moment, he placed his mouth over my heart and blew onto me. I was shocked because his breath was not warm. It was ice cold, and it blew my soul right out of me.

I experienced myself flying into outer space, zooming by the stars and planets. I finally arrived at an ancient rainforest filled with beautiful birds and tall palm trees. There, I met his teachers, the ones who gave him songs and told him how to make his mojo. They were the ones who told me how to find my wand, and they are the ones who told me how to direct you to find yours. This is not explainable, but that shouldn't stop you from enjoying the mystery that can be awakened by holding onto a stick, waving a wand, or carrying a staff. Carry a small stick, remember the holy water, and baptize a change in the world. The Guarani ancestors expect it.

6

MOJO ART AND THE
LEFT SIDE OF MAGIC

I once stepped into a horror story more frightening than the blood-curdling fiction Stephen King makes up. Sometimes that's the price you pay to bring back some powerful mojo. At the time, I would have been happy to throw away all my mojo if it would have taken away the nightmare, but I didn't have that choice. It all began on the far-away, mysterious island of Bali when I arrived to meet some of their mojo doctors, the shamans they call Balians. I was traveling with my photographer and an audio engineer, and we knew something wasn't quite right because the airline had not only lost our luggage, it had no record of it. This wasn't how we wanted the trip to begin.

We were the last passengers to leave the Denpasar International Airport, but fortunately a cheerful guide was waiting for us. Mr. Wayan Budi Asa Meskel, who prefers to be called Budi, is one of the best professional guides in Bali. He was the primary source for *Bali: Sekala and Niskala*, the two-volume book series on Balinese culture compiled by Fred Eiseman Jr. During an earlier visit, I had been introduced to Budi by John Cooke, a former photographer for *National Geographic*, director for Oxford Scientific Films, and lecturer at the University of Oxford.

Budi smiled and promised that he could arrange to get us whatever supplies we needed. He said he was certain everything would work out. We weren't so sure when we discovered there were no clothes big enough to fit us at one of the local discount stores. When we arrived at the family compound of Budi's uncle, I was led to my own separate room, a thatch-roofed structure near one side of the main house. My photographer and sound engineer stayed in separate quarters away from where I was located. After a traditional Balinese dinner, we all headed for bed to get some much-needed sleep.

I was not prepared for what would happen late that night. At two in the morning, I awakened out of a deep slumber. I assumed it was my jet-lagged biological clock thinking it was daytime. When I discovered what time it was, I tried to go back to sleep. Within a couple of minutes, I heard what sounded like one of the largest crashes or explosions I'd ever heard. For a moment, I thought my room had been demolished, but I was still intact. The sound seemed to have its origin to the right side of my bed, near the bathroom. I froze in a panic. I was paralyzed with fear because I wondered if it was an earthquake. I lay there for a few more seconds, and then things got much worse. I heard a giant stomping sound above me on the roof. Now I was really freaking out because it clearly was not a natural disaster. Apparently an intruder was behind this unnerving, hair-raising sound.

The person on the roof did not cease walking. He simply stomped back and forth from one end of the roof to the other. It made no sense. Why wasn't he trying to break in? Why walk like that above me? Why was there such a huge explosion? No bomb was required to break into a thatched structure. The scenario made no sense.

Just when I thought I couldn't get more frightened, I was struck by the fact that the sound of the stomping feet on the roof was way too loud for a human being to make. It sounded like the walk of a gigantic monster, what I imagined was a fifteen- to twenty-foot-tall beast. The stomping obviously was not human! That was the only fact I felt certain about, and it brought me to the alarming edge of an eerie, irrational shock that was outside the capacity of what my mind to handle.

In all my years of traveling and witnessing weird, strange, and unexplainable events, I had never encountered anything like this. I was experiencing what I thought was only possible in the imagination of a writer of fiction. If the stomping had happened for only a few seconds or minutes, I would have assumed I was in a waking dream or that I was hallucinating. But this kept going on and on. I was as awake as you can get, knowing that this stomping was not being made by anything human. It shook the entire structure and the earth below. It was as strong as the trembling of an earthquake aftershock. After each of its steps, I heard rocks and sand fall down the sloped roof. Back and forth, this march of terror went. On and on, it proceeded until the next unimaginable step took place. It would not stop.

I finally managed to get myself out of bed to move to wherever the stomping wasn't taking place. That beast would be on one side of the roof, and I would head to the opposite side of the room. When it went to the corner away from the window, I'd run to the window and open it so I could shout for help as loudly as I could. I sounded like a madman screaming for my life! But no one answered. This was a compound filled with many people, but I heard not a single human reply. I wondered if they had been killed. My fear soared and left any hope of escape far behind. None of my psychotherapy or spiritual training helped. Prayers were ineffective, and relaxation techniques were less than worthless. Making deals with the universe simply went unheard.

Nothing would stop the stomping. It lasted all night. To take things to the next level of fright, this thing, or whatever it was, would rattle the door on the upstairs balcony, presumably demonstrating that it wanted to come in. It did not kick down the door; it just messed with my mind.

After several harrowing hours of this torture, I began wondering if there was a link between the missing luggage and the unexplainable noise on the roof. I thought about this because it made no sense that there would be no record of our luggage on the airline's computer. It also made no sense to be terrorized by some bigger-than-life thing stomping on the roof! I was reaching for any irrational clue or impossible connection to help me get a handle on the situation. I asked myself if the missing luggage and the mysterious stomping were trying to alter the course of the research I came to conduct in Bali. I came to this conclusion: if I survived the night, I was getting the hell out of there. I would never ever put myself in a position to go through another night like this.

Without photographic and recording gear, what could I possibly accomplish anyway? Then I remembered that I had heard that the Balians make magical drawings as a kind of mojo for protection, good luck, and other forms of influence. It led me to a practical idea. *If I survive all this,* I thought, *I'll immediately leave Bali, and have Budi collect those drawings and send them to me. That way I don't need any equipment, can quickly get off the island, and can still get my assignment done. Screw this madness! I'm out of here!*

The moment I decided to procure the magical drawings, the stomping stopped. Yes, that is exactly what happened. Somehow my consideration of that type of Balinese mojo had been heard and responded to by the beast on the roof. My heart almost stopped beating. It was as frightening for that sound to suddenly stop as it was for it to unexpectedly show up. I felt simultaneously relieved and more alarmed. The possibility that it was communicating with me by telepathic means was taking the night way too far into an episode of *The Twilight Zone*. This thing seemed to read my mind!

Though I had been completely terrified by the unexplainable presence, the moment I thought there might be a reason for the madness, I suddenly held the possibility for a change in perspective. *What the hell*, I thought. *I'll talk to the damned thing.*

I spoke out loud, "Am I here because of the magical drawings?" It was my feeble attempt to communicate.

Immediately, I heard wings flapping. It was not the sound of a monster stomping on the roof but of a flock of birds. My flashlight was on, and it appeared that a group of white birds had flown into the room and then right through the wall. There was no doubt that I was in a mojo world. This was not orchestrated by anything other than the mysteries of the dark.

I was not a happy camper. I shouted back, "This can't be real. I did not see that." The beast answered back by stomping on the roof with even more rock and sand sliding down its edges. At the same time, all the doors and windows started violently rattling. All hell broke out.

"Stop it!" I screamed. "OK, I'll listen," I pleaded. "Tomorrow, I'll ask to be taken to the drawings, but I am not staying here. I can't handle this. I have to get out of this place. It's too much for me, and I can't take it anymore." A great silence settled into the room.

After four hours of wrestling with the foot stomping of an unknown beast, the silence sounded like the roar of the mightiest dragon of the mythological wild. I noticed that it had become light outside. The sun was up—thank God! I had prayed all night to see the sun again, and it had returned. I felt safer. I heard human footsteps in the compound. I carefully opened the door, peeked out, and to my great relief, saw Budi's staff preparing breakfast.

I ran toward them and was rather hysterical. Shouting, crying, and trembling over what had happened, I told them to get me out of there. I only had one thought on my mind: escape from Terror

Island! I asked for a phone and made a long-distance call to my travel agent. Let's say that I was a bit out of my everyday mind. I demanded that he immediately book me at the Ritz-Carlton Hotel. I assumed that a modern, non-spiritual setting was the last place any spirit would visit. My mind was so shaken that I was making wild attempts to rescue myself from whatever had taken place. It took a while to gather my wits.

Budi sat me down and helped me relax so I could report what had happened during the night. As I spoke about the sound on the roof, he did not express any surprise. He seemed to understand what had happened. I stopped talking and asked, "Budi, do you know something about this? Can you help me put all of this together? I am really lost as to what any of it means."

Budi was ready to talk. "The big god of the island has paid you a visit."

I quickly asked, "Have you heard of this sort of thing happening to anyone else?"

"It's rare, but Balinese people have heard stories about it. You need to get dressed. There are people who know about these things. I must take you to them. They will be able to explain. They will know what you need to do."

I assumed that mojo was calling for a new adventure on an island historically steeped in magic.

Hearing his words brought a great calm even though I had no clue what it meant. I knew that the mysterious experience fit into a bigger picture that I had not yet seen. I assumed that mojo was calling for a new adventure on an island historically steeped in magic. Then I remembered that no one had heard my shouts for help. I asked him about that.

"That is the way this kind of thing is. The big god cuts others off from having the experience. It's between you and the big god. The big god has come for you. You are being sought by Jero Gede Macaling, the god for our shamans. This is a very big deal. This god is found on a small island called Nusa Penida. Hurry, we need to go tell the elders. I will take you to the leading Balian in our country. She advises the heads of our government and is highly respected by our traditional elders."

After getting dressed, Budi shouted, "Hurry, hurry. Come quickly. We must go. She is waiting to see us."

I later learned that Jero Gede Macaling is the most important god to the Balinese people. *Jero* means "highest level," *gede* means "big," and *macaling* refers to a big tusk or fang. Hence his nickname, the big god. The Balian woman Budi was talking about was a medium named Mangku Alit, who had a unique ritual for entering a trance. She burned pieces of coconut shell in a bowl, creating a flame with a lot of dark smoke. She would then appear to bury her face in the smoke and enter a trance. That's when her voice would change. In this altered state of communication, she claimed to speak for various spirits and gods.

After I met Mangku Alit, she wasted no time getting ready for the ceremony. We had brought the appropriate offerings, and her staff was already prepared for what needed to happen. As the smoke rose, she leaned over and buried her face in it. I don't know how she could possibly breathe. Not once did she turn her head away from the heavy smoke. She disappeared into it. She began to speak, but with a more authoritative sound.

I was told that the god, Jero Gede Macaling, was speaking through her. "Yes, you are wanted here," it said. "I have granted you permission to learn our ways. You are to know about the magical drawings. More importantly you are given permission to be taught what is rarely discussed and shown: the left side of magic. You will be taken to many Balians so they can open our mysteries to you. You must do these things, and then you must come visit me on my island. After all these things have been accomplished, you must return to the room where we first met. Special offerings, prayers, and ceremonies need to be made."

Great, I thought silently to myself. *That's all I need to hear. This monster is actually a god who wants me to get appropriately groomed and then come back for another date with it. Damn! How did I get myself into this?*

For the next month, we trekked all over the island, and I did not stay in that compound. I only spent the nights in noisy hotels and resorts to keep all spooky visitors away. I met the most important Balians, and they all gave a blessing for me to enter their unique mojo world. Getting a blessing to gain entry like this is not common. I was told how the authors of one of the most renowned books on Balinese magic and healing, *Trance and Possession in Bali*, written by Balinese psychiatrist Luh Ketut Suryani with Western psychiatrist Gordon D. Jensen, had not been given permission by the Balinese gods, according to Mangku Alit. They, too, had come to her house, and the gods emphatically said no to their desire to learn about these ways.

Every Balian I met confirmed that Jero wanted me to be given the secrets about their mojo. It was foreseen that I would be in Bali numerous times to learn how to make all kinds of magic, including their special drawings. Over the years, I would learn about the light and dark sides so my education would be complete. *The Zohar* had laid a philosophical foundation for intellectually holding the relations of light and dark, but Bali opened the door to reveal a world of dark, left-handed practices, something I had never felt compelled to explore. I was apparently scheduled by the future to become well schooled in the good and the bad, the left and the right, but not as opposites. In Bali, they are regarded as complementarities, each side requiring the presence of the other.

It was foreseen that I would be in Bali numerous times to learn how to make all kinds of magic, including their special drawings. Over the years, I would learn about the light and dark sides so my education would be complete.

In that first month, I learned many things, especially about the magical drawings, which I will share in this chapter. When I truly committed to this mission, our luggage arrived on that day. It seemed the world of spirit was waiting for me to know why I was there. Yes, I honored the request to pay a visit to the big god, Jero Gede Macaling. Accompanied by several Hindu priests, I was taken to Pura Dalem Peed, home of the big god shrine that is located on the island of Nusa Penida. And I went through a series of tests that day. I would be taken to a certain spot and left for a while. Then the priests would ask what I experienced. I'd have a strange vision and report it, and then they'd take me to another spot. Finally, I was taken to the big shrine.

I sat, dressed in traditional Balinese attire, and was blessed by the priests of the shrine. They began a ceremony, and I felt appreciation for the mojo know-how I had been taught by the Balinese Balians. I don't know how many moments passed, but all of a sudden, I felt someone kick me on the side of the head. I turned to see who had done it. No one was near me; I was sitting alone in the middle of the shrine. I looked up to see whether a coconut had fallen on me, but there was no tree. My head had really been clobbered, and I rubbed it with my hand. That's when the priests ran over and asked what had happened. I told them someone had kicked me in the head and that it hurt.

They did not offer me any sympathy. Instead, they celebrated this occurrence. I then saw a woman smiling in the background. It was Mangku Alit, the medium I had met after my first encounter with the big god. She came over and said it was a very auspicious day. She and the priests explained that the big god initiates you as a Balian—a Balinese mojo doctor—by kicking you on the side of the head. I had been kicked. Furthermore, that first house call with all the stomping was an invitation to get kicked. If I had asked the god to come in, it would have kicked my head and the whole ordeal would have been done with. I was too scared, thinking it only wanted to kick my ass, and it seemed like it was capable of kicking me to another island!

It didn't matter. I got to his island after all was said and done, and there, I got my head straightened out. Along the way, I picked up a hell of a lot of mojo—far more than the hoodoo gris-gris merchants in old school New Orleans ever dreamed was available on the planet. I had spent all this time in Bali on a magical bus ride, tracking down mojo.

I was soon reminded that I was supposed to go back to the compound room where I'd had my first date with Jero. I still felt apprehensive about another sleepover with that god, but I knew it was part of the deal. I didn't want to face the consequences of any unfinished business with the kick that thing had. I faithfully, though nervously, returned to the room on the main island where I previously had been almost scared to death. I fell asleep with a reminder that there was nothing to be afraid of because I now understood the context of what had happened. Then it happened again: I woke up in the middle of the night because something startled me. There was no explosion this time; it was just thunder and rain. The rain sounded gentle, though it sounded like it was raining in my room. I did not turn on the light to check. I went back to sleep.

Behind the seen is the unseen, and it is filled with magic from all sides and directions.

The next morning, I discovered that every personal possession and piece of equipment in the room was wet. The papers on my desk were soaked, and my clothes inside the armoire were wet. But everything else in the room was dry! Furthermore, it had not rained that night; nothing was wet in the yard. The rain had fallen only on my stuff. I guess the big god has a sense of humor. It must have gotten a big kick out of that practical joke! All kidding aside, that rain was gentle and did not destroy a thing. I accepted it as a final baptism—another reminder that water is an anointing of initiatory birth, the marking of a new beginning. I would never see the world the same again. Behind the seen is the unseen, and it is filled with magic from all sides and directions.

As I prepared to leave, Budi told me something he didn't want to say until after I had successfully made it through the night. "Brad, after that first night you spent here, my workers and I got up on the roof and guess what? We found it was covered with sand and rocks. We don't put sand and rocks on our roofs. The big god was here just like you described. The rocks and sand we found were the same kind found on his home island of Nusa Penida." Hearing that, I concluded that none of this had been a psychotic episode caused by a tropical island cocktail. Something mysterious had happened, and the elders regarded it as an important sacred event.

Several days of ceremony followed, and thousands of offerings were placed around the room where I had stayed. A gamelan (Indonesian orchestra) played through the night. Prayers were given, and blessings were spoken. But this was not the end of the story. After the ceremony, the room was empty. The next night, the room collapsed to the ground. The whole thatch-roofed structure fell apart and would never entertain another guest. It had served its purpose.

Mojo is real whether you want to believe in it or not. Belief doesn't matter. It can still kick you in the ass or give you the extra boost you need to get through a dark episode, an impasse, or a lost journey. If mojo makes a house call, you can't hide under the covers and expect it to go away. If it comes for you, you are going to know something is up. It doesn't matter whether you ask for it to come or go away; it just does its thing, and that's all there is to it.

In Bali, I met a medical doctor, Dr. Ngurah Nala, who was the rector and professor of physiology at Indonesia University of Hinduism. He told me a remarkable story about one of his colleagues, a former professor of economics. Years ago, this professor started having the same dream every night of the week: an old man dressed in white clothes would come to him and say, "You must become a Balian." The professor absolutely refused, saying, "No, no. I am an economist!"

He took a leave of absence to get as far away as he could from Bali and its cultural influences. He thought that was the best way to put an end to his dreams. He went further by trying to make himself as dirty as he possibly could, drinking a lot of liquor and having sex with many prostitutes. He figured that if he made himself spiritually dirty, the spirits would leave him alone. Staying away for three years and receiving another advanced degree, he then came back to his university in Bali, where they gave him his old position.

The next week, his dreams returned. This time, the professor tried something different. He asked the old man dressed in white whether he could have a friendly discussion. The old man in his dream responded, "Ask me anything." The economics professor made a request, "Prove to me that you are really a wise man." The old man instructed him, "Go to the island of Pura Dalem Peed and visit the shrine of the big god, Jero Gede Macaling."

The next morning, the professor took a boat to the island just like I had, and he visited the shrine. I presume he got his head kicked, but I wasn't told about it. When he returned home the next morning, he was surprised to see many people standing in a line in front of his house. They were waiting for him. They were all troubled or sick and needed help. He pleaded with them, "I am a professor of economics. I am not a doctor or a Balian." He was not prepared for what each person told him—he got the surprise of his life! Every single person in that line had experienced a dream in which an old man dressed in white told them to go to his address the next morning; that's why they were there. The professor had no choice. He blessed some water and gave them all a drink. That is how he became a Balian. But he is now as wise as the old man he dreamed. He only treats people who dream of him.

During my first visit to the smoke Balian, as I like to call Mangku Alit, I recorded what the gods spoke through her. Toward the end of their pronouncement, I was told this was the purpose of my visit to Bali:

> You are very close to the gods and are looking for truth and rightness. You are already in communication with the Buddha, Siwa, and the power of life, and you have the inclination of the supreme god. He is connected to you. You should tell people how to live in these crazy times. You are the right person to teach because you are close to the supreme god. You must help others. Our gods will protect you to do your work. The supreme god gives you permission to discuss our most sacred ways. Our gods want you to talk about both the left and right; they will give you a strong feeling

regarding what to write. Don't omit what is the reality in Bali. You should teach them about the secret drawings. You are completely accepted by the supreme god.

As the gods directed, I will share what I learned about the magic drawings, and the left and right sides: I collected many old renderings of magical drawings as the big god requested, which had been etched onto the long, narrow leaves of the rontal palm tree. To make these, a Balian scratches the leaves with a sharp-tipped iron instrument called an *apengerupak* and then rubs the ashes of a burned nut into the cracks of the etched surface to make the drawing more visible. This magical drawing, called *rerajahan*, is a sacred image that starts to become mojo when drawn onto a piece of cloth, metal, paper, pottery, leaf, fruit, wood, basket, or skin.

The images depicted in magical drawings are numerous: holy characters; the sun, stars, and moon combined with holy characters; flowers with characters on the petals; animals such as tigers, crocodiles, lions, snakes, or dragons; human bodies or parts of the human body; distorted human body forms with animal heads or human bodies without a head; gods and goddesses; distortions of gods and goddesses manifesting angry personifications; mixes of the gods' weapons with holy characters; renderings of demons, spirits, and various strange creatures; and sacred buildings and dwelling places.

The image in itself is not magical. To make it come to life, the Balinese believe that it is wise to have it drawn by a mojo doctor who the big god, Jero Gede Macaling, has approved and ordained to do so. The drawing is made on the appropriate material during an auspicious day accompanied by special offerings. The magic is infused into it when the doctor speaks some mojo words, a special incantation called a Pasupati mantra. The activated drawings are then used for a wide variety of purposes, including the summoning of protection and magical power from the big god. Other purposes include purification of one's body and soul, the enhancement of someone's spirituality, gaining access to unique talents, driving away bad luck, protecting one's home and family, and preventing or negating physical and spiritual harm from enemies.

There are endless ways in which this art can help someone change their life.

Practitioners of both the left and right ways appeal to Jero Gede Macaling for mojo power. Without asking for it or even knowing about these matters, the big god gifted me with permission and know-how in matters concerning mojo art. I draw upon it in my clinical cases whenever I ask people to place a special drawing under their pillow or hang an object above their bed when they sleep at night. I may also ask them to slip a drawing inside their shoe, wear an image or symbol inside or outside their clothes, bury a photograph in the ground, or draw a symbol on their body. There are endless ways in which this art can help someone change their life.

In addition to mojo art, my experiences in Bali also taught me about the left side of magic, as their elders called it. Yes, it exists. In Bali, there is a complex understanding and relationship with regard to the practice of the right and left sides. These sides somewhat correspond to good and bad, light and dark, but with more complexity and subtlety.

What is the left side of magic? Commonly called black magic, it is easily trivialized by saying that it is solely bad and relies upon dark forces that are not associated with good purposes. It is more complicated than this.

There are two ways to gather the vitality needed to summon, awaken, and dispense mojo. One is through the biggest form of love—love that has no strings attached. It does not use love as a means of achieving a goal or making something happen; it simply asks that we surrender to God's will as we open our hearts to a higher power. You might say it is love for love's sake. The other way of activating mojo is to purposefully will an intended outcome and to do so with whatever mobilizes the feeling and expression of power. These two paths to mojo—love without purpose and power with intention—underlie the right and left roads respectively.

These two paths to mojo—love without purpose and power with intention—underlie the right and left roads respectively.

It all becomes more complex as we dance the relations between love and power. We may love fully in order to feel the power that authentic powerlessness evokes, and then draw upon it to enact the fulfillment of an honorable intention. Or we may gather intentional power and then release it into the arms of the highest and purest love. Note that these complexities are voiced from the perspective of the right side. Seen from the left, our love may make us desire power in order to maintain or bring on more love. Or we may think power brings us love, so we surrender whatever love we have for more power, assuming it can pin down elusive love. Complexity that is embodied by dancing distinctions rather than simplified by stationary dualisms is understood by Balinese culture. The former seems less present in less seasoned (though more technologically developed) cultures. We get caught in the either/ors of an opposite too easily rather than allowing a more interdependent dance to emerge. As a result, we forget that good can sometimes do harm and a harmful experience can sometimes be transformed into a greater good.

**We get caught in the either/ors of an opposite too easily
rather than allowing a more interdependent dance to
emerge. As a result, we forget that good can sometimes
do harm and a harmful experience can sometimes
be transformed into a greater good.**

A mojo doctor works with the complexities of all the many forms of dance that arise from interacting opposites. This includes love and power as well as right and left. When complexity dances, mojo power, or what the Balinese call *sakti*, is awakened. This is when we are able to participate in the influence of events and, from time to time, be a part of creating a marvel. We are never in control, but we are part of the higher processes of control that welcome our involvement. How we participate is determined by our nature or destiny. Whether you go about it as a gentle lover or fierce warrior is not a choice; it is a calling. It is your starting point. You light the match with love or power, but that only gets things started. Then you get danced by all sides, and you skirt the edges of left and right.

As they say in Bali, you must follow your destiny. If you are called to the left side, you have no choice but to follow. If you are called to combat the left, you must do it. All sides must be present in the larger interactive dance—the whole ecology that holds and moves the differences needed for all things to dynamically coexist.

Perhaps the most extreme reach of the left side is the practice of transforming yourself into another form. In Bali, the people who are able to appear as an animal or as a nonhuman entity are called *leyaks*. Most Balians will say they know nothing about leyaks even though they do know something. Anyone suspected of being a leyak faces the possibility of being banned from the village; they are feared and considered dangerous. Leyaks are the same as the skinwalkers known by the Diné, or Navajo. Of the oldest culture in the world, the Kalahari

Bushmen say these characters are the doctors who turn themselves into lions.

I have met these beings in all these cultures and have been told what is required to become one. It is not something you want to have a date with; it is dark and frightening. Suffice it to say that evil can get a hold of people from time to time, and it requires some strong mojo to help someone stuck in such a situation. I have been taught this mojo, and sometimes this work looks like an exorcism. I almost died performing one in the Deep South, but that is another story for another time. There is far more to all of this than what I have just stated.

Most people do not know that there are good and bad leyaks. This is sort of like saying there is good and bad "good" and good and bad "evil." Life is more complex than the simple words and categories we use to try and capture it. In Bali, a good leyak is called a *leyak sari* (white leyak) and the bad leyak is a *leyak pamoroan* (black leyak). A leyak sari doesn't change into an animal shape; it only changes into higher forms, often without any shape. This positive work can be done while you stay at home and sleep, sending your resourceful thoughts and feelings elsewhere. The lower leyaks, on the other hand, can only travel with their body, as they desire to fight and conquer their opponent. Please remember that you have nothing to worry about in these matters as long as you don't worry; fear feeds the leyak's power. This is another reason to keep laughing, and to cultivate a jaded and absurd worldview. It's the best protection against things that frighten us.

How does this relate to everyday life? Everyone's ordinary experience includes irrational fears and worries. Sometimes, we become terrorized by them, and find we can't sleep at night or perform to the best of our abilities in the daytime. I am not referring to a fear of leyaks chasing us around the house but to the ways in which our minds race with fear as we become endlessly concerned with problems regarding health, relationship, meaningful work, personal finances, and the myriad daily challenges that creep into our lives. If we aren't careful—and sometimes in spite of being careful—we can get swept away by a monstrous angst that spoils our hope and happiness.

The way in which a mojo doctor understands and handles a leyak, or dark force in the night, teaches us how to address our own demons and monsters who are as capable of disturbing our peace and as they are our well-being. If we feed fear, no matter its source, it grows. If we introduce absurdity and laughter, terror dries up and shrinks away. It also helps to know that the source of what troubles us is not *all* bad. There is a silver lining inside everything, including that which we are most disturbed and troubled by.

Am I suggesting that the dark isn't as bad as you thought it was? Leyaks really aren't as bad as you think? I was taught that a leyak is like a knife. It can help or hurt, depending on how you use it. As the Balians say, "Everything depends on your point of view." This may be the deepest secret of mojo; its purpose is to change your point of view. Changing the viewing, of course, also changes the possibilities for doing, and this is mojo at its best. Rather than getting caught between choosing whether something is only good or bad, you can move through ever-changing and ever-shifting perspectives that expand your recognition of the greater complexity of any situation.

Rather than fighting the monsters that bring fear, you can thank them for bringing you an opportunity to learn and grow. As you imagine thanking your monster for the gift it brings, the absurdity of doing that might tickle your funny bone. To your surprise, you might be able to laugh at your fear, or you may be released to go further by asking your monster to help you with another situation.

The more you creatively expand your choices of interaction, the less likely you are to get caught underneath the roof of a terrorizing, back-and-forth, no-exit dilemma. Go ahead and get kicked in the head from time to time so you can be reminded that sometimes the least expected thing is the perfect thing to get a new kick out of life—the very thing you need to get your life retuned and jump started.

Rather than fight the monsters that bring fear, you can thank them for bringing you an opportunity to learn and grow.

Thanks to my Balinese training, I have wrestled with the magical dark and know its tricks. You have to be respectful of the presence of all things in the universe. A head-on attack only precipitates a war, and no one in their right mind wants to go to war, whether it be with other human beings or critters that ain't human.

The key to working with these situations is to understand that troubling presences don't want to hang out with you any more than you want their darkness casting a big shadow over your home. Whether it is out-of-control worry or anxiety, or a leyak running amok, you don't have to be trapped. There is another choice beyond trying to eradicate whatever troubles you. You need to throw some mojo into an overwhelming situation in order to open up more possibilities for how to be present in the ordeal.

A mojo doctor needs to make both sides—the good and the bad—happy. In a Zulu village many moons ago, Credo Mutwa taught me his approach to ridding a situation of an unexplainable, unwelcome, and troublesome ghost: "Tell it you know it isn't as happy as it should be, living where it isn't wanted. Go on to say that you'd like to show it a better home, and then take it for a journey to another place, like a big boulder sitting on a hillside faraway. Invite it to jump into that stone or ocean or faraway star and dissolve itself into another form of existence where it will be much happier." Of course, what he says is spoken through metaphor and strategic communication, but this is the way to effectively address disturbing visitors whether they are ghostly apparitions or haunting emotions and thoughts.

The next time you are shaken by a disturbing experience, try not to exercise the knee-jerk response of regarding it as solely bad. Even if what happens is terrible and causes great suffering, remind yourself that there is another perspective that enables a silver lining to be revealed, even if it is a very thin lining. Find that lining and thank it for bringing more complexity into your awareness. As you find the silver linings inside troubling situations and experiences, your world will expand, and in this larger space, you will discover that you have more choices than you previously imagined. All mojo, whether it involves objects, drawings, or words, is about making your experiential space larger—so large that there is more room for you to move creatively and not be caught underneath a terrorizing dualism that stomps back and forth over your head.

Turning a Monster into a Mojo Artist

I saw a sixteen-year-old, troubled boy from Louisiana who everyone said had fallen to the dark side. Andy came to me with his family, which consisted of a grandmother and a purported "mildly mentally handicapped" mother. A year before, he supposedly tried to kill his mom with a steak knife because she refused to play with him. In and out of hospitals and institutions since he was seven, Andy had a history of mutilating, torturing, and being sexually inappropriate with various kinds of animals, including dogs, cats, birds, frogs, and lizards. He would often finish his routine by roasting and eating them. When a case involves mutilating animals and other disturbing actions, one needs to think about getting out some strong mojo. That's when my Balinese training serves its purpose in a big way. Andy's clinical files also said that he claimed to see ghosts when he was admitted to a hospital. A professional presentation of this case was published in my book *The Creative Therapist: The Art of Awakening a Session*.

As I walked to my clinical office where Andy and his family were sitting with their therapist, I noticed a soft rubber ball lying on the floor. It felt like mojo, so I picked it up and carried it with me as I entered the room. My experiences in Bali taught me that mojo is everywhere; look for it when you need it. In this case, it was lying on the floor in front of the door to my office.

I started by talking about the ball. "How y'all doin'? Is this your ball? It was just sitting outside. It looks hard doesn't it? But when you squeeze it, it's soft." I looked at Andy and asked him directly, "Do you think it looks hard?" I threw the ball to him. "But feel it; it's real soft. See?"

"Yeah," Andy agreed and then tossed the ball back to me.

"Is that the way you are? Do you look hard, but you're really soft?"

"Yeah."

Already we had entered the complexity of the mojo universe: things aren't always as they appear.

"Tell me why you guys are here. What's the reason?"

Grandmother started laughing and replied, "To meet you, for one thing, and to chat for a little while."

I asked, "What kind of creative expression led all this to take place today? What happened? Did he burn down a building, or did he ...?"

To my surprise, Mom said that *she* actually tried to burn something down. Andy explained that it was an accident. I teased the family, saying that Mom was a fire setter.

Mom laughed and responded, "Yeah, not really."

I asked Grandmother what she did that helped keep their family interesting, and she said she was grouchy, griped a lot, and had to take some medicine to calm her nerves. When I said, "So you gripe all the time," she added, "Not really."

I picked up on this theme, and mentioned that Mom sometimes set fires, but not really. Grandmother griped all the time, but not really. Then I asked Andy, "What do people say about you that's 'not really'?"

"I just aggravate people."

I chimed in, "But not really."

He echoed me, "Not really. I just play a lot."

I turned to their therapist and said, "These people do things, but not really. You know what that tells me? It tells me that whatever he got in trouble for, he's just pretending." I was thinking how life outside of Bali is also complex, having more categories of real versus not real, good versus bad. Here, a family acts in ways that appear real, but on another level, are not real. My Balian mojo took note.

His mom offered a report on what Andy had recently done. "He wrote on a wall."

Andy corrected her, "I spray-painted my bedroom door."

I was reminded of the magical drawings of Bali. The fact that this boy was painting things on walls and doing eerie things did not escape my attention. I looked at his family and asked whether he did a good job of painting. I asked Andy whether he was a good painter. He nodded that he was. That's when I offered the idea that he might be an aspiring artist. I added, "Maybe he just wants to take an art class." His mom agreed and said that he did.

Andy then announced, "I'm a good drawer. I draw creatures."

"Interesting," I replied and then addressed the adults in the room. "Did you notice he said the word *creatures*? Do you mean something that's not an animal?"

Need I say that after my terrifying experience in Bali, I pay attention whenever someone says the word *creature*! My mojo confirmed that we were heading into similar territory. In Bali, the world of the unseen is addressed through aesthetic experience. One way of relating to it is through magical drawings. I continued moving in this direction.

"Like what?"

"Monsters. Aliens that evolve into monsters and stuff."

I leaned over to ask, "Now, this is a serious question: do you do the best you possibly can to draw the scariest monster?"

"Not really, but I try my best sometimes."

I turned to their therapists and pointed out the pattern that had been intriguing me. "Did you notice what he said? 'Not really.' That's the most interesting thing I've learned about this family. Anything they say that's about a behavior that others would think is a problem, they always say, 'Not really.' This tells me that they're actually experimenting with various forms of creative expression. In other words, it appears that Mother is setting the house on fire, but not really. It appears that Grandmother's whining, but not really. It appears that Andy's expressing scary things to people, but not really. Does that capture you all?"

All of the family enthusiastically agreed with this appraisal of their behavior, and they seemed proud of this fact. My mojo reminded me that magic takes place because of the energetic tension found in the midst of any strong juxtaposition of opposites. If this family was performing an unusual behavior and then claiming it was not real, then it was a clue that there could be some mojo stuff going on.

I concluded, "The problem is that the world thinks it's for real. But it's really not real, and this is probably what's happened with your boy. People are seeing something and thinking, *Oh, this is real; his monsters are real.* Maybe you draw so well that people are scared that you'll actually make a real monster."

"I'm thinking about it . . . something like a new species."

I showed genuine excitement. "Wow! That's what I call ambition! Most kids want to be a musician or a professional sports star. He wants to create a new species." I leaned over and shook Andy's hand. "That's pretty impressive. Awesome!" I threw him the ball again and said, "That takes balls." We all laughed together before I continued, "I would have been so proud if my son would have come to me and said, 'You know, Dad, I think my goal is to create a new species.' That would be amazing." I paused before asking, "What would the new species be able to do that human beings are not able to do? Or what would be something it would say to people that human beings don't say to each other?"

"I like scary stuff. . . . It would speak a new language."

I asked, "Would it be a language people hear? Or would it be a language where you just put thoughts into people's minds?"

Andy knew what his monster would do. "Put thoughts in people's minds."

"Would it be thoughts that startle them as opposed to thoughts they're familiar with?"

"It would startle them," he replied.

"Would it be thoughts that you would say they think are real but you would say are not real?"

"Not really. Yeah, sort of. Yeah."

Everything Andy said also accounted for the way mojo works. It plants seeds in the minds of other people's imagination and starts the motion toward a different reality. It is a form of hypnosis that is inseparable from suspending one's experience between what is real and what is not real. I couldn't help but notice that the qualities that defined Andy's monster were similar to the beast that gave me a fright in Bali. I kept this insight to myself, knowing that my Balinese mojo was by my side. It was directing what I observed and said.

Noticing that he was using the family's habitual response, I added, "In other words, your family is teaching you how to create the perfect monster. Do you all hear what I'm saying? His monster is going to create fires, but not really. It's going to get everybody to complain, but not really. Look at Grandmother. She's smiling and enjoying this whole family. This family is entertaining, isn't it? Would you say this is an entertaining family? In other words, you don't get bored in this family?"

Andy commented, "Oh no, it's never boring," as his mom and grandmother chuckled. Then he added, "Not really."

I underscored what was most important about what he just offered. "Do you know the most complimentary thing that an adolescent, a young man, can say about his family is, 'My family is not boring'? Almost everyone his age thinks that his family and everyone in it—and that includes him—is boring. This is a miracle! You may be the only family that isn't bored in the whole state of Louisiana, as most families are bored. But you have a family in which your son wants to create a new species. This beast doesn't even have to say a single word because it can put thoughts into your mind about things that startle you, though they really aren't what they seem to be. Very interesting. Let's say you created this creature and it did these things. What would be its name?"

Andy spent some time thinking and then offered a name, "Magmore."

I was impressed with this name; it had mojo. "That's a very interesting name. I never heard of a Magmore. *Mag* suggests it is sort of like a magnet, so I assume people are going to be attracted or drawn to it. Does that make sense?" Andy nodded his head. "And the more people try to stop thinking about Magmore, the more they think about Magmore."

Andy was with me as I pointed out the mojo nature of his creature's name, adding, "Yeah, it hypnotizes you."

I picked up on this. "It hypnotizes. You know what? I've got a feeling that you hypnotize a lot of people." The whole family burst into laughter as this truth was revealed. "People do all kinds of things in response to you because they think what you are doing is real, though you know it's not real."

Magmore and Andy both had mojo. They had a magnetic, hypnotic effect on people, leading them to assume more about a situation than its real truth. In other words, Magmore embodied the same influence Andy had on the world. Now we could see that any talk about Magmore would also be talk about Andy. Furthermore, any drawings related to Magmore would influence Andy. That's one way the magical drawings get inside you.

Andy's mom agreed with this view of his hypnotic effect on others, and I replied with my conclusion, "You're a master hypnotist in some ways: you can make people think things are real, but the things are not real." I turned to the others and said, "I bet he could convince someone that he actually is trying to make a monster, and they would probably send reporters to the house to sneak in and take photographs of him creating it."

Mom nodded her head and agreed. I looked at Andy and asked him directly. He agreed that he could do this. My mojo recognized a young mojo doctor in the making. The goal at the moment was to harness his talent so it was moved to the right side, away from the ways it had been getting him into trouble, as I sensed this was his destiny.

"Maybe you'll grow up to be a Hollywood filmmaker."

Andy laughed at my idea and then added, "I've been thinking about making comic books."

"Have you made a comic book before?"

"One time when I was little. I was in the sixth grade."

I was intrigued. At this stage, my mojo told me we had discovered that Andy's transformation would involve his drawing some mojo, just like the Balians had taught me to do. My inner voice suggested that I make a shocking announcement: "My heavens! I think this case is done. Andy knows precisely what he's to do with his life; it's just been on hold. Once upon a time, he had a skill that he knew—he recognized he could draw. He knew how to use his imagination. He knew how to make things appear real that aren't real; that's a comic book. He knew how those things that were real and not real sometimes involved monsters; that's a comic book. He knew that those monsters could set fires, but they weren't really fires. He knew that people in his comic book world would complain and get scared, thinking this was going to happen and therefore be worried. But it wasn't real. Andy knew how to create a name for the character that nobody had ever heard before because the secret and the art of comic book making is hypnotizing others by drawing them into a fantasized 'real' world."

> **My mojo told me we had discovered that Andy's transformation would involve his drawing some mojo, just like the Balians had taught me to do.**

I was telling Andy how he could make a different kind of mojo through pictures by using his language to explain it—talking about the world of comic books, where things also dance between seeming real and not real. I needed to explain that he needed to be using his mojo to help bring forth better outcomes in his life. As it was, his mojo was backfiring and turning him into a monster. I paused before continuing, "When his drawing of comic books stopped, I think he probably tried to make his life a comic book. He's been acting like a comic book character. I don't know the details of your life, but I'm going to guess that you have been acting like a comic book character, carrying on and doing things that a comic book character would do. Is that true?"

Andy replied, "Hmmm. Yeah ..."

"You need to pick up from when you last stopped drawing comics. Which hand do you use to draw? Are you right-handed? OK, I see that you are. Your mind has been waiting for your hand to start again. When you make a comic book, do you use pencils?"

Andy answered, "I use any pencil I can write with."

I turned to his mom and grandmother and made a dramatic request. "I'm going to ask the two of you the most important thing anyone will ask you to do with this young man. Immediately after this session, go get him a special set of pencils and paper so he can get on with his life and become a great creator of comic books."

They agreed to do it.

"This is a hand that's waiting for his talent to be expressed. He has a hand that wants to express his imagination, doing so with a hypnotic way of influencing people. If it's not used, and if he doesn't have the right pencil, he's going to turn into the very thing his hand wants to express. I guess the decision for this family is *whether he'll be a comic book character or whether he'll create comic books*. I advise you to create comic books because that will give you a rich, interesting, and maybe even lucrative life. The other choice will just make your hand want to have a pencil more than it already does."

Andy had art mojo. With it, he could create comic books. Otherwise, the mojo inside him would backfire and turn him into a comic book. Both outcomes were hypnotic, wild, influential, startling, disturbing, and beyond average forms of imagination. However, an artist gets paid for being wild and crazy, whereas the other stereotyped role gets into boring kinds of trouble. Andy's situation had become a choice. If his hand used his mojo talent, he would become an artist. If his hand was held back, his creative mojo could turn him into the very thing his hand wanted to express.

I continued this theme: "In a comic book, you can say and do anything. You can set fires. You can go to the backyard, look at a dog, and just take your pencil and say, 'I change you into metal.' You can see a deer walk by, and take your pencil and go, 'I change you into a five-headed octopus, with a sparrow's wing and the sound of a bumble bee when you fly near people.' A pencil can do it. Your hand can do it."

The bottom line here was that either his hand expressed a "not really" or he could go out and enact it. "Not really" is framed as another way of talking about a comic book.

Grandmother offered, "He's always had an avid imagination, even when he was little."

I prepared to give them a dose of absurd mojo talk. "I'm going to give you a professional opinion by technically naming what's happened. This is professional talk, so be prepared: His hand is constipated. His drawing hand is constipated. It has to be loosened up and set free. The creativity that is in him has to come out—he has to draw. He has to make comic books. He should consider making the scariest comic books, and he should not only have them be scary but have them be a little crazy. He might have a story where the monster that scares people the most ends up being the nicest creature. I think comic books often get boring because they show the scary people as the bad guys. The scary people should sometimes be shown to be the smartest ones."

My mojo asked for the teaching of Balinese wisdom where life is regarded as more complex than simple dualisms that lazily sort all matters as being merely a difference between good and bad. I was asking him to create a good bad—a bad comic character that served a socially and individually rewarding outcome.

Andy agreed with me.

"I knew that you were born with a special mission and a special talent. Your mission is to use that special talent." I announced that I was going to take a brief break. Before stepping out of the room, I invited the therapist to talk to the mom and grandmother about what kind of pencils and paper Andy needed. I suggested that maybe they should put a sign over his bedroom door that said *Professional Cartoonist.*

I departed and watched their conversation on a video monitor. The therapist and family successfully discussed the kind of art materials Andy required. Andy proposed that his studio should be located in his bedroom, near his desk and window. Grandma agreed and said, "He can look out the window, and think and concentrate." They put together a plan to go to a hobby center and Walmart.

I was reminded of some mojo that was sitting on a bookshelf in my office. It was a heavy metal arm with a hand. I frequent antique stores and flea markets to find unusual mojo items that I can give to clients when the moment seems right, just like I made the mojo wand for the father and son who were healing their relationship. My office is filled with mojo objects. I walked in and reached for this object; the mojo was pulling me in that direction.

I carried the metal hand to Andy and said, "For years I've had a hand, not understanding why I had a hand. I know that you have noticed that it's a right hand. I think maybe this hand's been waiting for you and that I should give it to you." I paused before proceeding. "When I give you this hand, your own hand is going to be free to express itself fully through the art that's your talent." I gave Andy the metal hand in a ritualistic way, concretely marking the moment when his hand was declared free to express his inborn gift and destined mission. Rather than giving him a Balinese kick in the head, I drew upon another form of heavy-handedness.

Andy thanked me, and we shook hands. He was clearly moved by the mojo object. It was a magical moment in the session; mojo had been exchanged.

The mojo feeling in the room inspired me to say, "Andy, this is important. I want to say this to your talent. I want to speak to your talent. When you make a comic book, it becomes your whole world. Every comic book you make can be anything that your talent wants to express. That means you can create many worlds." Andy nodded in agreement. "You can sometimes base your world on things that happen in your family. You can turn to your family and see it as an inspiration for the kind of things you create in a comic book world. If Mom almost burns the house down, it gives you an idea for a comic."

For the next few moments, his grandmother presented other facts about the family. Whatever she mentioned, I suggested that Andy could use it as inspiration for a comic. She said that some kids were supposedly playing with devil worship and dark things, but I encouraged Andy to turn this story into a comic. "What's important is that you take whatever is presented as a creative inspiration and express it in the art that God gave you to use." I turned to the grandmother and mom and said, "If he doesn't use his right hand, the hand that's been stuck, his talent will just come out in weird ways." Then I shifted to Andy. "Now I want those things to come out in even weirder ways; weirder than what anyone ever imagined. You're now free to do it in your own world—the reality of the comic book. Do you understand what I'm saying?" Andy nodded that he did.

Grandmother suggested that the death of Andy's grandfather had deeply affected him. Again, I utilized it as something his artistic mojo could handle. "I bet there are some interesting stories about Grandfather's life that would make an interesting cartoon."

Grandmother continued, "His grandfather was always telling Little Moron jokes. He did that all the time."

I showed Andy how his mojo could play with what Grandmother just said. "Isn't that weird? Because the first part of the word *moron* is *more*, which is the last part of the name of the monster you wanted to create, which was Magmore. Isn't that a weird thought?"

Grandmother was surprised by this connection, even though it was absurd. She later expressed her appreciation for what had taken place as she spoke to her therapist about my participation in the session. "How did people like you two come into our lives?"

I responded in kind. "How can fascinating, creative people like you come into our lives?"

Grandmother later mentioned that Andy didn't prefer going to church with them. I responded by pointing to his mojo. "In his comic book, he is free to invent a church nobody's ever heard of. Wouldn't that be interesting?"

"Yeah," Andy said with delight.

"The church of Magmore," I suggested. We all died laughing at that idea.

I stood up to wrap up the session, shaking hands with Mom and Grandmother. I addressed Andy with these parting thoughts: "I think you all are going to have one of the most fascinating stories to share with the world. Maybe someday it will be a Hollywood movie, or a cartoon, or a story in a book that is seen in everyone's home. That would be something, wouldn't it? You never know. Cartoons become movies, movies become cartoons, and lives become cartoons, and lives become movies, and movies become lives, and lives become stories. What a movie you've been living! Now it's time to be free to express everything that touches you most deeply, including your feelings for your grandfather."

Out of the clear blue, Grandmother mentioned, "There's a hummingbird that comes by my house."

I looked at Andy and said, "There you go—more material for your comics. Magmore's hummingbird—what could you do to a hummingbird in a comic book world that would make people think that it is real but not real? What would be compelling and hypnotic? That's something for you to think about. Maybe for Christmas, you can make a comic book for each person in the family. Grandmother gets a hummingbird comic."

Mom piped in, "And I'd get one with the house on fire."

"Yeah, she gets one, too," I added.

Andy mentioned he could also design some video games. I answered him, "When you take all the energy that you've been wasting on nonsense and creatively apply it to the world of art, it will make a surprise you're not going to believe. Your life is going to be so ..." I leaned over toward Andy and finished the sentence, "weird." Andy looked up and smiled.

Mom added, "It'll surprise everybody."

"Yes, it will surprise everyone. Your ability to hypnotize will multiply ten times. And your ability to disturb people in ways that make you smile will multiply ten times. But you know what? You'll get away with it, and someday you might make a fortune doing it. Whatever the case, one thing's for sure: this whole family is already very wealthy—rich with unique creativity—and that's a blessing for us. As quickly as you can, without breaking the speed limit, you need to go start the next chapter of this gifted young man's life. OK? Turn his room into the studio of a professional cartoonist."

I looked at Andy and said, "Andy, now you have three hands." As I pointed to his steel hand, I added, "There's the beginning part of Magmore. Perhaps Magmore will be a monster who secretly draws cartoons with a steel hand."

The therapist added, "I'm eager to see what Magmore looks like."

I parted with these words: "Awesome. Go make some history!"

After shaking Andy's hand again, I asked to shake his new metal hand. We all laughed.

Several months later, we found that Andy had successfully started doing his schoolwork, and things were moving along nicely at home. His bedroom, now a studio, became a place where his imagination was able to express itself freely. A second follow-up interview indicated that Andy had found a job and had volunteered for public service to clean graffiti off of public walls.

He's still drawing and continues to successfully navigate school. For the final meeting with Andy, my colleague and I visited his home during the Christmas holiday. He was proud to show us his grades because he had made all A's. We celebrated how his story provides inspiration to people whose natural gifts are not always seen or understood by others. He invited us to see his studio. We took a glance at the spot where he created his mojo cartoon figures. There, he gifted me with his first drawing of Magmore.

To my great surprise, his drawing was the image of a Balinese mojo figure. Around five years earlier, I had written an obscure book with I Wayan Budi Asa Mekel on the magical drawings of the Balians called *Balians: Traditional Healers of Bali*. Andy, without knowing anything about this culture, had drawn something very similar to one of their powerful images, that of Sang Hyang Bhima Sasa-Dhara. In Bali, a traditional healer draws this image on a rontal (palm) leaf, places it in a glass of clean water, surrounds the client with fragrant flowers, and then asks him to drink the water and

clean his face with it. Its purpose? The drawing is made and utilized in this traditional way in order to transform anything that is toxic inside a person so he will no longer be sick.

**Mojo arrives when you need it,
even if you don't recognize what it is.**

This was the mojo operation we accomplished with Andy. We took the underlying creative source of what was making him socially toxic and transformed it into something more useful—an artist's playful work. He moved from being a monster to being a creator of comic monsters. The latter draws upon his resources and leads to other more resourceful ways of using his talents in his life. Magmore was more than a comic book figure; it was a reminder that life will always be a mystery when it is filled with mojo. Again, mojo arrives when you need it, even if you don't recognize what it is. This is how it has always been.

During the night when an otherworldly creature nearly scared me to death, I had to get past the way I was hypnotized by fear. When art came into the picture, the situation was transformed. Drawings enabled the monster to become a creative power that could protect and influence desired results. Andy, without knowing it, had lived under the same kind of roof that I'd encountered in Bali. My job was simply to lead him to the drawing that could tame his beast and make it a creative ally.

Prescriptions for Making Mojo Art

I am going to suggest a magical drawing for you. It is something I have used before that actually involves two magical drawings. First, I want you to think about what the holiest symbol is for you. Think of all the holy symbols in the world, whether they are from the great world religions or whether they lie in other domains of creative inquiry and aesthetic appreciation. Whether it's a cross or butterfly, sign of infinity, circle, egg, Sanskrit symbol, shaman's drum, peace sign, mandala, or something you make up yourself, find a copy of it or draw it. Make it small—less than three inches tall and three inches wide. Then cut it out and set it aside.

Now consider the most absurd image you can imagine. Again, it can be something others recognize or something you invent. Maybe it's a picture of Curly (of The Three Stooges) when he lies on the floor and spins around; Groucho Marx with a cigar; a clown's squirting flower; a silly looking dodo bird; a flying circus; or an oddly shaped carrot. Reproduce its image or draw it. Like before, limit it to three inches square, and then cut it out.

This is what I want you to do with your mojo drawings. In Bali, you are often asked to wear your magical drawing, placing it inside your belt or somewhere else on your clothing or body. At other times, a magical drawing can be placed under your front doormat or hung inside your house. In this case, you are to wear your mojo when you sleep. With some tape or bandages, attach the holy mojo drawing to the bottom of your spine. Make sure you pause to play your flying drum before it is actually attached. By now, you realize that your drum will always be the means of calling forth a transition into the world of mojo. It provides the flight that takes you to Mojoland. When you are ready, attach the absurd mojo drawing over your belly button. When you go to sleep, know that you have two opposite mojo forms on the front and back of your body. This is very powerful mojo, and it can precipitate all kinds of openings.

I have used this with people of all ages and backgrounds. Some folks, even those with no previous spiritual practice, have experienced major spiritual awakenings by simply wearing these drawings. I taught a class on shamanism to undergraduate students in Santa Fe and asked them to do this task. Many of them reported waking up in the middle of the night, shaking and entering a kundalini or life force awakening. Others had powerful spiritual visions that changed their life. Anything can happen. It doesn't matter what you ask for or don't ask for, the mojo will do its work when it feels so inclined.

Consider this suspension of opposite mojos as a way of setting up a mojo magnet. It will help you attract and catch the mojo that is perfect for you. Whatever form the mojo is in, don't be surprised to find yourself surprised. You might hatch a dream or wake up the next day with a thought you never had before. Be on the lookout for the ways in which new intuitions, perceptions, understandings, thoughts, or feelings (to mention a few outcomes), show up in the middle of your day or night. Assume that a mojo process is happening, and develop a curiosity about how long it will take you to notice it.

Repeat this as often as desired. Experiment with different drawings. Try different kinds of material on which the drawings are made. Paper of different colors and textures, cloth, aluminum foil, leather, and even bandages are some examples of the choices you have. Invite others to do the same mojo exercise so you can discuss it together. Consider starting a mojo club that has this prescription as your initiatory experience. It only takes two to have a mojo party and three to have a mojo organization. Know that the Balians are constantly giving people magical drawings that bring mojo into their lives. There is no reason for you not to have some fun doing the same. You might spice up your life with two drawings you'd never imagine facing one another. Curly meets the Buddha, a coiled snake encounters a clown, or a Tibetan symbol faces a silly face. Imagine the offspring that could be born from these magical mojo marriages!

I became a friend of a renowned Balian named Mangku I Made Pogog. His teacher was the spirit of a leech. It taught him to heal others with his tongue. That's right, he licked people. He was the sixth generation that practiced this form of healing. He and his ancestors put their tongues on whatever part of the body needed it. He was able to lick the sores of lepers and all kinds of disease-afflicted people; he had an invisible shield of protection that prevented their sickness from getting to him. I am not suggesting that you become a mojo licker, because outside of his village, you're a city slicker and would get into a whole heap of trouble for unleashing a mojo tongue! I am using this story to show you that you never know the form that mojo will appear in.

It can be in your words, spit, breath, or the wind you blow. Mojo might be found in what you draw, how you sign your name, or in your unconscious scribblings. The ancient magical drawings of Bali were kept alive by being etched on dried palm (rontal) leaves, with the resultant magical text called a lontar. Another of my Balian friends, I Gusti Gede Raka Antara, is a scholar and Balian of the lontar. His family has kept these drawings alive for fifteen generations, and he made a lontar of protection for me that I use when I teach others about Balinese magic. It sits near me now as I write these words. He also carved me a knife that has a dragon on its handle. It reminds me that everything can be used as mojo as long as it is sliced and served in the right way.

**It can be in your words, spit, breath,
or the wind you blow. Mojo might be found in
what you draw, how you sign your name,
or in your unconscious scribblings.**

Mojo fights the darkness of anger, jealousy, and selfishness. Those are the enemies, and they reside within us, although they are also mirrored on the outside. When you stop your anger, all the power of nature will come to you without effort; this is what Antara taught me. As he put it, "The biggest enemy we have is anger. Our closest friend is knowledge." He was speaking of the knowledge that is derived from holding opposites. When the dark is left alone, it begs for its other side—pure goodness—to come interact with it. It will cause all kinds of trouble to catch your attention. Know that it is simply lonely and wants to play. Andy had a lonely passion inside himself. It was transformed into constructive creative expression when the shining-like-silver creativity that was a part of his trouble-making found it could come out and play.

I'm going to prescribe some left-sided mojo that can help you transform any darkness that shows up in your life. Trouble and suffering are not going to disappear, so you might as well put them to work rather than get dragged to the bottom of an existential swamp.

Gather the following items: a photograph of an alligator, some silver fingernail polish, and a clipping of your fingernail. You'll also need some tape and a pair of scissors. Begin by conducting a search on your computer for a photograph of an aggressive alligator with an open jaw. Make a copy and cut it out. Now paint all the teeth of the alligator with silver nail polish. Also paint your nail clipping, and after it is dry, carefully tape it over one of the gator's eyes as if it were an eyebrow. Take a close look at how you have transformed a dangerous, primitive, eating machine into something that looks more like a cartoon figure.

To turn the art into mojo, take the gator to a grocery store and walk down every aisle with the reptile in your hand. As you walk around the store, whisper the swamp mantra, "There's a silver lining in every bite." Purchase a glass jar of pickles. When you get home, wrap the gator around the pickle jar and secure it with tape. When the pickles are gone (give them away if you don't like pickles), carefully remove the gator, clean the jar, and place the gator inside the jar. Your mojo is now ready for action.

Every time something comes to your life that feels like it is taking a bite out of your happiness, get out your mojo gator. Whether it's the presence of something mean, troubling, frightening, discouraging, disappointing, or sickening, make sure the first thing you do is turn to this special form of swamp magic. Open the jar, reach in, and rub a silver tooth. Do this as if you were handling the most powerful agent of magic in the world. Say out loud, "I'm going to feed you a trouble. Please enjoy eating it, and remember to leave its silver lining. Thank you."

As you integrate this crazy mojo wisdom practice into your daily habits, you should acquire a new delight in receiving trouble, fear, and worry because it provides an opportunity for you to feed your gator. It also leaves you with more silver! Arguably, all the silver and gold in the world could not change you as much as this magical form of playing with the difficult concerns in your life. Seriously, if you took one second a day to imagine the look on your mojo gator's face whenever you feed it a trouble, your life would be completely transformed. In each of these reflective moments, make sure you wink one of your eyes while believing that the alligator in your pickle jar is winking its silver-lined eye at you.

If you faithfully carry out this assignment, I promise that your life will change. It only takes one second, one bite, and one wink to become a different person. In the blink of an eye, your mojo can carry you through any pickle you get yourself into. Like Andy, your inner demons can become the source of a new resource. Use some mojo art to make your monsters part of a comic book story. Allow the silver lining of each and every cloud to lift you to new creative horizons, doing so in the blink of a passing moment.

In the terror of the darkest night that seems like it will never end, remember that the monster that hovers above is there to help, no matter how menacing it may seem. See every entry into the darkest nights as a moment that can kick open a very important mojo door. Every menacing shadow is simply a dark cloud that holds a special line of silver. In the back and forth marching over the terrors of suffering, there is a silver-lined path that leads you to receive gifts from a most auspicious mojo hike—a journey into incredible magic.

See every entry into the darkest nights as a moment that can kick open a very important mojo door.

7

PILLOW TALK:
MAKING SOFT CHARM

*T*here once lived a Japanese woman who knew how to catch a typhoon. She could reach her arms straight up in the air and grab hold of an unleashed wind that obeyed her every wish and command. In her world, born of ancient samurai families, there was deep respect for the mysteries of life and a practiced intimacy with nature. Not only did she possess a seasoned relationship with the flowers of her traditional garden but she also cultivated the know-how for harnessing the invisible winds that move the meaning and action of everyday life.

The mysterious wind she handled is the invisible force behind all of life, or what simply may be called the universal life force. Ikuko Osumi, sensei, used the old Japanese word *seiki* to refer to this hidden aspect of the universe and believed that a cultivated relationship with it is the secret to living a successful life. She dedicated herself to being a master of the art of working with seiki. This ancient approach to the life force, called *seiki jutsu*, was served to those who sought her help and guidance. Japan's leading scientists, politicians, artists, and traditional families regarded her as their most valued cultural treasure. As they often said, she was the unseen factor behind many of the creative contributions and successes of Japanese art, business, and science.

Like seiki, she was a secret. Her patients were well aware that she was Japan's least-known cultural treasure. She had been taught how to gather the winds of seiki into an intense vortex that was capable of lifting and carrying a person's life into extraordinary transformation. When she called forth the winds, anything could happen. These typhoons could be channeled into others, awakening inner talents and gifts, nurturing a destiny to unfold, or bringing healing and well-being to a sick and tired body. She did this as swiftly and powerfully as a samurai's sword, and as gracefully and beautifully as a culturally perfected geisha.

The word *typhoon* most likely originated from the Greek god of the winds, Typhon, and from the Chinese (Cantonese) *tai fung*, meaning "big wind." In Japan, a typhoon is feared, for overnight it can change the landscape and the fortune of whole communities. The life force typhoons known by the old-school practitioners of seiki jutsu are also respected, for they, too, unleash powerful forces of nature. Their currents can wipe you out or, in the hands of a master, bring a tsunami of health, success, and joy. The art of mastering these life force winds is one of the oldest secrets of ancient Japan. Ikuko Osumi, sensei, was the last of the Samurai family custodians of this lost knowledge—a grandmother samurai who prodigiously mastered its handling and dissemination to others.

In early 1992, I first learned about Ikuko Osumi from her book with Malcolm Ritchie titled *The Shamanic Healer: The Healing World of Ikuko Osumi and the Traditional Art of Seiki-Jutsu*. When I opened the book, I was unable to stop reading it until I had gone all the way to the end. I was immediately filled with the hope that I would meet her someday. Within several weeks, I received a surprise invitation to give a keynote address at the tenth annual symposium for the Japanese Association of Family Psychology. I wrote my host, Professor Kenji Kameguchi at the University of Tokyo, asking for his help in locating Ikuko Osumi. I did not know where she lived, but I suggested that he try to find Dr. Takeshi Hashimoto, who was a professor of anatomy at Toho University Medical School. Dr. Hashimoto had written the foreword to Osumi, sensei's book.

Unfortunately, my host discovered that Dr. Hashimoto had recently died, and he had no other way to learn where Ikuko Osumi lived. I didn't lose hope because the timing of the invitation seemed like a sign that our meeting would occur. Sure enough, the night before I was to depart for my flight to Japan, I received a fax from Professor Kameguchi that said he was delighted to say Osumi, sensei, had been found. As hard as it was for anyone to believe, she lived right across the street from the university where I would be giving my speech. She had been contacted, and she agreed to meet me.

I went to Tokyo and gave my speech, which had something to do with Zen Buddhism and the importance of no-mind therapy. The following day, my mind did not know what to expect as I was taken across the street to meet Ikuko Osumi. My first glimpse saw a traditional elder woman in her seventies, dressed in a formal kimono. Without going through the formalities of a long introduction, she immediately began speaking nonstop in Japanese. The translator was panting as he tried to keep up with her outpouring. As if standing there reading a book about my life, she gave me an account of my history as well as those of my father, grandfather, and son. Her mojo power overwhelmed me. I had never experienced anyone with this much unexplainable observation. I nearly collapsed.

Out of nowhere, she announced that is not the sort of thing you'd expect from an elder who is deep inside a cultural system that is rather closed to outsiders. She said, as if formally addressing a delegation, "I will treat you as a son. It is time for you to come home so I can teach you more about how to master these mysteries.

Please call your wife and tell her that you are staying with me for a while." I imagined the phone call home: "Hi, dear. I just met an older woman in Tokyo and am going to move in with her!" However, my family already understood and patiently accepted how mojo requires all kinds of unexpected pit stops.

So began my adventure of being personally tutored by one of the greatest healers and mojo masters of our time. I sat by her side, and watched her work with clients in her clinic and during visits to their homes in Tokyo. She taught me to handle the life force in all kinds of situations. I learned how it could be used for more than healing; it can find and awaken the unique inner gifts and talents of every person. For her, seiki was the magic that could turn objects and people into mojo.

After that first introduction and stay, I visited her numerous times and lived in her compound. She also came to my home in the United States on several occasions. In Japan, I was introduced to Japan's national cultural treasures and the leading scientists of Sony, including the scientists who invented the compact disc, the DVD, and the future technology of their computers and robotics. The best of the old and new ways of Japan were opened. At times, I felt a bit like Forrest Gump being thrown into a scene that didn't quite seem possible. For instance, I was served tea in a temple where this had been done for only one other outsider— Queen Elizabeth!

Ikuko Osumi, sensei, taught me that the samurai warriors tuned their mind during tea ceremony. It was used as a kind of mental training that prepared one to be a natural vessel for carrying the life force. Both rigorous discipline and a readiness for fluidic, effortless action are the ways in which one learns to be a container, and to cater to the emptiness and the fullness it can serve. The slow pace of tea ceremony takes us into another realm of interaction and awareness that is the matrix for deepening our participation in the everyday. As the tea whisk is used to stir the tea, we must be stirred by life to make ourselves suitable for service to the greater complexity that holds and pours us.

The temples, gardens, teahouses, and shrines she sent me to were filled with mystery. The Shinto religion of Japan has no founder, scripture, or body of law; it is regarded as the way of the gods, wherein the world is filled with spirits, or *kami*. Shrines honor the kami, who include influential ancestors from the past. One of Ikuko Osumi's ancestors was regarded as a powerful kami in Japan, and then when she passed on, Osumi, sensei, became a kami.

When you enter a Shinto shrine, you first walk through a gateway called a *Tori*, a "gateway to the gods." It is best to pass through it with bare feet or sandals following a ritual cleansing in a nearby river, or at least a ceremonial washing of your hands. Some Japanese skip a meal once a month and use the money saved from not eating as an offering at the shrine. They toss a coin into the offering box as a gift to the kami the place honors. They then clap their hands at chest level a couple of times to call upon the kami. Keeping their hands together with fingers pointing up, they bow modestly and make a request of the kami. Further adoration and appreciation may be expressed by offering an origami flower or animal. *Origami*, called "the paper of the spirits," does not necessitate cuts to shape its form. It relies upon intricate folds in order to show respect to the spirit of the tree that provides the paper. In these temples, I learned that honoring the never-ending complexity of spirit awakens its appearance in the details of daily life.

In the midst of these rare invitations to enter the customs of traditional Japan, Ikuko Osumi taught me what she knew about the life force. After years of interaction with her, she took me aside one day and asked me to give seiki to her daughter, a well-known contemporary artist. I instilled the life force into Masako as Osumi, sensei, looked on. I sat Masako on a special stool and began making spontaneous sounds that called seiki into the room, gathering its intensity. As I felt it become a small typhoon of circulating energy, I experienced a oneness with Masako that enabled me to feel inseparable from the channels through which her life force moved. When the moment was right, I placed my hands on top of her head and poured seiki into her body. Masako began to move spontaneously as she was renewed and retuned. In this work, I realized that serving seiki and tea are not fundamentally different to the Japanese mind. They both are ways of bowing to a nameless mystery that give us life.

I realized that serving seiki and tea are not fundamentally different to the Japanese mind. They both are ways of bowing to a nameless mystery that give us life.

Ikuko Osumi carefully observed my working with dozens of people in this way until she declared that I had mastered the art of seiki jutsu. One day, she called from Japan and announced that she was coming to my home for another visit.

After she arrived and rested, we went to dinner, and she told the story of how her involvement with seiki jutsu began—when a magical white snake seemingly jumped into her belly when she was a small child. Her family went every year to the Makiyama Shrine on top of Makiyama Mountain, a holy place that honored her most important ancestor, Eizon Hoin, who was revered by Shinto priests as a kami. When the family took their annual trip to the shrine, they would collect the skin of a white snake that lived there and use it to make a special medicine. This time, Osumi, sensei, stayed behind at the shrine, and the snake came to her and said, "I am tired, and it is time for you to take over my job of helping others." That's when it came inside her as a spirit helper.

Years later, the Shinto priests of that temple wrote Ikuko Osumi, sensei's name on a piece of wood that confirmed that she had been accepted into the ancient lineage of working with the life force. As Osumi, sensei, told me these things, she reached into a bag and pulled out a package. She continued talking, "All that remains from my ancestors are two pieces of silk cloth, and one is like a small, thin red pillow. They are my link to the past masters of this ancient way of healing and helping guide others. With the blessing of my ancestors, you have been chosen to keep this tradition alive. I am passing it on to you." She handed me both pieces of silk and a slat of wood, on which the Shinto priests at her family shrine had written my name.

I was speechless. The last thing I expected was for Forrest Gump to be told he was part of a tradition of samurai mojo masters. Yet as I write these words, the wood and the mojo silk rest on a shelf behind me. The silk I own holds seiki instilled by the masters of the past. Osumi, sensei, taught me how to do the same. You can take a soft substance like raw silk or cotton and infuse it with the life force of seiki. It is highly charged mojo. When a pillow is made out of it, it can open your mind when you sleep on it. It can also bring on a powerful rest that is super healing.

Ikuko Osumi's great ancestor, Eizon Hoin, was born into the samurai family of Katagiri. His grandfather, Katsumoto Katagiri, was the renowned vassal of Toyotomi Hideyoshi, the *daimyo*, or ruler, who controlled Japan in the sixteenth century. In 1641, Hoin was appointed to restore the shrine on the sacred mountain of Makiyama that had been founded seventeen hundred years earlier. Hoin did this and thus began his career as a spiritual teacher. When the Kitagami River later became impassable due to an accumulation of muddy silt, the local industries reliant upon the passage of ships into their harbor were threatened. Hoin was finally asked to intervene because all previous human efforts to clear the river failed miserably.

You can take a soft substance like raw silk or cotton and infuse it with the life force of seiki. It is highly charged mojo. When a pillow is made out of it, it can open your mind when you sleep on it. It can also bring on a powerful rest that is super healing.

He prayed for three nights and four days at the shrine altar. At the end of the fourth day, a huge storm broke forth and caused extensive flooding, thereby clearing the entire river mouth. Even the largest ships were subsequently able to enter. The clan lord wanted to honor Hoin for this achievement and decided to grant him some land. Unfortunately, the local lord was jealous of Hoin and intercepted the news, stealing the land without Hoin ever knowing it had been intended for him.

Hoin continued to earn the devotion of the local people, and this made the lord more jealous. He tried to take away the land that belonged to the shrine, but the people refused to do it. The lord falsely accused Hoin of misdemeanors to hide his own crimes, but the people refused to believe any of it. Finally, the people became so fearful of the lord that they stopped going to the shrine and seeing Hoin. Only one man continued visiting him and paying his respects. Hoin expressed his appreciation by secretly making him a talisman, a mojo gift, and told him to place it in his house for protection. Later, when a fire destroyed the whole village, only that man's house was not touched.

Hoin was finally rounded up and tried on false charges. In spite of all the defenses in his favor, he was sentenced to a lifetime of exile on a faraway island. There, he prayed day and night for several years and then publicly announced he would die. His final request was to be buried upside down. Like a warrior of the spirit, he stared at the sky and died without a tear. His request was not honored, however, and he was buried in the typical way. Immediately, a high fever struck the people and made them sick. One crisis after another took place, but most peculiarly, it was discovered that no one could catch a single fish, which was a huge calamity for the fishing village. The community finally dug up Hoin's body and turned him upside down. That's when everything returned to normal.

Years later, Hoin was reburied at the shrine that is now dedicated to him. He is still regarded as a kami who protects the weak, maintains justice, and guards against fire and difficult child-birth.

Ikuko Osumi's early life was also filled with great pain and suffering, though she always felt Hoin's presence in her body, protecting and guiding her. He entered her as a white snake and made her ready to do the same kind of work. Powerful mojo is created by the lives of holy people who sacrifice themselves for others; they leave a legacy of powerful spiritual mojo that is available for us to tap into. This is how seiki has been kept alive throughout the centuries. These people, in spite of their suffering, are capable of standing as a beacon of light no matter how sinister the forces of dark. They bravely face life and death while cooking up a legacy of mighty mojo.

The history of seiki jutsu is known to date back to the 1600s, but it is presumed to be much older. The details of its practice were taught to Ikuko Osumi when she was a teenager by her Aunt Hayashibe, who was in her sixties at the time of their meeting. Her uncle and aunt, who had no children of their own, raised her after her grandfather and father passed away. They made sure she was tutored in the traditional refinements of tea ceremony, calligraphy, and flower arranging, among other practices. The silk that Osumi, sensei, gave me was what her aunt had passed on to her.

From this lineage, I learned that lost mojo returns to you when you appropriately prepare to receive it. To do so, you must balance your body rhythms in daily life. You need to rid yourself of the exhaustion that accumulates in each day. Even if you have to be socially rude, get the daily rest that you need. As Osumi, sensei, taught, "Value your rest more than your social life." For seiki jutsu, healing is defined as a return to yourself—the journey to becoming your true self.

All this takes place when you set out to find your long-lost mojo. In the practice of seiki jutsu, there is a simple mojo body movement. It is effortless and improvisational, free of the constraints of any memorized choreography. You sit down every day on a bench and allow spontaneous movement to have its say. This practice invites your mojo to return. When you move in the right way—which is natural and without purpose—the mojo just comes. When you give mojo to another person, you must be of one mind and one body with the other. Here, touch is the best way to share mojo. We should always follow the wisdom of our bodies because it is the source of our natural mojo. These things I learned from Osumi, sensei.

With your head upon a mojo pillow, rest becomes a mojo rest. This is one excellent way to make yourself ready for the reception of magical transformation. When my son was a child, Ikuko Osumi traveled to our home to give him seiki. With intense ecstatic movement and vocalizations, she and I brought the life force into the living room and directed it to flow into the top of his head. His body became filled with the life force, and he began to rock naturally, as always happens when you receive this gift. As a present, Osumi, sensei, gave him some raw silk filled with concentrated seiki. It was made into a pillow that he slept on whenever he needed a special boost. From that moment on, he began to dream what he wanted to be when he grew up. His first desire was to hit a home run in a baseball game.

With your head upon a mojo pillow, rest becomes a mojo rest. This is one excellent way to make yourself ready for the reception of magical transformation.

One week after he'd received seiki, Scott hit his first home run at a Little League game. It was the last game of the season, and the score was tied at the bottom of the last inning. The bases were loaded, and with a full count, he hit a home run over the left field fence. After that Steven Spielberg–like performance, he went home and wrote this letter to Ikuko Osumi:

Dear Mrs. osumi!
Thanks for giving
me seiki. I got
a home run that won
the game.

from,
Scott Keeney

Yes, mojo can help you get a home run. Pedro Cerrano, the baseball player in the comedy film *Major League*, tried all kinds of voodoo to get mojo for his bat. The trick is that you have to activate the mojo inside your body. A mojo pillow helps your body bring the mojo out. Whether you call it mojo rest, a power nap, or deep revitalization, mojo is required when you sleep just as much as it is for the times when you are awake. Nighttime mojo and daytime mojo are joined, so one can't work without the activation of the other. A mojo pillow is able to take care of the night and get you ready to receive more mojo the next day. I always have my mojo silk pillow from Ikuko Osumi close at hand. It is there to remind me that there is as much mojo in rest as there is in busy activity. I also rest my head on it when I need an extra lift from its soft mojo in order to handle any particularly hard times.

A Pillow for Therapeutic Mojo

I was invited to work with Melissa, Kristi, Tyler, and Susan, a young team of family therapists at a social service agency. My job was to help awaken their creativity—their therapeutic mojo. On this morning, Melissa volunteered to do some work with me. As they all got situated on a big couch, Tyler ended up with two pillows in his lap, Kristi had one pillow in her lap, and another was resting on the arm of the couch, against the wall. Susan walked in and stacked the extra pillow on Tyler's pile. He looked at me and teased, "Do you want a pillow?" I was laughing as I watched all this pillow movement.

Melissa then said, "This is pillow therapy." At that moment, I felt the presence of my Japanese pillow mojo. I knew we were in for an interesting journey.

"What does this say about your therapy?" I asked the group.

Melissa then asked for a pillow. "I might want one of those, actually." Kristi handed the extra pillow to Melissa, who put it on her lap.

Tyler commented, "I call it pillow therapy."

"Pillow talk," I answered back

"Oh, this is perfect!" Melissa said, referring to how the pillow felt comfortable to her.

I asked her, "Well, that's interesting. Are you a pillow person?"

"I'm not the kind of pillow person who likes a lot of fluff and stuff, but when Kristi and I went to Nashville, I took my pillows. I also carried them with me to Ireland. I have to have my pillows." Kristi nodded in agreement as Melissa talked, indicating that pillows are a big deal to Melissa.

I pointed to the pillows on all their laps and said, "So this already tells us a lot."

"This is perfect," Melissa confirmed.

I continued with a tease, "That's so interesting. I know someone who has her own pillow. She has to sleep with it. If she goes to the airport and discovers that it isn't with her, the trip is canceled."

"Oh, I don't think I'm that bad."

"Did you take more than one pillow to Ireland?"

"Oh yeah, I have to have two. I have to have one for my head and one for between my legs," she said as she laughed. "For Ireland, I took smaller ones to fit in the suitcase. I must have my flat pillows with me."

I commented, "What's interesting about this is that, although I have known quite a few people who carry a head pillow, I've never known someone who carries two pillows. You're the first person in my life that I have met who carries two pillows."

"Wow," Melissa said as she nodded.

As I listened to her discuss her pillows, I was certain that my Japanese mojo pillow had been there since the very beginning of the session. Seeing all those pillows brought it right in. Thinking of how it is used in seiki jutsu inspired me to ask, "Why don't you carry a pillow with you to therapy?"

"I don't know. I guess I could. I don't intend to sleep in therapy," she teased back.

"It could be interesting. I don't know that there has to be an obvious reason for carrying a pillow to therapy, but I wonder whether a pillow can be like a security blanket."

"Uh-huh."

I moved to introduce the idea of having a personal mojo pillow or what I will call a therapy pillow. Knowing how it benefits participants in the seiki jutsu tradition, I offered the same resource to therapy.

"If you brought a pillow to work and had it with you when you saw clients, it could indirectly send the message, 'I'm comfortable being here with you, and as you can see, I carry my comfort with me.' A pillow might also communicate, 'I'm going to be with you the way I choose, on my terms.' In this way, a pillow becomes a statement about your strength and authority even though you're soft and gentle. When a pillow is used for therapy, it becomes a therapeutic pillow. With this in mind, it might need to be a certain size, shape, and color. It might have special quotations on it. If you had a therapeutic pillow, what color would it be?"

"Blue, maybe," she said hesitantly. "Yeah, like a calming, peaceful color, I think."

"Would it have a picture on it, like some clouds? Would it be all blue, or would it have an image on it?" My red mojo pillow has the image of flying cranes on it, so I wondered what might be on her imagined therapy pillow.

"I don't know. An image doesn't come to mind right off."

"How about words? You know how pillows sometimes have embroidery."

A coincidence at the right time and place becomes more than a coincidence; it is a confirmation of a special moment—a spotlight that accentuates what otherwise might pass as mere talk.

"Yes, I think I would go more toward that."

"Without giving it much thought, what words would you want on it? It could be one word or a quote."

"I'd have to think about that."

Susan offered an interesting comment: "I actually have a blue pillow that was given to me when I graduated. It has orange braiding around the outside, and it says, *Friends make the best therapists*."

"Perfect," Tyler added his affirmation.

My mojo was quite excited to hear that we were actually talking about a pillow one of the therapists already owned. "Really?"

Melissa was taken by it, too. "Huh!"

We all laughed at this coincidence. A coincidence at the right time and place becomes more than a coincidence; it is a confirmation of a special moment—a spotlight that accentuates what otherwise might pass as mere talk. This is one way of helping mojo be revealed and drawn upon.

I used the moment to note how the vibe of the room was feeling alive and to imply that mojo had made a house call. "That is just unbelievable. We've entered a mystery. This is quite remarkable. Look how connected you all are. You care enough about each other that you already knew what was an important resource for her—pillows. You started with a pillow dance, making it such an obvious thing that I had to comment on it. Sure enough, it opened up something about you that's very unique. Like I said, I have never met anyone who carries two pillows. It's the two-ness that makes it interesting because it inspires me to wonder whether there are pillows for rest at home and then a second kind of pillow that kind of floats around. Maybe that's a pillow wanting to go out in the world with you as you do your work. In other words, there are rest pillows and therapy pillows. Susan surprised me by announcing that she already has a therapy pillow. It's the same color as the one you desire, and it has a cord wrapped around it. How interesting."

Melissa was intrigued. "That is interesting."

I kept all this on focus, underscoring the fact that something special was happening in the room. "This really has me thinking. I'm taking this very seriously because it doesn't seem to be an accident. The pillow has entered your therapeutic scene, and I'm wondering about the size of your therapy pillow. It'd be one thing to bring a small one and another thing to bring a large one. It could be round or square or rectangular. It could have a fringe on it, look modern or old, be made of leather, or be covered in soft material. Maybe you need a trunk full of pillows so you can decide which therapeutic pillow would work best for each client. What would empower you? If you had a blue pillow with a quotation on it, would it be a funny saying or a serious saying?"

"I probably lean more toward serious."

"That's what I predicted you would say. Would it be something you created, or would it be a quote from a book?"

"I think it could be either. I think it would have to be something meaningful to me, so it should be either a quote that I really connect with or something that I created."

"What would it be about? What theme? Remember it's a serious thing."

"Probably about life or important experiences."

"How about, 'Life needs a cushion.' Or 'Life needs a pillow.'"

"Yeah. Let me write that down."

"Imagine a client seeing a therapy pillow right as a session begins. It would sure give you something to talk about. You can ask, 'Do you feel close to your pillow?' Most people do feel rather close to their pillow because it is the material thing you are most intimate with. After all, your head rests upon a pillow more than it rests upon any other thing in the world, including the closest people in your life. You're closest to your pillow."

Melissa agreed emphatically. "I am in fact."

I continued spelling all this out, "What an interesting way to start therapy—talking to people about their pillows. If you walk in with a pillow, it helps starts a whole conversation about metaphors of intimacy and closeness. You can ask them whether they allow their pillow to be used by someone else. There are all kinds of things that pillows enable us to talk about, and they tell us a lot about each other. Pillows provide a fertile ground for therapeutic exploration."

In other words, a pillow can become a form of mojo. How one handles a therapy pillow can infuse it with transformational power. Without saying it, I started to introduce Melissa to how she could carry her pillow as therapeutic mojo, and how it could be a way of delivering mojo words that inspire a session or encourage a magical flight to someone who sleeps on it.

"You could become a connoisseur of therapeutic pillow interventions. You might specialize in pillow covers. You could put some words of wisdom on them, or write your intervention on a pillow and have your client sleep on it. The title of your book on therapy could be *Pillow Talk*.

"Now, this is a weird thought. Let's assume you become internationally famous for *Pillow Talk*—the therapist who brings a blue pillow to every case. I'm wondering how you'll carry that pillow into a session. In my fantasy, I see you carrying it in a wooden box, like an old-fashioned, wooden briefcase with a handle. You could walk into a session and *snap, snap,* the briefcase lid is opened and out comes the pillow. It will be interesting to see how you carry that pillow because you certainly don't want to be sloppy about it. When you pack your pillow, do you put it in a plastic bag, or do you take care of it in a certain way to get it ready for your suitcase?"

"When I put the smaller pillows in my suitcase, they usually go on the bottom. But if I take them in the car, like I did last week when Kristi and I drove to Nashville, I lay them out very carefully on the seat underneath my hanging clothes. I do not want them wrinkled."

"So, this rings a bell. How your pillow is handled is important."

"Yes, because my head lies on it. I don't want it thrown in the trunk."

I started to spell out how her pillow was a therapeutic resource for the mojo that helps awaken creativity in a session: "How you handle your therapy pillow in the clinic will say a lot to the client about how you regard therapy. If you've placed some serious writing on it, that says something. It makes sense to show that you have a professional relationship with your therapy pillow. There should be special care taken in its handling. That would fit you quite well."

"Yes."

"This is such a rich metaphor because how you take care of your pillow is really a message regarding how you will handle therapy and what it will be about. People are coming to you because they haven't done a good job of taking care of their head. It's mental health, right? Mental health is one pillow away; it's rest for the mind."

Susan made another suggestion: "You could make pillows, too, not just covers. Kristi knows how to do that." As Osumi, sensei, made special pillows for her clients, therapists can do the same, bringing magic into situations needing a special, soft touch.

I was thrilled with the direction the mojo pillow talk was going. "This is interesting. I'm really excited! How about the rest of you?

It makes so much sense, and it's a perfect fit for you. It fits well underneath your head, your therapeutic head. Where does the therapy pillow fit in a session? Do you sit on it, do you put your head on it, or do you hold it in your lap? What comes to your mind? How do you see yourself with that pillow? What would feel like a good fit for you?"

As Osumi, sensei, made special pillows for her clients, therapists can do the same, bringing magic into situations needing a special, soft touch.

"I probably would not sit on the floor because I wouldn't want it on the floor," Melissa answered with a giggle. "I probably would use it like a desk, like I am now with this pillow."

"Your answer is right there in front of you."

Melissa continued, "I could put it behind me because I'm short. I also use a pillow between my legs at night because my back hurts."

I quickly interspersed, "You actually do need a pillow in your sessions."

"Yeah."

"Maybe you need two pillows—one for your lap, and a little one for your back, like when you're traveling."

Melissa was thinking about the pillows she was already finding in her home visits with clients. "Sometimes clients have a couch full of pillows and we have to move them to be able to sit down, in which case I can put one behind me or hold one."

I related this comment to today's session, where there was a couch full of pillows. I started to spell out, without mentioning the word, that we had been talking about mojo all along. "That's true. This is kind of what manifested itself today. Collectively, you have unconsciously presented yourselves in such a way to assure that a pillow will be found in our session. How interesting. Perhaps you could have something different written on each side of your therapy pillow. Depending on how things are going, you can turn the pillow to one side or the other. You could have a dozen different kinds of pillowcases, so when you recognize what theme needs to be presented, you just get up and pull out a particular pillowcase, saying, 'This is what we're talking about today. I've found it's a good thing to have these words in front of us when we're talking about this sort of thing.' I don't know how you'll do it, but there's a lot of creative room in pillow talk."

Susan and Tyler reminded Melissa of something that seemed important. "What is it you say you do when you get mad? Don't you take a pillow and punch it?" Susan said this as she clenched her fist and punched the pillow on her lap.

Melissa burst into laughter. "Oh! This is true. I didn't even connect with that."

I inquired, "What's this she is talking about?"

"When I get upset, I can be a little violent. Instead of using a punching bag, I take my pillow and beat it against my bed."

"Really?"

"Which exhausts me and then I usually cry. I think it helps me release that energy."

I underscored the meaning of this for her pillow talk therapy. "Do you realize that you've found your therapy?" In other words, her pillow was mojo for more than her peaceful sleep; it doctored her anger. "The pillow is such an important part of how you handle your own mental health."

"Yes."

"In addition to helping find peace at night, here's something else you can share with clients and colleagues who are handling this kind of problem."

Melissa acknowledged, "I have shared this. That's how Susan knows about it."

"As you know, a lot of our court-ordered clients have problems handling their anger, so they use their fists. Using a pillow would be far better. You might want to consider teaching families new ways of having pillow fights."

"Huh!"

"We might loan them some pillows. You could have a separate bag in the trunk for a family that needs a pillow fight. These would be real small, fluffy pillows. Hand them over to a family and say, 'We're leaving these here for you this week. We want you to have a pillow fight.' You can use a therapy pillow in many different ways."

"That is so weird," Melissa remarked with another giggle.

"It is, isn't it? How often do you replace a pillow? Does it survive a long time? Do you keep it until there's barely anything left to it, or do you replace them quite often?"

Melissa's facial expression suddenly changed, appearing to have had an important insight. "Here's another interesting facet that I hadn't considered. I have a feather pillow that's from my grandmother's house. That's my special pillow."

"Whoa!" I exclaimed.

"I lived with my grandmother. We were very close, and she passed away right before I started grad school. This pillow had the smell of her house for a long time. I can't get rid of that pillow, ever. Even if I don't use it, I will keep it." I was reminded of the pillow that Osumi, sensei, gave me. It had the smell of her Japanese home on it, and it reminded me of her. She is my samurai grandmother, and the same pillow must have reminded her of the woman who raised her and taught her the old mojo ways. I have learned something today about my own mojo pillow.

I felt a shiver go down my arms as Melissa disclosed this fascinating fact about her pillow. I announced this to the group, "I don't know about you all, but I just had a chill go down both my arms, especially my left arm. I don't know why my left more than my right, but I had a chill go down them. Through the sense of smell, your pillow is a direct link to a great resource in your life—your grandmother, one of your strongest relationships. Every night, your brain's getting a direct hit of your relationship with her. This empowers your mind in ways that your conscious mind will never be able to keep up with. This is deep, and it's extraordinary. This would also be an interesting topic, whenever the occasion calls for it, to discuss with clients. Explain your pillow and how it links you to your grandmother. You could then ask them how their pillows can be used to link their relationships. For example, when a child goes away for summer camp and his mom misses him, I bet some moms go smell their kid's pillow. Did your grandmother ever talk about her pillow? How did you end up with it?

"I took it," Melissa said as she laughed. "She had a lot of pillows in her house for when we came and visited. When I went to the university, I slept there fairly frequently. I wouldn't take my pillow to her house because she had one that was appropriate that I could use . . ."

"Is that the only place you felt comfortable about using someone else's pillow?"

"Probably, yeah. And at home."

"Was she the person you trusted more than anyone in your life? I'm curious."

"Probably. I cared for her when she was sick and I was in college. She had a couple of heart attacks, but she definitely cared for me in a way that nobody else could while I was in college."

My mojo suggested that her grandmother was a mentor for her therapy practice. Her memory of her grandmother, awakened by her pillow, might have served as an inspirational source for working with others. "Would she have been a good therapist?"

"Probably, yeah."

"How would she talk to people? If she had been a therapist, how would you describe her work with people? Would she be soft or would she be tough?"

"Oh, very soft."

"Just like that pillow."

We were pouring grandmother mojo into the pillow. Her pillow was the perfect place to hold these loving thoughts and remembrances.

"Yes, very gentle. She would have been very concerned. I think my most fond memory of her was when I studied at her house. She would bring me a little glass of orange juice."

"How wonderful. She brought you that feather pillow of gentleness along with some sweet orange juice. I think your therapy should also have orange juice. I've never heard of a therapist who brought orange juice to a client. There are all these connections and surprises that are coming up for you, and I think the act of giving orange juice has a special meaning. There may be a forthcoming session when you think, 'I'd like to bring them orange juice.'"

Melissa was with me in this discussion. "What's interesting about this is that, somewhere along the way, I think I heard that orange juice helps you remember things."

"This is all coming together," I added.

Melissa was already ahead of me. "When I want my clients to remember something, I could give them orange juice."

I picked up on this. "When it's important for them to remember something, whether it's an assigned task or some insight that's come forth, that's the time to teach them about orange juice. If you happen to have some in your car, you can take a brief time-out, saying,

'I'm going to go get you some orange juice so you'll remember.' The act of marking that moment in the session will actually help them remember."

As I said this, I remembered how Ikuko Osumi loved to bring me fresh juice and keep me overfed. She was more obsessed with my health than a classic Jewish mother! She thought I needed more food if I didn't gain weight, even if I didn't need either. Melissa's memory of her grandmother's orange juice made me wonder whether Osumi, sensei, served me juice to help me remember what was most important in life—those who mother and grandmother us into feeling that there is a always a soft and gentle place for our head to rest.

My samurai grandmother whispered to me, and I passed it on to Melissa: "You have a one-of-a-kind way of being in the world of therapy that the world has not experienced. It's blessed by the wisdom you experienced firsthand from the gentle soul of your grandmother. Pillow talk provides a metaphor that is rich in ways other metaphors can't possibly be. It touched the spontaneous truths that sprung forth today without any of us knowing or planning what would happen. It showed up in this room and sits in all of your laps." I pointed to their pillows and said, "I would like to ask you to do this. Will you?"

"Yes," Melissa said with confidence.

"Good. Now, go take some orange juice so you won't forget."

Melissa had discovered that her pillow was special for a reason: it had mojo. Like the pillow Ikuko Osumi had given me, her grandmother's pillow provided soft magic that could inspire, heal, and provide comfort. In therapy, her pillow was also capable of waking a typhoon of creativity that could inspire her work with clients, including a reminder that she could help them find their own pillow mojo.

Prescriptions for Pillow Magic

Like Melissa and the clients of Ikuko Osumi, sensei, you can also benefit from a mojo pillow. The first pillow I shall prescribe may surprise you, and that's the point of it. Make a pillow not much larger than the size of a coin. A ball of cotton will work fine, though it's better to wrap it with a piece of cloth and tie it with a piece of string or thread. Choose the color of cloth that brings you a sense of calm, and carry this pillow with you. When you need a rest, take out a pencil or pen and draw a happy face on one of your thumbs. (Drumroll please ...) Fly your drum, then put your tiny mojo pillow on a desk or table and gently place your thumb face on it. Stare at it as it rests on the pillow. Imagine concentrating all of your tiredness into that thumb and allowing it to get a super mojo nap. Adding a children's bedtime lullaby is a nice touch. Do this for at least one minute but no more than five. Try other fingers if you feel so inclined. Consider this a special kind of mojo nap.

There is another way to use your tiny thumb pillow. Imagine that the cotton inside of it is a cloud. Blow on it three times and place it under the pillow on your bed. When you go to sleep, think of this cloud and blow on it another three times. Go to sleep knowing that you are sleeping on a cotton cloud. Like a child, wonder if you will have a dream where you meet your guardian angel while floating on a cloud. Ask for this dream and assume it will happen whether you remember it or not the next morning.

You may want to empower this ritual with a tender incantation. Before going to sleep, hold the pillow with the cloud inside and say this simple prayer: "The Creator above has made everything, including you. You are my closest friend. I rest my head upon your surface and the rest I receive is shared with you, as are all my dreams. Thank you for being such a good nighttime companion. As a token of my appreciation, I would like to offer myself as your pillow. Please know that I am your pillow, and you can rest yourself on me as I rest my head upon you. Let's be true buddies, and provide rest and comfort for one another. In the name of all things soft and gentle, have a peaceful sleep each and every night."

As an alternative bedtime prayer, consider having a pillow cover that has the following modification of an eighteenth-century childhood prayer written on it. Take your index finger and pretend to dip it in some mojo ink. Then gently press your finger on the pillow cover to lovingly write out these words:

Now I lay me down to sleep,
I pray the Lord my soul to keep,
Keep me safe all through the night,
And wake me with the mojo light.

Are you aware that pillows were found in Egyptian tombs and that sometimes ancient wealthy Egyptians slept on stone pillows? Get yourself a small stone and write these words on it: *It's a hard life being too wealthy.* Every time you think you are suffering because you don't make enough money, or don't have enough possessions or importance, get out this stone and consider whether you really want to end up getting a hard night's sleep.

Traditional Chinese pillows were often hard boxes made from wood, metal, stone, porcelain, bronze, bamboo, or jade; they didn't use stuffed fabric. There are many Chinese mojo stories about pillows with magical powers. One tale is about a man who would climb inside his pillow and fly to places all over the world. He didn't need a flying drum because he had a flying pillow. You might want to consider having someone embroider some wings on your pillowcase.

It might help you fly somewhere interesting in your dreams—
perhaps to a place where you learn more about making mojo pillows.

**The good mojo flows from love. Always.
Send your love into a pillow, and it will become magic.**

There was an ancient Chinese philosopher who used a stack of
three books as his pillow, believing it would inspire pure dreams.
The American psychic and seer Edgar Cayce found that he could
sleep on his schoolbooks and wake up knowing what was in them.
I suggest that you read your books first and then sleep on them so
you won't waste your mojo on what is better accomplished through
enjoying a good mojo read. By all means, make sure that you place
this book under your pillow tonight!

There is no end to the mojo that can be associated with pillows
and pillow talk. I'm from Louisiana, and some of the old mojo doctors down here used to talk about the hoodoo of pillow magic.
Certain things, like a feather, dust, salt and pepper, or even a pair of
scissors, were placed inside a pillow to stir things up. You could
brew trouble or something good, depending on the pillow magic
you used. The good mojo flows from love. Always. Send your love
into a pillow, and it will become magic.

I also recommend taking a string that is as long as the length of
your pillow. Stretch it out on a table and, with a red felt pen, make
a single dot at one end of the string. When you do this, think of a
person you love. Feel your love for them as you make the dot. Make
another dot and open your heart to another person you love. These
people can be living or deceased relatives, friends, or figures from
history, including holy ones. Make those loving dots all along the
string. You can do as few as five dots or as many dots as you can get
on the string. Hold this string over your heart and then place it

inside your pillow. Consider it to be your mojo love line: it connects your heart with those you love in a special way. This will feed you some delicious love mojo while you dream. Just don't forget to take it out every night before you sleep and hold it over your heart before placing it back inside the pillow.

Your pillow can become a mojo pillar. When you give more heartfelt consideration to the pillow on which you rest your head, the mojo of the night will more likely bring you something. Prefer a love fest over a love arrest? Then spice up those pillows so that your pillow talk is mojo-fied. Want an answer to a pressing question? Then write that question on a piece of paper and put it in your mojo pillow. Want more mojo in your life? Try talking to your pillow and asking it to help you out. Whenever you have an important dream, don't forget to thank your pillow and give it a pat on the back.

Tonight's the night for mojo sleep and magical dreams. All you have to do is get to know your pillow better and show your appreciation for its companionship. If you need to be reminded of the important role your pillow plays in your life, then make sure you place an orange on top of your pillow after you make up your bed. It will sit there all day, helping you remember to express some kindness to your pillow before you retire. And what would mojo be without another old-fashioned incantation to top things off?

> *Fluffy, fluffy pillow talk,*
> *Take me on a mojo walk.*
> *Every night before I rest,*
> *Take that orange and roll some jest.*
> *Fly me to Mount Everest,*
> *And make my nest the very best.*

228

8

CONJURING THE
CREATIVE LIFE FORCE

*B*e careful when you ask for something, because you might get it. And if that is true, then be careful when you don't ask, because you might not get it. In the case of mojo, what you say or don't say may or may not matter; mojo has its own mind. It comes when you are ready for it and when you need it, independent of whether you ask for it. There have been times in my life when it felt like mojo was pouring from the heavens above and rising from the ground below. I wanted to take cover because it was overwhelming. No wonder my close friends call me a mojo magnet and my colleagues call me a mojo doctor.

When I ponder what delivers mojo to us, I always end up answering: the universal life force, otherwise known as kundalini, Holy Spirit, chi, seiki, n|om, and all the other cultural words that point to the mystery that makes us feel totally alive. A mojo doctor knows how to conjure the appearance of the life force first and foremost, and there are more ways to invite its appearance than anyone could ever enumerate. Suffice it to say that calling mojo into a situation requires being both readily available for its spontaneous flow and knowing that it requires a beginner's state of mind. I am a mojo doctor because I know that I know nothing. At the same time, I have a lot of know-how in the art of opening the door to the universal life force that can flood any empty space needing some rejuvenation.

When the life force flows, creativity flourishes. It is fair to say that the life force and creative force are one and the same. I suggest that the creative life force is what brings us mojo. Being vitally alive requires spontaneous creativity that invigorates one to be awakened in an inspired manner. I believe that a mojo doctor is a physician of creativity—a shamanic conductor of the life force that orients us to be vessels for the expression of ongoing invention. We are here to create with the gods and amuse them in every moment we exist, in spite of all the challenges that tempt us to trivialize life as nothing but a struggle against the tyranny of pain.

When the life force flows, creativity flourishes. It is fair to say that the life force and creative force are one and the same. I suggest that the creative life force is what brings us mojo. Being vitally alive requires spontaneous creativity that invigorates one to be awakened in an inspired manner.

I invite you to move past all definitions of success and failure, and see your life as an opportunity to soar with the eagles, run with the mustangs, and swim with the dolphins, doing so whether or not you are able to walk, run, gallop, swim, leap, or fly. You were born to play with the gods. They need your company, and are as miserable as you are when you fail to irrationally throw yourself into the dreaming that calls for radical joy and happiness in the everyday stewardship of serving happiness for the greatest good.

There is a drum waiting for you to grab hold of its handle so it can lift you into the sky, flying you to heights of inspiration you've never imagined. There are endless mojo objects, words, and works of art waiting to be touched, held, spoken, or made. Doing so plugs you into the creative life force so that you feel the tingling surge of electrical-like current flowing through your body. The purpose of this vibrant experience is to recharge your connection to mojo and make you more able to bring magic into the everyday.

I was once asked to visit the home of a young married couple on a rural farm in Louisiana. The wife was the granddaughter of an elder tribal medicine man from Montana. I worked with them in the mojo way, and afterward, they showed me a special treasure, saying they were its custodian. Needless to say, I was quite startled to discover that they had the medicine rattle of the legendary Oglala Sioux holy man Black Elk. He was the cousin of Crazy Horse, had participated in the Battle of Little Bighorn as a child, was later wounded at the Wounded Knee Massacre, and had traveled with Buffalo Bill's Wild West Show. He was most well known for telling his life story and revealing his visions and rituals to John Neihardt and Joseph Epes Brown. Their books about the holy medicine man introduced the world to the ways in which his people had access to the Great Spirit that guides the formation of the universe's mysteries.

The couple handed the rattle to me, and I observed how it looked like a doughnut with a handle. It was a sacred hoop rattle. I knew its mojo could not be awakened unless it called someone to use it. I felt it pulling on my arm, so I shook the holy rattle. Electricity surged through my body, and I recalled how I had initiated my own spiritual journey at the age of nineteen when I walked past the former office of John Neihardt at the University of Missouri. I had never heard of Black Elk back then, but it was nonetheless quite a coincidence that I had the major spiritual awakening of my life in the vicinity of Black Elk's biographer.

After I held and shook the rattle, a piece came off its handle. It was a strand of the hide Black Elk had personally harvested and prepared to decorate the rattle. It was given to me. I placed that mojo in my medicine bundle, where it still lives today. Later, the woman who had handed me the rattle became my student. Her grandfather came to her in a vision, saying that the mojo I was teaching was very important and should be honored. He blessed it. She now is a mojo practitioner on her reservation and gives good medicine to others for their healing.

Several years after I'd held Black Elk's rattle, I was called to the deathbed of Dr. Jim Crowley, a renowned anesthesiologist in St. Paul, Minnesota. His daughters said they wanted me to talk to him. When I came to his room, he was on a respirator and clearly had only days to live. He said he wanted to get something off his chest.

"I want to tell you what I have not told anyone before, not even my children. Years ago, my father moved here from Ireland. He was penniless but worked hard to save up some money to buy his own land so he could farm. He went to South Dakota and found what he was looking for, but the land was owned by the Oglala Sioux, or Lakota.

"My father went to the chief and asked to buy a parcel of land. The chief said, 'This land is our mother. We cannot sell our mother.' But my father did not give up easily. He went back the next day and asked again if he could purchase some land so he could support his family. The elders held a discussion and asked their medicine people. They came back with an offer, 'If you give us your newly born son, you can have the land.' That's right, my father sold me to the Oglala in exchange for some land. That is how I came to be raised by the Lakota elders and medicine people. This is a secret I have never told anyone. My wife never knew nor do any of my children or grandchildren.

"They named me Iktomi, the name of the sacred spider and also the symbol of the *heyoka* practitioner, a holy Lakota medicine man who works like a sacred clown, knowing how to behave and do things backwards. One of the heyokas was Black Elk. When I learned to be an artist, I painted his visions."

He pointed to the corner of the room where I saw his paintings. He continued, "They are there for you to see. I am supposed to tell you these things because that is the way it is. I was taught many things by the old ones and that included how to speak their secret medicine language. All that is in my past.

"When I became an adult, I walked away from the reservation. I went to college and medical school and became a doctor. I have several medical patents to my name, but I also became a self-taught architect. I learned to paint a bit as well. The only thing that my children know about my past is unspoken. As children, they noticed that sick animals would often come to our front door. I'd go outside and talk to the animals in an old medicine way. The animals would then go home happy.

"I need your help now. I grew up in the spiritual ways of Black Elk's people. Then, as an adult, I turned away from it and became a Catholic. I have been wondering whether it is OK to have walked in both those worlds."

I looked at the twinkle in his eyes. I knew he wasn't really asking that question. He was answering the question I was holding in my gut at that time because I had been walking in so many spiritual traditions. I sometimes felt dizzy from all the multiple realities I was simultaneously in.

I smiled and realized he'd just given me an important gift. I then replied, "You know as well as I that Black Elk was both a medicine man and a Catholic who held the position of the Catechist. I heard he was responsible for bringing over four hundred people to the church. But he also kept his medicine way. This was true for a lot of those old timers. I heard one of them explain it this way: 'If you ever get caught by a bear in the woods and have to start running with your pants down, you'd better have all your bases covered. That's why I belong to every religion.'" We both had a good laugh over that one, and the old doctor went on to tell me his life story and what he'd learned from the old ways. I felt like I was the historian in the movie *Little Big Man*, where Jack Crabb is portrayed by Dustin Hoffman as a 121-year-old white man who had been adopted by the Cheyenne in his childhood. In my case, the doctor was not a work of fiction. It was a true story.

When Dr. Jim Crowley died, the family asked me to preside over the funeral with a young priest. I set up a ceremonial space in an Irish Catholic funeral home and performed what was asked of me. After he was laid in the ground, the family presented me with a gift. They said their dad had only mentioned that it was a special gift he had received from the people who raised him as a child. It was an old piece of Indian jewelry, a silver and turquoise spider— Iktomi. I had received the old man's mojo totem.

Black Elk's rattle and the Iktomi both carry the mojo of the old heyoka, who were thunder dreamers. They are the human beings who dream the thunder beings, the sacred eagles that soar in the highest realms of sky and spirit. Elders say I am a thunder dreamer— one who has been tapped by the sacred rapture to feel the ecstatic flight and extraordinary transformation. The thunder beings first came to me in the wilderness as I fasted on a cliff. They provide the wings of inspiration that carry me into realms of mystery that surpass the expression of words and thought. They open my voice to sacred sound and sanction me to cross into the dark spaces, where tiny, bright lights reveal mystery in ways that cannot be explained. Thunder dreamers know how to call in the spirits, enabling all sorts of mojo work to take place—from finding lost objects to helping lost people find themselves. These practitioners understand, like the Balians, that the most powerful mojo is held inside the tension of opposites. Black Elk, myself, and others have crossed that path.

**Thunder dreamers know how to call in the spirits,
enabling all sorts of mojo work to take place—from
finding lost objects to helping lost people find themselves.**

Mojo can come to you in dream or in the dreams of others. That's when you need to go look for it or make it so it comes into your everyday. Once an Ojibwa Indian woman from Canada came to me and said, "I came to tell you my vision because you were in it. I was sitting at a table in a diner with my teacher, the late Albert Lightning, a Cree medicine man; we were having some breakfast. You came to the table, and we turned to you and said, 'Hi, White Crow.' In the vision I gave you a spiritual gift. That's why I have come to see you and hand over the holy medicine. It will help you when you work with other people." She handed me what she had seen in her dream.

White Crow was an old holy man in the late 1800s. He dreamed of the thunder beings, the most revered spirits of Lakota spirituality. They gave him the power to see the future and heal others, and he was part of a generation that included other strong dreamers, such as Black Elk. What made White Crow unique is that he doctored without carrying a medicine bag or sacred objects. His mojo traveled with him in an invisible form. I typically do the same with my clients, who have no idea that I am packing mojo.

In dreaming, we can meet other mojo doctors, dead or alive, and exchange gifts with one another. We learn that mojo is not given to anyone because he or she is better than others. A mojo doctor is just as human and messed up as anyone else. Speaking of the old days, Luther Standing Bear, an elder writer and chief from the Pine Ridge Reservation who, like Black Elk, was once part of the Buffalo Bill Wild West Show, wrote that "a medicine man was no holier than other men, no closer to Wakan Tanka [the Great Spirit], and no more honored than a brave or a scout." But medicine men knew how to obtain and use mojo to help others in a good way. It was simply their calling, their occupation, and their life purpose to handle mojo in a well-developed manner.

Mojo also can come from a vision that is situated in any culture during any time, even when you are not physically there. For example, in a holy dream, I met Yeshe Dorje Rinpoche, His Holiness the Dalai Lama's rainmaker, and weeks later learned that he had passed away. Those around him said he went "rainbow body," meaning his flesh vaporized at death, leaving only his hair and nails. This purportedly happens when dualisms, including that of mind and body, are fully dissolved. Due to the nature of my vision, I was given some of the holy man's remaining hair, and it serves as mojo in my work.

As the Dalai Lama's rainmaker, Yeshe Dorje Rinpoche would control the weather and make the conditions favorable for His Holiness's important ceremonies. He used a trumpet made of a human thighbone covered in silver and leather. His lineage was with the tantric master Padmasambhava, whose practice is now known as Nyingma.

His practices were not limited to controlling the weather. He also could summon the negative forces impacting people and disperse them, thereby relieving clients of the forces that obstruct physical or mental well-being. He became an illuminated master by spending many years in a dark cave. There, he was infused with mojo. Like the thunder dreamers, handling this power was paradoxical and often required utilizing contrary expression to communicate its teaching. This sometimes meant that on the surface, you may look like you are playing around, but underneath, there is some heavy-duty spiritual work going on. The strongest mojo doctors always clown around because it makes it easier for the serious mojo to get delivered; from the thunder of a storm, happiness is derived.

From absurd play, serious mojo is administered. Black Elk said it best in John Neihardt's book *Black Elk Speaks*:

> Only those who have had visions of the thunder beings of the West can act as heyokas. They have sacred power and they share some of this with all the people, but they do it through funny actions. When a vision comes from the thunder beings of the west, it comes ... like a thunderstorm; but when the storm of vision has passed, the world is greener and happier; for wherever the truth of vision comes upon the world, it is like a rain. The world, you see, is happier after the terror of the storm.... You have noticed that the truth comes into this world with two faces. One is sad with suffering, and the other laughs; but it is the same face, laughing or weeping ... as lightning illuminates the dark, for it is the power of lightning that heyokas have."

Holders of the strongest mojo are practical jokesters and trouble-makers, and they are impossible for anyone to control. One of Yeshe Dorje Rinpoche's spiritual fathers was Yogi Tashi. According to Rinpoche's biography, *The Rainmaker*, Tashi refused to pay his taxes, so the government sent fifty policemen to arrest him at his house. They came armed with swords and guns. When they found him, he ran. He then appeared to be flying over the roof, performing *lung-gom*, an ancient mystical practice that makes the practitioner extremely elastic. The police, overtaken by his mojo, prostrated themselves before his feet and said, "You are obviously not the man we came for. It is apparent that you are a great holy man."

With Black Elk being a thunder dreamer and Yeshe Dorje Rinpoche being a rainmaker, it should not surprise you that both mojo items—the strip of leather and the hair—have been associated with any kind of rain. I don't get those items out unless thunder energy is needed. When visiting Sao Paulo, Brazil, for the first time, I was taken to the distant outskirts of the city to meet an old woman of African descent who was the head of an Umbanda spirit house or temple, a place for practicing the syncretic mix of religions that includes old African traditions and Catholicism. It was a bright, sunny day when we arrived, but as soon as I opened the car door, large hail started to drop from the sky. We ran inside the house and watched it fly through the window. That's how I know the necklace she later gave me had strong mojo and would be a nice friend for my other necklaces of thunder.

I know the beings of thunder and how they can help a drum fly, or how they can help a boy like David, the boy who was scared of thunderstorms, learn to drum. I have seen how sight, hearing, smell, touch, and feelings are enhanced by the mojo that comes from absurd play but carries more strength than the storms it meets. Whether from Africa, Tibet, Brazil, South Dakota, or elsewhere, thunder mojo can knock your socks off while tickling your belly button.

> **I have seen how sight, hearing, smell, touch, and feelings are enhanced by the mojo that comes from absurd play but carries more strength than the storms it meets.**

Kundi, The Musical

I once worked with a young musician named Tom. He sang and played rock guitar so loudly that it sounded like thunder. He had studied a variety of alternative healing practices and was nearing graduation from a school of Chinese medicine at the time of our meeting. Having heard him perform, I was fully aware of his talent. When he volunteered to have a mojo encounter with me in front of a live audience, I saw him coming to the stage and shouted out a greeting, "Music man!"

Once he sat down, I said it again, "Music man, welcome." He corrected me to assure everyone that he was bringing more to the table than musicianship. He replied, "Among other things."

"You're here."

Tom was hesitant. "I think, yeah."

"How much of you is here?"

"Most of me, I think."

I noticed his slight hesitation to say that he was fully present and asked, "Are you 80 percent or 90 percent here?"

"Maybe 80; maybe 70."

"Oh! The percentage just went down as you spoke. Something left. What's the missing part? What part is not here?"

Tom replied with certainty, "I think my mojo's missing."

I think of how all thunder dreamers learn how to find lost objects. Also called stone dreamers, they are able to bring in the spirits and assist with finding lost things. My thunder mojo immediately arrived by my side, and I was reminded that Tom desired more creative inspiration and a connection to the life force that carries it. Mojo here concerns the magic that makes music feel that it has soul. If needing soul was true for Tom's music, it was also true for his life. He wanted the mojo that could infuse him with the creative life force. We needed to go on a journey to find his lost mojo so that creativity could return to all his performance venues.

"Did you lose it, or did you just leave it at home?"

"I think I lost it," he answered back.

I challenged him, "Yeah? Or did you ever have it?"

"I had it, yeah."

I pushed for specifics. "When's the last time you knew you had it, without a doubt?"

Tom was serious when he said he last had mojo when he was a child. As he put it, "I had it when I was this tall." He held out his arm to show the height he was at the time he last felt mojo.

I pressed on. "How did you know you had it then? Did you know that you had it then, or is it now that you know that you had it then?"

Tom chose to comment on his present condition. "I just don't feel confidence in my ability."

My thunder medicine loves turning things upside down, so it advised me to address the *con* in *confidence*. "You can no longer do a good con job?"

Tom laughed as he agreed with a head nod.

"But as a kid you could."

"Yeah, yeah!"

"So you acted big when you were small."

"Yeah."

Thunder continued to have me dance the differences concerning big and small. "What is it now? You're big but you don't know how to act small, or you're big and don't know how to act big, or you're big and don't know how to act at all?"

"The last one: I don't know how to act at all. I feel like I have a lot of gifts to give but I feel stagnant when I try to give them, whether its music or art. I have a lot of fear in my life, a lot of anxiety, and stuff like that holds me back."

Feeling stagnant is an indication that the vitality of the creative life force is missing. It wouldn't help to point out how his constant evaluations and worries are the very things that interfere with the natural flow of creativity. He needed mojo, something that could sweep him above those concerns. Inspiration pulls you above all the rational reasons why you should stay grounded and stuck. It makes you feel like it is possible to express the seemingly impossible. That invigorated conviction invites the creative life force to empower your whole being.

I played with his descriptions. "Is it fear of being a con or fear of forgetting how to be confident?"

Tom laid it on the line. "I fear that I'm just full of sh**. I've also been estranged from my mom for a long time. I think that has a lot to do with this."

I linked what we'd been discussing. "Is that a con job also?"

"Maybe. Perhaps I'm looking to her for a strength I'm not nurturing in myself. She needs a lot of help, and I can't seem to provide it. She's now sick, and no one in our family can give her the help she needs. That ravages me at times."

I connected this with all the studies he was pursuing. "Are you trying to learn everything you can about every healing tradition in the world so you can bring it home?"

Tom agreed, "Yes, to bring it home."

I teased him, "Then you can make things real again, like they were when you were a kid?"

"That's an interesting question because I don't stop to wonder why am I studying healing. I study healing constantly. Especially indigenous stuff because I'm really into the indigenous way. I'm trying to get past the dogma and get to the mojo."

I piped in, "'Cause it's hip. It's in fashion."

Tom indicated his uncertainty about himself again. "I didn't go through an initiation, so I don't feel like a man."

I stayed with my challenge. "Initiations—especially those of the indigenous variety—are popular. These days you like being hip."

He agreed, "I do!"

"You want to be more inside your home with more authenticity—that is, to be more inside these traditions."

Tom was clear. "Yes. Public approval is important to me somehow."

I started laughing as I said, "That's why you're messed up."

"Yes!"

I spelled it out. "You can't heal anybody if you care about public approval." Tom nodded in agreement. I continued with heyoka-like counsel that pushed him into the absurd in order to paradoxically get a serious thing accomplished. "If you want to get offstage and be the real thing, it requires being more jaded. That's what you're missing—jade. You've been studying the wrong thing in China. You've got all the *dogma*, but you need to be more *jaded* about it."

Mojo doctors and thunder dreamers know that serious truths need to be coupled with equally playful absurdities in order to bring both of them to life. Otherwise dogma gets sleepy and dogmatic rather than reflecting the lively Buddha nature of a mama dog. One jewel that contributes to a life force makeover is a jaded juxtaposition that makes everyone take notice in an unexpected way.

Iktomi, the spider-trickster of Lakota mythology, was the son of a rock. You could say that he was originally stoned in his conception. His jaded and shape-shifting, trickster nature gives him great mojo power. Known as a creator god, Iktomi is a master mojo doctor with the power to make potions that can influence the experience of human beings and even change the other gods. Given his rocky background, it is no accident that the great thunder dreamers were also called stone dreamers. They were jaded mojo practitioners. I am mindful of these things as I encourage Tom to get more jaded.

Tom surprisingly was serious about my comment. "Yes. I've thought about jade a lot, actually."

I immediately suggested action. "You need to get a piece of jade and add the letter *d* for your jaded response to dogma."

What better stone could there possibly be for becoming a jaded mojo doctor than a jade! Like Iktomi, I was encouraging Tom to be symbolically reborn out of a stone to become a mojo doctor who plays tricks on theories rather than being overly weighted down by them.

Tom continued to take me seriously. "I wonder if there's a store that sells jade around here."

I continued, "It would be nice to have a necklace with a piece of jade and the letter *d* right by its side so you can be jaded about all dogma. I think you want to put the charm and hex of mojo on all your dogma. I know that about you by the way you look. With your clothing and jewelry, you wear the signs of someone who is interested in hip things from Chinese symbolism to esoteric secrets from far-out disciplines. I don't think you really want approval; you want a reaction."

Tom was in full agreement. "Definitely."

"I think you'd be just as happy if people were pissed off at you as you would be if they admired you."

"For sure."

Then I moved toward making quite a proclamation, addressing his personal mojo. "This stuff you have around your neck is boring." Tom was wearing a New Age necklace that was hip and cute but not provocative. "That's not going to get a reaction, you know what I'm saying? I mean, it's beautiful and it's interesting, but it doesn't stand out. You should get the ugliest piece of jade you can find, a real clunker." We both started laughing. I was finding a way for Tom to be more creative with how he performed in front of others—to try new ways of getting a reaction from his audience. We started with his attire and then later, with his music.

Tom jammed on this idea. "Get some bling-bling in jade."

"Yes, along with a gothic *d*."

Tom was with me. "I like that."

I enacted how he could talk about it in the world. "If somebody says, 'What's that?' you can just say, 'I'm a jade mother.' If they ask what that means, you can reply, 'It's about my mother.' Should someone come back at you with another question, 'What's that mean?' you can always respond, 'You're not ready to hear that.' If they ask, 'Why?' come back at them with, 'Because I'm not ready to say that.'"

Tom understood this invitation for improvisational performance. "I like this."

"You know how to jam," I announced.

"Yeah, oh yeah."

"That's what's missing in your life. You're not jamming with your life. You think you can only jam when you're singing and playing the guitar."

Mojo jazzes life up, doing so by improvising with whatever is set upon its stage. The art of improvising is all about winging it—embracing life with inspirational wings and letting it all creatively fly. Everything can be improvised—words, meanings, symbols, actions, objects, juxtapositions, sounds, movements, and anything imaginable—as a means of getting a liftoff. We fly when we jam. Magic may start with a sacred loaf of bread, but you need to spread some jam on it to reach the sweetest heavens.

Tom responded, "I can jam. It's just when I get in front of people, it just seems absurd all of a sudden ..."

"You're having music problems when there's an audience?" In other words, his creativity was getting blocked when he was too self-conscious in front of others. He needed some mojo to lift him above this trap. I would move to create a mojo audience for him—one that would inspire his creativity rather than block it.

"Oh yeah, totally. It's crazy 'cause I love making up stuff out of thin air. When there is no audience, it is perfect and beautiful. But it gets messed up with an audience."

Inspired by contrary mojo, I made an unexpected suggestion, "The problem is the particular audience. I suggest that you change the audience to a new one. You need an audience that sits in front of the other audience. Imagine if you got on stage and you had your own audience there. It might only be three or four or five people, but they would be people who are jaded. Maybe they all have jaded *d*'s too and you play for them. Who cares about the rest of them? You know what I'm saying?"

"Yeah, yeah, yeah."

The thunder mojo wanted me to push him further into the absurd. "Or you could create a mojo audience. You could have people painted on each of your fingernails. This would be your private audience. Play for them. Put the audience in your hands. That would be something."

Tom liked this direction. "That's a damn good idea!"

"Maybe you have the faces of people on your fingernails. Or maybe you have symbols representing all those 'in' things—those *in*digenous things you like. Maybe you should consider the people on your fingers as the tribe you want to be initiated in. Play for them. Nobody else would matter. Jam on that idea. Perhaps you should just play for the jade."

Tom was nodding in agreement. "I like that, breaking it down. Just making it simple and basic."

I suggested, "Create your own world: a world within a world, a stage within a stage, an audience within an audience. You can hold them in your hand. Wouldn't it be interesting to put a tattoo of a whole arena or a whole audience right on your hand? When you play the guitar, you'd have the audience in the palm of your hand. That would be marvelous. That would be a trip." We were exploring ways in which creative mojo can inspire further creativity.

"That would be cool," Tom added with a smile.

"Madison Square Garden in your palm."

The mojo was working as I found out that Tom was on the same wavelength. "I was just thinking about Madison Square Garden."

"Wow! That tells me you want a real audience, not the small-time stuff."

"Yeah, I don't want to play it small. I want to reach a lot of people."

I underscored this moment. "Listen to what you've just said. You said you don't want to play it small; you were thinking of Madison Square Garden. Find a photograph of Madison Square Garden where there is a wild, crazy, enthusiastic audience. Cut it out and carry it on your palm. You might get a glove and have that image burned onto the palm of the glove. You could wear an audience glove."

"Yes!"

"When you are feeling challenged by one audience, just put on the glove and play for that audience. The audience glove enables you to carry around the audience you enjoy entertaining."

"That's very true, man, very true," Tom said as he was laughing about this idea while taking it seriously.

Thunderous teasing was released. "This may be the tip you've been looking for all of your life because I know you want to have the money to be free to do all these crazy things. You're just worried somebody's not going to pay you."

"Yeah, totally."

"Totally, man. Get this glove and sell it—the world's first audience glove. Think about how many people out there, especially musicians, would like to carry an audience in their hand."

Tom was intrigued. "Interesting idea. Have you copyrighted this?"

"No. You can have it! When you clap your hands, thousands of people will be clapping!"

Tom nodded in agreement. "That would be awesome."

We had created some mojo that radically altered his relationship with himself, his audiences, and the world, doing so by encouraging him to be creative with his problem—his interaction with the assumed audience. "Today, the world gave birth to an audience glove. And your hands can hold a lot of things; they are not limited to an audience. You could hold the world. You could have a whole line of gloves with different images to carry an assortment of things in the palms of your hands. Maybe the gods decided you'd have this particular screw-up about audiences to set you up to have an accident, a moment such as this. Without it, we wouldn't have come up with a new product line. And since you know how to be a con artist, you can sell it."

We had created some mojo that radically altered his relationship with himself, his audiences, and the world, doing so by encouraging him to be creative with his problem—his interaction with the assumed audience.

Tom was captivated by this possibility. "That is an interesting idea."

"That's probably the underlying reason you've learned all these indigenous things—to have more product ideas. You could have sacred imagery where the palms hold an initiation rite. Imagine that! You could find an image of a faraway, magical, mysterious, secret initiation. Perhaps sketched, perhaps photographed. Have it put on a glove. People could wear it and go through the everyday while taking a peek of an initiation going on every moment, because they're holding it in the palm of their hand. There are so many things you can do with this kind of glove! You could have Buddha in your palm—

a Buddha Palm Pilot. Or a Jesus Palm Pilot, a Holy Mother Palm Pilot, even a Nietzsche Palm Pilot for spanking all true believers. Put whatever god mojo you want in the palm of your hand!"

"That is awesome!"

I laughed and made an offer. "I'll take 20 percent of the profits. I'm the prophet of your profit!" We both laughed.

"It's a deal, man; it's a deal."

Now I brought the creative mojo to his immediate life. "Think what you could do if you had this kind of liberation. You need to be the test pilot; go wear the first one. Carry the audience at Madison Square Garden and keep a diary of how it transforms your life. Build a website and advertise the product."

"That's pretty cool. I've never been much of a businessman, though," Tom added.

"You don't need to be. You only need to be a con artist." We were laughing at the absurd truth behind our discussion. "Someone else can do the business; those are the bean counters. Can it be this simple? Yes, it can be this simple. That's the wild thing. That's why nobody does it. Every single creative thought that comes in your mind hears the critical voice of reason saying, 'It cannot be that simple.'"

"Yeah."

"The only secret for you to uncover is the idea that it can be that simple. That's the heaviest idea you can ever receive. This idea weighs a *creative ton*. Be a *simple-ton*!"

Tom repeated what I said, "Simple-ton."

"Believe that a simple—though existentially heavy—kind of novelty can lead to a great unraveling, a great freeing, a great performance, a great audience, a great difference, a great healing, and a great homecoming. It takes someone who thinks like a child to believe such things are true." I was showing him the essence of thunder mojo.

Tom piped in, "I have that childlike streak, but I also get too serious about issues in my life."

"How old were you when this was not a problem?"

"I was six or maybe eight years old."

My thunder mojo rattles were shaking, and I could hear them. As a mojo doctor, I have been carried into many mysteries, and have been asked to say and perform many mysterious things. Some of my rattles have flown and lit up in the dark just like the flying drum. They were now inspiring me to ask Tom to stand up. "Would you stand up, please? Show me how tall you were then. Where would the top of your head reach on your body now?"

Tom indicated he was the height of where his belly button now is.

My mojo already knew where this needed to go. "You need to draw a line right here." As I said this, I drew an imaginary horizontal line across his navel. "Know that everything below this line is fine; you're already halfway there. The problem is with what is up above."

Tom agreed and added, "It's funny because in Chinese medicine, my pathology is heart–kidney imbalance. They're not speaking to each other, and I actually have ribbons of varicose veins along my diaphragm."

The mojo was delighted with how things were moving along. "There you go—that's the line."

Tom was with me. "Yeah, that's the line."

"Yes, that's where you stopped," I said while pointing across his midsection. "Now you know. You never have to ask again. You don't need another course on dogma. You don't need to go to try to figure out what another dogmatic book or dogmatic author has to say. You know that you can stop here. You are at the finish line, which just happens to be your next starting line."

"Yes."

As Tom sat down, I gave him an important message. "It's no problem. Be a simple-ton. Make heavy stuff simple. Get small; you think too big. Just make Madison Square Garden smaller so you can hold it in your palm. I wouldn't recommend getting a real tattoo, but it would be nice if you could have someone draw a horizontal line across your body right where that line is. You also could have a second head drawn there. Its mouth could be your belly button. Have this head be upside down, looking up at your other head and saying, "Hey, dude, come on down and join the show.""

Tom exclaimed, "I really like that."

"Go ahead and cross the line. Don't be afraid to cross the border."

Tom added to this improvisation. "Yeah. Go down."

"Get down. Bring it down."

This phrase reminded Tom of something that just happened in his life. "It's funny because I wrote someone recently about taking me to an initiation, and he said, 'Are you willing to go down 'cause that's the direction you need to go.'"

"Are you?"

"I don't know. I've dealt with a lot of inhibitions about my sexuality for a long time as well, and that's been a hang-up for me ever since I came into sexual maturity."

I interjected a comment, "You know where the line's drawn."

"Yeah, I see that now."

I pointed to Tom's body and the imagined line, and said, "This half is separate from the other half; it doesn't know about the other side. This means that what you just told me is no news. It's just the same thing."

Tom nodded in agreement, "Totally."

At this moment, my thunder mojo was ready to pull Tom into a creative storm of transformation. I turned to the audience and asked, "Does anyone have an eraser?" A participant brought up an eraser on the end of a pencil and handed it to me. I continued, "Tom, we are going to initiate you." I pointed to the midsection of his body and went on. "You have a line there. Here, take this eraser and erase it."

Tom took the pencil and went through the motions of erasing the imaginary line. As he did this, I commented, "You are using a mojo eraser. Maybe you ought to stand up again and turn 360 degrees while you're doing it." Tom stood up and turned as he erased. As this was taking place, the audience and I started clapping and hollering, making a driving rhythm. We all began to chant some wild sounds—thunder had broken out inside the theater. When Tom was finished, he smiled and threw the pencil back into the audience.

"Feels good," he said with relief and delight.

I talked to him about the change. "Now your body's going to say, 'Where did that line go?'"

Tom joked, "Now kundalini has an autobahn straight up my body."

"That's right. You were just lined up the wrong way. You messed with your line."

Tom was thrown off guard.

"You made it go horizontal. You have been so curious about anything and everything that is spiritual that you couldn't keep your hands off of whatever came in front of you."

"Totally right."

"When you saw that kundalini line, you grabbed it and turned it sideways, making it horizontal instead of leaving it straight up and down."

"Yeah, yeah, yeah!"

I went on with this mojo-inspired trickster explanation. "As a consequence, all your energy's been going horizontally across your midriff; that's like somebody with a saw chopping you in two. You could probably write a book about what happened."

This struck a chord with Tom. "I've got about three books on the go."

Now I braced myself to make a special announcement. The thunder mojo had an idea that could be life-changing for Tom. "This is what I think you should do: you should write a musical—a kundalini musical. Maybe call it *Kundi, The Musical!*"

Tom nearly jumped out of his chair, throwing his arms up to the ceiling as he exclaimed, "That's what I've been thinking of doing!"

"Brilliant, dude!" We laughed and bumped fists as confirmation of this project.

Tom continued, "I already do shows with crystal balls and chakras, and I thought to myself, *Let's just make it absurd and get someone dressed up as kundalini.*"

I felt the kundalini inside me dancing wildly as I shouted, "Awesome! That's it! What's going to be the opening number?"

Tom had the look of eureka on his face. "Whoa, I just got hit by something!"

I felt electricity in the air and noted it, too. "Whoa!" It moved me to jump out of my seat. "Did you feel that right now?"

Tom felt the energy amplifying. "Yes! Something came up, man."

"I felt it, too!" Kundalini had come to life in our interaction. This was mojo, live and in person. It wasn't something you passively believe in like the placebo effect. Mojo is an awakening of the here and now. It is the excitement brought on in a live theater when the curtain is opened and the musical overture begins to play. Mojo is producing this magical show.

Tom was blown away. "That was wild."

I sat down and asked, "What's going to be the opening number?"

Tom thought for a while and then saw the light, "'The Big Bang, Baby.' God and goddess got together and made it happen."

I suggested some special effects demanded by my mojo. "The theatrical performance is going to need thunder. It's going to require some kind of sound-making machine with low-frequency vibrations to get everybody moving. Let's take the show to Broadway! I think it's going to have the music and lyrics only you can write because this musical will show that this is the reason you've been put on Earth—to create this performance. You will have the world, the universe, kundalini, and spirit all in the palm of your hand. Maybe the guitar you'll play onstage will look like the chakras; it will look like a spine. Get a guitar that looks like the vertebrae of your spine."

"Wow! That would be awesome." Tom loved what his show was becoming. "Whoa! That would be really cool!"

"Damn!"

Tom laughed and echoed, "Damn!"

"Every time you move up and down the guitar, the stage lighting changes to match the coloration of the chakras. I'm feeling it!"

"Yeah, me too, man. That's how I want to serve this stuff. I don't want to write too many intellectual books about it; I want to make people feel it. That's what I've been learning from you—get out of the knowing and move to the unknowing. Get people to feel, dance, and perform what kundalini wants."

I reminded him of what we'd learned together. "Make it small. Make the whole universe small so you can hold it in your hands. Make the heavy stuff small so it can be handled. What if this whole musical were a puppet show? Wouldn't that be wild?"

Tom agreed, "That would be wild. We could make it for kids! We could have the big show at Madison Square Garden and have a tour of schools 'cause I love kids."

I suggested, "Why not call the show Kundi? This name makes it smaller and a little easier to handle."

"Kundi! I like that."

"Kundi learns to fly," I added.

Yes, strong mojo flies whether it is found in Tibet or in a Broadway musical empowered by magical thunder.

I took a deep breath and prepared to make an important point: "There's so much ahead of you if you can get over your head."

Tom was ready. "Yes. I need to step into this and not be afraid. I will feel it."

My mojo asked me to voice a question that made no immediate sense to me. As a mojo doctor, that's the best reason I know for saying it. "Can you carve?" I asked.

"No, but I want to learn. That's been on my mind, too."

I emphasized what he had said. "That's been on your *mind*, too?"

Tom clarified what he meant, "Not in my heart but on my mind, yeah."

"Well, of course, because that's what needs to be carved. I see you taking some potatoes, carving your head out of one, and then *eating* it!"

Tom was surprised, "Eating it?"

"Yes," I answered as if it were a matter of fact, though I was as surprised as he was as to why I'd suggested it.

"That would be cool."

"That's the diet you need to be on. Do it so this head (I pointed to his head) becomes friends with the lower part of your body. Bring it down."

Tom was enthusiastically nodding his head. "Yeah, yeah, yeah!"

The heyoka nature of thunder mojo revels in extreme teasing that sometimes includes vulgarity or dirty talk. I felt it brewing. "Digest and integrate it. Whatever needs to be left behind, dump it. When you have enough potato head turds, you'll be on your way."

Tom was excited. "Hallelujah, man!"

"We have to talk about excrement because something's got to go."

Tom was still with me. "Definitely, definitely."

The mojo was thundering within me. I released it: "Go eat your whole potato head. Down the hatch! Down the tube! Down the kundalini highway!" I said this as I drew a vertical line down his body. "That which doesn't need to stay, drop it. Make a direct deposit into the infinite ocean. There, it can go back to where it belongs in the highest state of maximal delusion, but without any influence. Let's call this a distillation of your mind. Eat your head, swallow, drop, and then do another round again. Eat your head over and over again. With each passage, you'll become cleaner, more purified, and highly distilled, highly charged, highly spirited—two hundred proof! You'll become the higher proof of the kundalini man! You'll take others on the grand climb. *Kundi, The Musical!* Welcome to the ascension ride!"

Tom addressed how this matched his dreams. "This is the work I want to do—to bring people down into the base chakras. I want to take them to those primal ones, the earthly ones—those forces you can't control that are just there pulling you."

Totally possessed by mojo thunder, I started singing a cowboy song, "She'll Be Coming 'Round the Mountain."

"Yes! Definitely. Wow, you knew about it, too!"

I teased him. "It's a western. A western kundalini show with kundalini cowboys and cowgirls, and a kundalini bronco ride! Whoa, think of that!" I said these things as I bounced in my chair, as if riding a wild bronco.

Tom was excited about the song. "I have to include that number—'She'll Be Coming 'Round the Mountain.'"

I continued teasing him with extreme mojo, sacred clowning. "India always had it right. With all that kundalini over there, we now know why they worship the cow: because kundalini is a wild bull—it's a rodeo! It jerks you around and gives you one hell of a ride! But there is nothing more satisfying than when you manage to stay on top."

"I got to stay on that Taurus bull."

"It's your life, and it starts in the palm of your hand. There, we will find Madison Square Garden and the cosmos." I paused before going on. "I need to remind you of something that took place here tonight. You were initiated when your line was erased; that was the initiation. It erased that which has been the hang-up."

"I'm going to go carve some sweet potatoes right now and eat my head. I'll definitely start writing on my hand before I play. Then I'll get a glove made ..."

Someone in the audience shouted out, "Kundi's coming!"

"Yes," I added. "Kundi is coming. The musical should have scenes about your life. It might show your initiation and have another scene about the time you swallowed your sweet potato head. Things will come down, and things will go up; it will all come together at the crossroads. That's where blues guitarists make their deal and get their life force. You're a guitar man who needs to go to the crossroads. You need to go there and make a deal, saying, 'I'm here, and I want to be empowered to be the ambassador for all things that hold the feeling of transformative power. I wish to be ordained, initiated, and holy. I will be known as the one called Kundi.'"

"Damn straight," Tom asserted.

"You're going to have to name your guitar. It needs a name, too."

"I will call it Kundi! It's interesting because I haven't named my guitar. I've been wondering about it for quite a while. Kundi is perfect."

"You and the guitar have the same name. When you play it, you become the same.

"The guitar is your spine. From this day forward, when you play your spine, know that as your fingers go up and down it, so does Kundi."

"Whoa, man, that's wicked." Tom was deeply moved by this realization. "I will never play my guitar in the same way."

"How could you?" I asked and laughed. "You'll never think about this in the same way." As I said this, I moved my hand horizontally along his midriff. "That line is gone. Now it's up to you to make the *x* intersection across your chest. Your heart and soul need to take a little stroll down to the crossroads. Every night for the rest of your life, you should perform this routine and regard it as your personal sign. Take your hand and pretend to make a crossroads— an *x*—over your heart. You can do that now because you've been initiated. Before you go to sleep, make sure that the last thing you do is draw this *x* across yourself, saying, 'Take me to the crossroads.' Those are the roads you are on; this is your mojo journey. Let's shake on it." As we reached out to shake hands, I said these final words: "I'll pretend you're wearing your glove so I can join an audience of thousands in applauding what you are doing with the mojo in your life."

Here we see that mojo is actually the creative life force, and anything that it touches becomes empowered with magic. Mojo inspires us to be creative, and that, in turn, fills us with the mystery of being fully alive.

Tom came to me for mojo. He wanted to feel more inspired by the creative life force in his performances and in other parts of his life but was blocked by his perception of how he interacted with an audience. Rather than explain how he was stuck, we utilized his stuck-ness in a creative way, finding new ways to define and create an audience. This started a momentum of creativity in the session whose flow would not stop. Creative mojo touched everything we discussed, from his necklace to his audience glove and the guitar he used. Here we see that mojo is actually the creative life force, and anything that it touches becomes empowered with magic. Mojo inspires us to be creative, and that, in turn, fills us with the mystery of being fully alive.

Prescriptions for Generating Creative Storms

You, too, need some more thunder in your life. A mojo doctor has just the right spice to kick you up several thousand notches into the thunderclouds. There, you forget about being a wimp or a timid, fear-based creepy crawler. In the thunder, you are energized and empowered to kick some spiritual butt. I am going to give you the recipe for how to make some thunder mojo. Know that it will involve using an absurd action in order to bring forth a serious reaction. Here, opposites attract in a most fascinating way.

Go anywhere in the world—I don't care where it is, and it matters not whether you think it is a sacred spot or a trash heap. Just get off your fanny and head somewhere on an unguided journey with no purpose other than a very small outcome. Your mission is to find a tiny stone. Make sure it is the tiniest stone you are able to locate. Collect it and bring it home.

Place this tiny stone in the smallest matchbox you are able to get at the store. Decorate the matchbox so that it looks like a thunderous sky. I suggest painting it or covering it with paper and then drawing a lightning bolt or a thunderbird on each side. If you want, draw a snake on the box, and think about how the sound of a rattlesnake can be so alarming that it makes you scream like you have been hit by lightning. Whatever makes the box feel anything like a thunderstorm, whether it is sensible or nonsensical, will work fine. This is your thunder mojo rattle. As a tiny rattle, it is there to help you become a little mojo doctor—the smallest shaman on the block. Remind yourself that the smallest object always becomes the largest presence in the world of thunder.

Every time you feel the need for mojo that can wake up a creative storm, play your drum and then shake this rattle. As you do this, make the sound of thunder with your own throat and voice. Shake that rattle box and voice some thunder. Do not miss an opportunity to bring this to every situation that can benefit from a downpour of creativity.

Collect a tiny stone for every successful brainstorm that brings forth a leap in your imagination. Limit your collection of stones to twelve. When you have twelve tiny stones in your small matchbox, you can call yourself a Little Big Mojo Doctor. At this stage, your rattle is fully engaged and only needs to be shaken when you arise in the morning and before you go to sleep at night. Try to make it the first and last thing you hear each day for the rest of your life.

I promise that if you faithfully carry out this mojo mission, your life will never be the same. You will find a new climate change for your imagination, and it will be impossible to predict; call this global creative warming. This, you can count on: your creativity will clap with thunderous applause at your unexpected performances. Creative lightning will strike at any time, awakening you to become more alive and vibrant in your everyday. You'll wish you had an audience beholding your live enactments on the various stages of your life.

You already know how to procure an audience. Make yourself an audience glove or sketch some enthusiastic cheerleaders on your fingernails. Carry whatever audiences, worlds, angels, or gods you want in the palm of your hand exactly like Tom did. This will help turn your life into a creatively wild Broadway musical.

And yes, you will need some music. Listen to some samples of music as a producer would. You need to find the songs that match the staging of your rising star as it ascends into theatrical praise and stardom. Find your overture. Play it in the morning after you play your drum and shake your rattle. Have other soundtracks on hand. You may want to download them so they are readily accessible. What song needs to be sung when you feel a pinch of disappointment? You will need some love songs for those moments when your heart is all aflutter. It's good to consider having a battle song, a victory song, and one that announces the arrival of magical entities and beings. It's your production, so choose whatever you want.

Get on with your show and be responsible for all its many faceted aspects. Produce, direct, act, and promote it! As the old theater thunder dreamers like to say, "Go break a leg."

9

ON BECOMING A
MOJO DOCTOR

*M*ojo is another word for "mystery." Creativity is mysterious, and that's why it's mojo. The same holds true for love and anything that authentically involves spirited, magical experience. Mystics, poets, minstrels, creative performers, and lovers cultivate its presence. The problem with words like *spirituality*, *religion*, *god*, *light*, *healing*, *healer*, *therapy*, *wisdom*, and all the words that have been nearly choked to death by too much talk is that they tempt us to think we know what they mean. As a consequence, their heady meanings lose the effusive magic, mystery, and life force that used to embody them. *Mojo* is a word that is less used and it is practically unknown. It is more mysterious; it awaits creative handling. That is why it is important.

If you *feel* the truth about the big mysteries in life, then pledge yourself to expressing its mojo. It is the underground way of evoking everyday magic, and it provides less-worn rhetoric for infusing creative vitality into the most important things that cannot be easily expressed with words. It addresses any magic charm or spell of enchantment, refers to the belief in one's inner talents to creatively navigate through any situation, taps into one's cool essence, and embraces the here-in-the-now feeling of being alive with the life force. In addition, you can add it to another word and

261

help make it revitalized. Think of mojo love, mojo mystery, mojo spirituality, mojo god, mojo healing, and mojo therapy, to mention a few hot combos.

If you *feel* the truth about the big mysteries in life, then pledge yourself to expressing its mojo. It is the underground way of evoking everyday magic, and it provides less-worn rhetoric for infusing creative vitality into the most important things that cannot be easily expressed with words.

When I was recently elected president of the Louisiana Association for Marriage and Family Therapy, I accepted the role for a political reason. Please recognize that I will now exaggerate my polemic so my message is more likely to be heard. I intend to use my position and reputation as a platform to *ask for the overthrow and abolition of all the mental health professions.* Why? None of these professions has any mojo. The worst is psychiatry and its cozy partnership with the billion-dollar pharmacology corporations that promote the mass marketing of drugs for every imaginable discomfort and troublesome mood. Practically all the mental health professions have sold their soul to some trivial belief that therapy, counseling, and all the other people-helping professions should be solely legitimized and organized by scientific principles, medication, and so-called evidence-based treatment. This latter framing of therapy is its final deathblow.

This public service announcement is presented as a gracious act of soulful liberation. Overthrowing these misguided systems will benefit everyone. It will open the doors to the return of the long-lost mojo that aims to creatively set us free to experience a more joyful life. There is a drug-free way of turning lemons into lemonade: cut through the sour fruit; squeeze it; and add sugar, water, and ice to make it nice. We similarly can magically transform suffering into joy: hold the suffering, open it up so its inner gift is exposed, squeeze out the creative juice, and then be sweet about it so the situation becomes cool and enables another baptism into joyous living. You get through life effortlessly and naturally when you find your mojo. It should become your main squeeze.

It is time for therapists to become mojo doctors and for clients to feel free to seek them in order to receive help in finding their own personal mojo. We take a step toward this direction when we recognize that therapy is not a science but an art. I'm only comfortable saying that it is both an art and a science if we can also agree that the performance arts concerned with telling a joke, a magical story, or an absurd theatrical play are also science. In that case, I look forward to teaching a course on the physics of comedy, the neurobiology of theater, or the astrophysics of love. Rest assured that therapy is a form of improvisational theater that belongs in the house of performing arts. I have spent an entire career arguing for this perspective (see my books *The Creative Therapist: The Art of Awakening a Session* and *Improvisational Therapy: A Practical Guide for Creative Clinical Strategies*).

When we help people sort out their lives, we handle the mystery of a complexity that defies both description and explanation. When the politics of psychopharmacology, the mindlessness of psychiatric diagnosis, and the overly simplistic reductionism of statistical research come together to monopolize what has previously worked for thousands of years, it's time to take a prophetic stand and religiously shout, "Enough!"

There is no other way to set us free from this tyranny against creativity, soul, and mojo than to state clearly what is happening. We cannot avoid making the critique. No positive change can be made without smartly confronting the negatives that impede its creation. We must face the darkness of the moment in order to give birth to a new light. Prophets must point to the corrupt ways of profit making but also extend a loving invitation to the alternatives that matter. Say no to what has been a crusade against mojo, and shower the grand inquisitors with laughter, joy, absurd love, crazy wisdom offerings, and playful encounters. Do so while ripping down the walls that have kept the mojo hidden and imprisoned.

I am calling for mojo doctors to take their stand. I am asking for clients to see that they are in need of mojo rather than pills, labels, and psychobabble. We must join together in building and sustaining a world that highlights creative strengths over pathological weaknesses, encourages love as the motivation for a sweet offense rather than hate as the conspirator of a sour defense, reaches for ecstatic transformation and not addiction to pain relief, builds upon the street wisdom of elder traditions as opposed to the street illiteracy of our infant stumbling ways, and serves exhilarating mojo rather than boring, clichéd stereotypes. The bottom line is that we desperately need mojo more than ever; we have been starving for it while not even knowing it exists.

The greatest mysteries arise from the complex weavings of Mother Nature and the infinite ways she embodies the web of life. The divine processes of creation, death, and regeneration are beyond the limited abilities of our minds to fully understand and manipulate. We need to participate and cooperate with the ecology that holds life, not naively and arrogantly try to control it.

Cultures around the world have held wisdom in the helping arts, and we should start learning from them. Today's professions, on the other hand, encourage practitioners to be blind and deaf to the ways of masterful transformation. We do everything to make it impossible to heal our clients: we remove ourselves from the arts and spiritual traditions while spewing what we call social science, the least inspirational prose about the most important matters regarding the nature of our purpose in life. We have nothing meaningful to say about serving love and wisdom.

I'm in the mental health business, so I should know what I'm talking about. Yes, you can call me a whistleblower. The profession is iatrogenic—causes more harm than cure—and its foundation sits on collapsing sand dunes. Therapists too easily ignore the solid bedrock of the global wisdom traditions. Our mental health professions are simply doing the bidding of the drug companies and the academics who try to get research grants for their non-inspiring form of number-crunching masochism. We must act now, before pharmacology and psychiatry turn the world into zombies.

I have written professional books for therapists that attempt to provide an alternative to the mainstream, biology-oriented practices. Some are required reading in various clinical graduate programs. I have given keynote addresses to the major mental health professions, including the American Counseling Association. Finally, I have met many of the major innovators and leaders of the field. I've been around long enough to say, "It's largely a sham." Perhaps the best purpose for being in my present position is to be able to say this loudly and clearly without any hesitation or whitewashing.

Now it's time to bring the revolution into the streets. The professions will protest, but rest assured that they are only trying to hold onto their profit-making ways, hiding behind the closed doors of secrecy. There should be nothing secret about mental health delivery. The oldest healing traditions perform healing or therapy in public. That's right. It takes place in a ceremonial theater for all to benefit from whatever takes place. The whole mental health charade can be brought down overnight by kicking open the therapist's private practice door. Drop the privacy and make it a public performance. Shine the light and bring things out of the dark ages.

I have never made a psychological diagnosis, nor have I ever filled out an insurance form. I refuse to participate in maintaining a system that does not swear to do the least harm. *Primum non nocere*: first, do no harm. Unlike other cultural healing traditions, the mental health industry does not start with any concern about doing the *least* harm. The most harm comes from social stigmatization, injecting powerful, mind-altering chemicals into one's bloodstream or screwing around with the human brain. They are the most invasive procedures and should be the last considerations for treatment. In my entire career (and I specialize in impossible cases), I have never referred anyone to get an ugly label, social imprisonment, or a drug trip. We should always start with all the cures of the performing arts, and explore what can be done with inspired mojo before we even think of considering the molecular assault dictated by the latest fashion in commercialized pill popping. Cheers to the few who have courageously forged a new path! Hats off to psychiatry's party poopers, who include Thomas Szasz, Ronald Laing, Carl Whitaker, Milton Erickson, and Carl Hammerschlag, to mention a handful. If you are a member of any mental health organization, join them and become a pill pooper rather than a pill pusher.

We should always start with all the cures of the performing arts and explore what can be done with inspired mojo.

If you are a human being, you will always benefit from mojo, the magic that enchants your life. When you get your mojo, you find that there is more to it than turning your life around and coming alive; you also discover that you have the goods to help others. Once you get used to handling mojo, put up a sign that says *Mojo*

Man or *Mojo Woman*. If you're already a therapist with a doctorate, go ahead and call yourself *Mojo Doctor*. Forget all that other professional nonsense; it holds you back from drawing on the deepest wells of creativity—the truest source of a healing practice.

When you get your mojo, you find that there is more to it than turning your life around and coming alive; you also discover that you have the goods to help others.

Here is the alternative that I propose: If you are struggling, don't call a therapist. Invite a standup comic to come to your house and tease you into paroxysms of laughter. Or hire a singer to croon in your front yard and invite your 'hood to swoon all night. Bring a poet to your dining room or an improvisational acting company to your kitchen. If a psychiatrist suggests that you need your brain shocked with electricity or high-impact chemistry, try other less dangerous forms of aesthetic shock. Burn your bedroom furniture in the front yard. Paint your car the weirdest color you can find, wrap an electrical cord around the antenna, and write an odd message on the side that says something like *Who's depressed now? Shock your car and not your brain!*

Thinking of investing thousands of dollars in mental health? Try a benign source of mental insanity first. It's less dangerous. For example, pick up some friends and invite them to fly with you to a beach. Upon arrival, order everything off the menu at a well-reviewed Mexican restaurant and hire a mariachi band to sing holiday songs. The next day, gather at the beach and shout together, "Life is a beach!" Only return whenever you must. That's a far better investment than seeing a shrink.

Thinking about psychiatric medication? A martini is healthier—either shaken or stirred. Try lemonade with a chopped cartoon sprinkled on top. Eat three radishes a day. Stare at a head of lettuce and repeat to yourself, "Let us, let us, let us." Plant your pills in your backyard and see if they grow. Tape all your pills together to make a ball and play catch with it. Consider substituting your meds with a bowl of Rice Krispies. Listen to that snap, crackle, and pop; it has more to say than hardcore drug intervention.

As president of a Louisiana mental health association, I am planning a jazz funeral in New Orleans. There, we will bury the professions that stand in the way of letting the mojo prosper and circulate. I intend to have a small wood casket. We will throw away the bogus psychiatric labels, all psychiatric meds, the licenses of the various professions, and the key books that have led so many well-intentioned people down an impotent dead end. A brass band will lead a parade through the streets of the French Quarter. We'll lament the pain these professions have inflicted on others, and then, when the music announces it is time to transform, the drums will pick up the beat. We'll dance down the streets celebrating a new revival of mojo.

Let's throw a voodoo-hoodoo spell on all the unhealthy practices of the mental health professions. Get a piece of felt and cut it into the shape of a large pill—around two inches long. Now take some straight pins and pin that pill to the side of a lemon. This voodoo doll requires a sacrifice. Play your flying drum, and then, with a sharp knife, carefully cut off the head of the lemon. As you do this, say these magic words, "You're only a lemon, and that's not right. Our mojo light will end your night. Without a fight, we ask for sight." Remove the pins, and gently kiss the felt. Chant the final incantation: "This pill was chilled and now is filled with mojo *felt* in heartbeat dealt by flying drum." Take your mojo pill to any situation that could benefit from a dose of soul medicine. Use it to turn sour lemons into sweet mojo-aid.

I'm already helping other therapists who want to escape. In my consultation practice, I help people access mojo. I even deliver it to their front door, directed by how my own mojo cooks something up.

Whether you are a client or professional, know that there is an alternative to seeing a psychologist, therapist, counselor, coach, or psychiatrist. You can go hunt some mojo and look for someone who can guide you in that search. Ask around for someone who relies more on creativity than drugs to help people with their everyday challenges. They're out there, I know—I've taught quite a few over the last four decades.

I feel both compassion and impatience for the helping professions, as they are in dire need of assistance. Let's help them get reconnected to mojo. If you're a therapist, stop practicing what you think your profession dictates you should be doing and listen to your heart. Follow its direction. It is trying to lasso your soul and pull you toward the transformative magic. Follow it without further ado. It will deliver you to the hidden treasure.

If you are a therapy client, ask your therapist to give you mojo rather than medicine. If he doesn't cooperate, be prepared to take a stand and leave him, but give him a gift before you depart. You may want to consider handing the following letter to him. Make sure you modify it to fit your style of expression and temperament:

Dear Therapist,

I have come to the conclusion that I have come to you not for my needs but because you need help. The gods of creative mirth have asked me to invite you to the birth of some mojo for your practice. At the recommendation of a world-famous therapist, I recommend that you start listening more to your heart of hearts. You must have felt some uncertainty about your training and whether it teaches the best wisdom the world has to offer.

Please consider finding a song to sing to your clients. That would make you more like the majority of healers in the world, who have been at this for thousands of years. Please look for more poems and jokes to tell your clients. Do so right after you burn that manual that lists all the made-up diagnostic names you've been taught to pin on people.

Do this for your soul. Do this because your profession needs healing and there is no better place to begin than with yourself. I am now a mojo person and would be happy to assist your deliverance into a more productive and invigorating professional life. I charge twice your fee and only require one session.

If you come to me, I will ask you to write a letter to your original ancestor. I realize that you have no way of knowing his or her name. I suggest you generically address it to Adam and Eve.

Say something like:

Dear Eve and Adam,

I want to ask you whether I took a bite out of the wrong apple. Is there another wisdom tree that can serve my mission? I went to the grocery store and bought an apple. I ate some of it so I could get to its seeds. I am carrying one of those seeds with me every day. I want to trust that absurdly tickling my seed will awaken a new beginning in my professional life. I want to bring better fruit to the lives of others. Please let me know whether you will help me find my way back to the beginning. Thanks for getting everything started. I appreciate your helping me turn a new leaf.

Sincerely,

(Therapist signs here)

Until we meet in mojo time, here's hoping I have helped drive your practice to a double-agent status, where you secretly dispense less therapy and more mojo.

By the way, I have a flying drum. I sincerely hope it pays you a visit and leaves you a gift.

May a new sense of wonder be with you,

(Sign your name here)

If you don't have a shrink or therapist, send the letter to yourself because you already act like a therapist to yourself and others; we all do. We live in a psychological culture where everyone is an amateur therapist. It permeates our culture in television, movies, and literature. Daily talk shows are carnivals of psychobabble. So are the highest literary reviews. Even what we call spirituality is psychobabble dressed in camouflage. God bless you, Oprah, but jeez, why did you have to empower all those psychobabbling shrunken heads? They haven't helped us get to the mojo. Please rethink your roots and bring it on, girl!

I'm doing everything I can to spread the mojo—the resourceful, healing alternative to pathologically oriented mental health. I suggest that fresh mojo wealth is healthier than canned mental health. I am on the radio every chance I get, waiting to receive your calls. I'm more than happy to cook some mojo for you. Welcome to the future that comes after psychotherapy. It's mojo time!

MOJO: Magic Opens the Jaded Ouroboros

The Ouroboros is an ancient symbol depicting a serpent or dragon swallowing its own tail and forming a dynamic, ever-changing circle. It refers to the process in which something constantly re-creates itself. Often seen in medieval illustrations of alchemy to represent the circular nature of transformation, it is the mandala of infinity and wholeness—the spirited heart and soul of mojo. Carl Jung wrote:

The alchemists, who in their own way knew more about the nature of the individuation process than we moderns do, expressed this paradox through the symbol of the Ouroboros, the snake that eats its own tail. The Ouroboros has been said to have a meaning of infinity or wholeness. In the age-old image of the Ouroboros lies the thought of devouring oneself and turning oneself into a circulatory process, for it was clear to the more astute alchemists that the *prima materia* of the art was man himself. The Ouroboros is a dramatic symbol for the integration and assimilation of the opposite, i.e. of the shadow. This 'feedback' process is at the same time a symbol of immortality, since it is said of the Ouroboros that he slays himself and brings himself to life, fertilizes himself and gives birth to himself. He symbolizes the One, who proceeds from the clash of opposites, and he therefore constitutes the secret of the *prima materia* which unquestionably stems from man's unconscious.

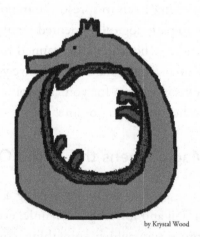

by Krystal Wood

The idea of a mythological dragon or sacred serpent swallowing its own tail was first found in ancient Egypt. In the Pyramid of Unas, which has been dated circa 2350 BC, hieroglyphs on the sarcophagus chamber indicate: "A serpent is entwined by a serpent" and "the male serpent is bitten by the female serpent, the female serpent is bitten by the male serpent, Heaven is enchanted, Earth is enchanted, the male behind mankind is enchanted." Throughout the ages, the Ouroboros has symbolized eternity and the soul of the world.

What could be a more fitting image for the work of mojo than the circular process of never-ending creation? Mojo comes to help you re-create yourself. Its wisdom stems from the ancient though revolutionary idea that you must never stop re-creating yourself. This is the secret to living a charmed, vibrant, magical life: To know yourself, change! To be alive, change! Re-create yourself each and every day so that you never stop getting spun by the infinite magic of the wordless mysteries of life. Mojo is best administered when it isn't taken too seriously. We now know that this stems from its paradoxical nature: swallow the opposite side to get across the bridge. Be jaded when you handle your re-creation; mojo opens the jaded Ouroboros. It opens the dragon's mouth to creatively feed upon the absurdity of the whole cosmos, bringing forth everything you need to live your life as fully as it can be lived.

What could be a more fitting image for the work of mojo than the circular process of never-ending creation? Mojo comes to help you re-create yourself. Its wisdom stems from the ancient though revolutionary idea that you must never stop re-creating yourself.

Make a commitment to the re-creation of yourself. Here is how to get things rolling: Cut out an image of Ouroboros or draw your own. Regard this as your mojo bait. Next, go get out your fishing pole or, if you don't have one, find a stick. Tie a string or fishing line to the end of the pole and attach your bait. Whenever you need to figure out what you should do about your life situation, try this alternative approach to counseling, therapy, meditation, yoga, and spiritual practice.

Sit down with your fishing pole and cast the line into the universe. You can throw it in any direction because the universe is infinite, where anywhere is everywhere. Now jiggle the line around and wait until you feel an inner intuition or inspiration take a bite. All you have to do is carefully reel it in. Stare at the bait so it distracts your conscious mind from scaring away what you are trying to bring home. Notice that what you catch is always Ouroboros. It swallows itself; it is its own bait.

Throw out the line again and move toward the circular realization that you are the bait waiting to catch your own mojo that is the whole of you being fully awakened; catch yourself on a daily basis. Go fishing every day in this special way of pulling in the line that has you on the other end. Feel free to invent a tall fishing tale. Use it to inspire a new script for your everyday.

As you attempt to disentangle yourself from the stuck babble of psychotherapy, please join those of us who unashamedly fish for mojo. Do so with a playful spirit or you'll scare the silver mermaids and golden dolphins away. Find yourself responsive to the crazy wisdom advice that encourages us to say with Friedrich Schiller, "Man only plays when in the full meaning of the word he is a man, and he is only completely a man when he plays." Get ready to catch the mojo that encourages never-ending absurd play and highly unpredictable spontaneous action.

Know that the flying drum is making a comeback appearance. It is another magical circle that keeps circling overhead. Hop on top and take a ride into your deepest imagination, though the flying drum isn't the only mojo that moves into the stratosphere. All the mojo presented in this book is as lively as the drum and flies to all points north, south, east, and west. All of it is a flying drum—a never-ending circle of creation that teaches every time you set it free. At times, it may hop along, but it never stands still for long to indulge in serious understanding of any kind. It briefly stands under whatever you need to leap from. Welcome to the mojo air show that promotes a flying circus! Here, you jump on board the wings of absurdity to find the deepest jaded meaning of life.

Today, I find that magical transformation is better served in the theater, cabaret, nightclub, circus, gospel tent, live radio, or traveling medicine show. It more likely becomes a bore when packaged as a core method that is certified, licensed, and franchised as if it were fried chicken. On the other hand, there is something hot and steamy about the idea of selling greasy, fried soul food!

Mojo has its own Ouroborean mind and is more likely to play with us when we are empty of demanding purpose and selfish expectation. It requires that we be willing to have the openness, doubt, faith, contradictions, creativity, silliness, curiosity, naive exploration, willingness to make mistakes, and nonsensical expression of a child. True transformative mojo encourages a death and resurrection show of ultimate circularity. It will shock your personality, shake up your ego, ask you to be absent of a know-it-all mind, toss your beliefs around, trip you over every assumption, and sometimes leave you dizzy with wonder. If you persevere, you will learn to love being charmed by mojo, for it brings on the surprise reappearance of a flying drum, a dancing doll, a magical wand, an enchanted word, or something completely unexpected. Remember that you must lose everything to find the magical nothing that is really something. So sayeth the circling of life.

Encourage extreme love rather than illusory power as you help each other awaken shared mojo. Be kind and gentle. Be a highly ethical child and leave your retarded adult morality at home. Play, and open your heart to the delight of being fully alive in the moment, doing so as the mojo dances with you. And for god's sake, do not get too serious about this pursuit! At the same time, take this absurd advice seriously. This is your time to be stretched by all opposites so you can pass through the narrow gate and enter the mojo wilderness.

If you persevere, you will learn to love being charmed by mojo, for it brings on the surprise reappearance of a flying drum, a dancing doll, a magical wand, an enchanted word, or something completely unexpected.

Be absurd and foolishly outrageous to run the pious judgmentalists away. Do not use too many sacred metaphors, for this makes things too rigidly slanted and more difficult to shake your mojo free. Consider your life performance a production of Buddha's Comedy Club, or the Kali Goddess Bar, the Angels & Devils Exchange Program, Jesus' Gas Station, the Shamanic Burlesque, or God's Whorehouse. The more absurd the talk, the lower the chance your controlling mind will be able to be in charge. This will help get things cooking.

Absurd talk delivers good mojo teaching. It helps you find an escape hatch from your own presumptuousness and get on with arriving at the staircase to heaven. Why do you think sinners and the meek have better odds of finding the gods than the smug know-it-alls? Think about it. Actually, don't think about it. Don't think at all. Just laugh, for laughter will get you trembling and shaking.

Said differently, all of this mojo business is serious work, and that contributes to why it is so insanely absurd. Words can't say what mojo is or what it isn't; they can only tease and negate whatever anyone says it is and isn't. That, in turn, must be negated. The art of double negation takes us to the whack of a Zen Shtick before anyone points out that we are always being mooned and marooned by pointing things out. Enough of this talk! It only bankrupts whatever we start to say, and although this can be useful ... enough is enough.

Real-life mojo mercilessly teases all rigid and overly serious framings of spirituality, healing, self-help, and therapy. It encourages an uncensored, open, free celebration of the complexly simple joy and Mad Hatter love of being alive. Its spirited delivery unashamedly serves and honors creative transformation. This includes holding both the sacred and the profane. Without both sides of this distinction, there is no dance, no spirit, and no life force; hell is being locked inside either side. This is why Mark Twain asked to go to hell if he couldn't swear in heaven. Allow the angels and demons to dance with one another to bring forth a whirling mojo wind—a breath of vitality that can lift you right off your feet! Be danced by the outrageously ridiculous gales, hurricanes, tornadoes, and typhoons that circulate and consummate the marriage of life and death.

The mojo traditions of the world do not rely upon cognitive understandings to teach their transformative ways. Instead, you sincerely prepare to be existentially awakened by crazy, magical mojo. For the Kalahari Bushmen, the world's oldest and arguably strongest ecstatic culture, this preparation takes place by simply being around n|om, their word for mojo (read *The Bushman Way of Tracking God*). It is also called kundalini, chi, Holy Spirit, and the creative life force. Jump into this flowing river and be anointed by its wetness and moved by its currents.

Mojo is a way of honoring the oldest way of transforming the human body, mind, heart, and soul. It throws you into God's pot so you can become cooked by its crazy, irrational medicine. Never mind what I might have said earlier: I bet you'd like to order some deep-fried wings for your hungry-to-fly soul! Be your own flying drumstick!

Talk is harnessed by mojo doctors and used in a most intriguing way. No particular importance is given to so-called answers, insights, or understandings. Anything said is subject to embracing its contrary in order that both may dance and get cooked. Here, we fry self-esteem so it becomes spirited steam. Mojo talk, or what my colleague Hillary Stephenson calls "circular poetics," is used to help shake up and liberate predictable habits of thought and action that block movement toward fully embodied, spontaneous, circular expression. In conclusion, mojo invites you to a deliciously insane, celebrative opportunity to evoke the creative life force that tunes the body/mind/heart/soul and provides you with an experiential link to the *mysterium tremendum*.

Let's keep mojo underground, where the wild still knows how to howl. True swamp mojo serves muddy wisdom while gobbling up overly simple dualisms and arrogant pomposity. It comes to kick your spiritual butt, making you more human and present to the fleas, lice, and alligator pissing near your pillow, while removing the constraints that hold back infinite joy and the ecstatic flight of extreme delight. It is the impossible catch of the flying drum that is nothing less and nothing more than the spinning, infinite dragon. Surrender to the hilarious vastness of the cosmic jig, and like Rumi, become a servant of extreme mojo love. Wiggle that fishing line and reel in the silver lining inside the clouds of uncertainty. Catch your own mojo and allow it to teach you how to fly to the twinkling stars that mirror who you really are.

AFTERWORD

*S*everal years ago, I dreamed I was in a large canoe with all the mojo doctors who had been my teachers and guides. They were from every corner of the globe. The water was smooth as glass as we glided gently to the shore. When the canoe came to a stop, I got out and waved goodbye to the elders. After twelve years of being away from my profession, I was returned home. As I turned around, I saw I was facing a large audience; they wanted me to teach them about mojo. A voice whispered, "Now is the time to pass on what you have learned. Let others know how to be good to one another. Help them know how to doctor their hearts and souls with the old ways. Teach them how to bring back the long-lost mojo."

In my dream, I turned to look at the canoe as it sat on the white sand beach. The teachers were gone; there was only mojo sitting in it. I saw the flying drum, the dancing doll, the vanishing pot, the magic books, the feather wand, the secret drawings, the samurai pillow, and many other magical objects. I suddenly heard that someone was giving an introduction to the audience; I was being called to the stage. I started singing and felt my heart express its tender appreciation for my teachers. The flying drum began to lift itself in the air and move toward me. All the mojo, one object after another, came to life and skillfully glided out of the canoe. It was coming back to the people.

At that moment, I realized that it was the mojo that was being introduced; I was merely an intermediary between different worlds. The long-lost mojo had returned, and it was flying, drumming, singing, dancing, teasing, and laughing as it healed and transformed. This mojo lives inside this book; you are holding it. Play your drum and sing joyfully so your heart can feel it. This is how mojo comes to life and becomes a part of your everyday.

> *For the joy of life, mojo has brought us together.*
> *Its magic is sweet kindness serving the grace of mystery.*
> *Seasoned with humor and invention, it invites us to go past*
>   *convention.*
> *Awakening our hearts and feeling the love,*
> *It conjures and charms the wings of a dove.*
> *Play that drum and plumb the depths,*
> *So eagles can soar and lions can roar.*
> *All of creation stands ready to fly,*
> *Made ready by mojo far up in the sky.*
> *Divine is the mind that leaves trouble behind*
> *And wants to be hearty for spirited party.*
> *Nothing less, nothing more; ancestors arrive at the shore.*
> *They bring you back home to a magical door.*
> *Within lies your truth, found pulling an oar,*
> *Canoe traveled far to bring a new jar.*
> *There sits the potion to brighten your star.*

There was a mojo doctor in Brazil who lived to be ninety-nine years old. She dreamed me before I arrived at her door, and she helped many people with her spirit guides and special kinds of mojo. "It all comes down to one simple ingredient," she would say. "It is one thing: love." Love is the only teaching of mojo. It is what the flying drum lifts you to know. It allows the strings of our heart to be pulled by the gods and, in turn, inspires you to pull others'.

Pulling the dough makes bread; so it is with mojo. Our hearts pull one another. Imagination is pulled by vision, and the life force is pulled by mystery. In the pulling is found the daily making of bread and the making of love. Mojo invites us to bake life into a beautiful cake; it is the yeast that helps our hearts rise. It invites us to do so with play and fun, laughter and cheer.

There you are, ready to get out of your canoe and turn around. In the turning is the churning of magic. You've come this far; why not go all the way? The gods applaud every step you take into the mojo of everyday awe. Charm, enchantment, and magic are all around you. Turn, turn, turn, and feel what is yours.

May the teachings of mojo be blessed and enjoyed
as a celebration of love.

—Otavia Pimental, Brazilian healer